PAPRIKA PARADISE

PAPRIKA PARADISE
TRAVELS IN THE LAND OF MY ALMOST BIRTH

JAMES JEFFREY

HACHETTE AUSTRALIA

HACHETTE AUSTRALIA

Published in Australia and New Zealand in 2007
by Hachette Australia
(An imprint of Hachette Livre Australia Pty Limited)
Level 17, 207 Kent Street, Sydney NSW 2000
Website: www.hachette.com.au

Copyright © James Jeffrey 2007

This book is copyright. Apart from any fair dealing
for the purposes of private study, research, criticism
or review permitted under the *Copyright Act 1968*,
no part may be stored or reproduced by any process
without prior written permission. Enquiries should
be made to the publisher.

**National Library of Australia
Cataloguing-in-Publication data**

Jeffrey, James.
    Paprika paradise : travels in the land of my almost birth.

    ISBN 978 0 7336 2070 6 (pbk.).

    1. Jeffrey, James - Family. 2. Jeffrey, James - Travel -
    Hungary. 3. Authors, Australian - Family relationships.
    4. Authors, Australian - Biography. I. Title.

070.444092

Cover design by Sandy Cull, gogoGingko
Cover artwork by Rosanna Vecchio
Cover photography by Neil Lorimer
Map drawn by Kinart
Text design by Bookhouse, Sydney
Typeset in 12/17.4 pt Adobe Caslon Regular
Printed in Australia by Griffin Press, Adelaide

Hachette Livre Australia's policy is to use papers
that are natural, renewable and recyclable products
and made from wood grown in sustainable forests.
The logging and manufacturing processes are expected
to conform to the environmental regulations
of the country of origin.

For Bel

Contents

Spice Cadet and the Sacks of Doom	1
Big Bang Theory	5
Projected Yearnings	15
Salami Side	25
For He is an Englishman	33
The Owl versus the Wizard	39
The International Language	47
Swine Buffs	55
To the Goose Fatmobile	69
Intergalactic	81
If I were a Bumblebee	91
Instruments of Satan	97
Terminal Condition	103
The Incredible Shrinking Country	113
Now and Then	123
The Road to Istvánakna	143
Round the Bend	157
Chews Your Relatives	181
Mercury and Melons	207
A Gathering of Goat Squeezers	221
Land of the Long Black Pudding	241
Coming, Going	259

Spice Cadet
and the Sacks of Doom

It was by all accounts a quiet midsummer morning when János Köszl arrived at work on Széchenyi Square for the last time. A paprika merchant who rented a shop in the southwest corner of Pécs's town hall, Köszl unlocked the door and prepared for the day's business by snipping the end off his ritual morning cigar. Outside, there was probably little more than the brittle tinkle of coffee cups at cafés around the square and the cobblestone clatter of horse-drawn cabs to disturb the hungover heads of some of the more festive guests at the Nádor Hotel. And then of course there were the bells from all those churches, on the hour, every hour. It was 1896 and the city of Pécs, along with the rest of the nation, was halfway through celebrating Hungary's millennial year, a thousand years since the seven Magyar tribes under Great Chief Árpád had ridden out of the east into the Carpathian Basin and taken a shine to it.

It was a big year. Emperor Franz Josef – equipped with facial hair that seemed a touch excessive even by Hungary's exuberantly bristly standards – had made it all the way down from Vienna to drop in on Pécs just a few months before, trailing medal-encrusted lackeys and preposterously fur-cloaked, scimitar-dragging nobles in his wake as he visited the four-spired basilica and, keeping more in the spirit of the occasion, the champagne factory.

It was a year of celebration, elevated that little higher into giddiness by Hungary's newly burgeoning wealth, spearheaded by a madly blossoming Budapest. If there were a few extra hangovers or a few more cigars quietly puffed to ash that year, so be it. Köszl may well have thought as much as he leaned against his shop counter that July morning and contentedly sucked the first mouthful of thick, blue smoke from his glowing stogie. Millennial fever, in a roundabout sort of way, might even have gone part way toward explaining why he kept four hundred and forty pounds of gunpowder stashed under the counter. (Exactly, it would later be noted, one hundred times the legal limit.) Perhaps Köszl had just interpreted his role as spice trader a little too broadly, who knows. No one knows how many morning cigars the gunpowder mountain had survived until that point, or just how many puffs Köszl got out of his cigar that particular morning. What isn't in question is the size of the explosion that followed, big enough to kill seven and injure thirty-nine, Mayor János Aidinger included, and apparently loud enough to wake anyone still sleeping in Pécs. It also put paid to the town hall that had survived a number of direct hits during the War of Independence against Austria earlier that century and the earthquake that had followed at an indecently short interval, only to fall victim to a shopkeeper's exotic collecting habits.

Back in the realm of mystery, Köszl – a bit like those drunks who cause the most appalling car accidents but walk away unscratched – survived the blast and was given eighteen months in prison to reflect on his choice of hobby.

Just over a decade later, a replacement town hall – an art nouveau design by Adolf Lang in the favoured Habsburg shade of custard yellow, with perhaps just a dash of mustard – opened for business, without the benefit of Köszl's spice shop.

Then on another July morning several decades after that, my parents walked in and got married. Maybe it's just me, but it all seems strangely symmetrical.

Big Bang Theory

The way my mother, Eszter, used to tell it, we fell out of Hungary the way some people (if not Mum herself) fall out of love – ruefully, ambiguously and wistfully, and with way too many a backward glance. Other times, more often than not as her years lived in her homeland were eclipsed by the years spent outside it, it became the paradise we had all rather carelessly tumbled out of.

Not that I had anything to say about it at the time. It was late in the spring of 1972 and I was just a wriggling bump in Mum's belly as she packed her bags for England, gathering together the two children from her first marriage and the passports the communist regime had reluctantly given them. Mum says it was only because she was scared the authorities might change their minds and keep her from her new English life and her new English husband that they left in such a hurry. My brother, László, and my sister, Eszter, aged nine and ten respectively and with scarcely a word of English between them, were whisked out of Pécs without a chance to say goodbye to their father, Mum's first husband, before flying out of Soviet Europe to the West where my father, Ian, was waiting to set up home with his ready-made family.

Thanks to the dismal British climate, Hungary began to grow in Mum's stories into a sort of heaven in hindsight, and rightly so. Any place that managed to bring my parents together, however briefly, was clearly a place of miracles, or at least a place to be reckoned with. It was only a matter of time before it would begin to lure us back.

I was born in England, as was my little sister, Olivia, who followed at a polite interval, but Mum wasn't taking any chances, regularly taking us across the continent for doses of Magyar immersion. Even after we left Europe altogether for Australia, we were kept connected by a constant tide of dark-haired, brown-skinned relatives who washed in and out of Hungary over the years, filling our house with their stretched vowels and soft consonants, smuggled salami and lurid green Zsolnay porcelain – a Pécs speciality, we were reminded. 'You will never find anything so beautiful in Australia,' Mum would inform us as she caressed each new piece into place in her crowded china cabinet.

Mum filled our heads with her language (Dad was in charge of English) and loaded us up with stuffed cabbage and chicken paprika while puzzling over antipodean eccentricities, such as the penchant for barbecuing lamb ('I don't know how they can eat it when it stinks of death') and opening presents on Christmas morning, when proper people knew the correct time to do this was the night before.

I was aware, in a foggy sort of way, that we were a little different to our neighbours. By accident, we'd finished up in the Sutherland Shire, the most resolutely Anglo-Saxon part of Sydney. Then, even more than now, it was the sort of place where flamboyantly Middle European behaviour stuck out like an orang-utan on an iceberg. Nevertheless, as her marriage to Dad turned to ash over the years, Mum consoled herself by keeping her ears tuned for compatriot voices. And there were a few: the man who ran the takeaway at Cronulla beach, the couple who owned the boat hire on the Woronora

River, the brawny woman behind the counter of the milk bar in Caringbah. There was always joy and relief when Hungarians found each other in this far-flung place; they weren't like the Greeks or Italians, who were so plentiful in Australia they were practically tripping over each other. Hungarians at least had scarcity value, especially in the Shire.

The milk bar woman – Edit – was especially excited, and invited us to a pool party she and her husband (also Hungarian) were throwing. We went without Dad, which was handy for Mum as she met János, the man who would become her third husband. Unhandily, János was still married to Edit. But no matter, Mum was very goal-oriented.

Despite everything, it wasn't until the next pool party, specifically when Edit offered to cut out János's heart and giftwrap it for Mum, that I truly began contemplating what it might mean to be Hungarian. It was a moment that neatly knocked the post-barbecue drowse out of the afternoon, a depth charge of Magyar passion in the leaf-smothered bowels of whitebread Sydney. Even at the age of eight, wreathed in a fug of chlorine and barbecued sausage, I understood the smug niceties of the Shire wouldn't be getting much of a look-in. Not now that Edit realised her new friend was stealing her husband.

'I'll cut his fucking heart out here and now,' Edit told Mum with an explanatory flourish of a large knife. As awful as it all was, I couldn't help feeling a strange pang of gratitude to Mum. If like so many of her compatriot émigrés she had taken the decision to not teach us her native tongue, I wouldn't have understood any of this. It just would have been an angry noise as Edit carried on.

'Why don't you take it with you, you shameless thief? Go on, take it, you whore. It's not as if it's of any use to me any more.'

It was hard to figure out what felt weirder – Edit's almost operatic performance in front of her mesmerised guests, or seeing Mum knock back a freebie. Either way, János's heart was still beating safely, albeit erratically, as Mum bundled me and my sister into the car and sped us away from the flaming wreck of one marriage and back to the fireball of her own.

Mum had only known János for a couple of weeks, but already they were planning to start their lives anew with each other.

Dad, who would later state that he didn't ever marry again as he'd learned his lesson quite well first time around, could have happily spent that time dithering over whether to buy new socks. Yet Mum and János had managed in that handful of days to meet, fall in love, start an affair, concoct plans for escape and divorce, and narrowly dodge a public disembowelling. It struck me that Hungarians were fast movers. While Dad's motto used to be a sigh and a vague promise of 'I'll think about it', Mum seemed to be pure impulse and emotion, one of the most natural candidates for spontaneous human combustion I have ever known. Not that Edit seemed too far behind. She took to stalking Mum – her little silver car with its sinister tinted windows became a familiar sight as it squatted at the end of our street – and even ambushing her at a local intersection, screaming imaginative sentiments as she charged at our Kombi and, using nothing but her brawny, brown arms, smashed the windshield.

I pondered the same questions that troubled so many others. Were all Hungarians like this? And if so, how come there were any still alive? More to the point, how the hell did my father, of all people, a man unlike my mother the way a penny-farthing is unlike a cluster bomb, get drawn into their universe? It was a mystery as enduring as it was baffling, yet once upon a time, somewhere beneath the layers of melodrama and hysteria, there had been love. Or at least there had been in Hungary. Even Mum and Dad admitted that. The relationship that breathed its last one Australia Day, as a pair of bored constables trooped into our house to add one more summer domestic to their list, had started out as a tongue-tied Cold War romance.

MY PARENTS' MARRIAGE was a year old when I was born and nearly ten when it ended, but I can barely remember them being together. My earliest memories in life are from before my third birthday, but the images I carry in my head of Mum and Dad as a couple are so few, it's almost as if a worm has gone through my brain and selectively eaten all the cells that held them. I can see them separately in my mind, but rarely together. There are moments here and there, but the clearest ones are from the closing months of what had long been a dead marriage. Fuzziness shrouds so much in my head, but not the final acts of that farcically doomed union. Neither the shouting nor the banging doors, nor the wedding ring ricocheting off the walls of an off-season ski lodge and coming to rest at the end of the hallway with a strangely piercing clatter as the rest of us closed bedroom doors and tried to will away the horrid, cascading inevitability of it all. It was late spring and the shouting was followed by a hot summer of cold silences, finally cracking open on a humid January night as I stood with sea salt crackling on my sunburned skin, and my little sister, aged five and overwhelmed by the vision of slapping, screamed for our mother's life. There were police badges and moustaches and heavy shoes clomping through the house, while across town fireworks sprayed prettily over Sydney Harbour to mark Australia Day. Olivia and I huddled together in the bed our parents would never again share, a cop tapping gently on the door frame and checking to see that we were okay. No, not really, but thank you for asking.

As my parents waged a raging custody war through expensive solicitors – perversely boosting for a child's ego – a battle Dad ultimately won, I understood that once there had been togetherness. It's almost as hard as trying to imagine the universe before the Big

Bang, but once upon a time my parents were in love. My eternally, helplessly doting English father, stuck somewhere between soft-spoken caution and an overbearing pragmatism, somehow sparked with my mother, an impulsive, compulsive, emotional Hungarian tempest, a woman whose personality had grown so large, it was like one of those huge corporations that splinters into different departments that don't always talk to each other.

It was Hungary that brought them together and Hungary that held them together. Hungary the small, Hungary the anomalous. It was only when they slipped from Hungary's gentle grasp that things began to unravel.

Years after we all left Europe for a life in Australia, pint-sized Hungary – a country that other Europeans speak of as if it were some exotic island dropped onto the heart of the continent by a passing spaceship – continued to loom large in our lives. All of Mum's fits of strangeness and operatic drama were tied, in my head, to her Hungarianness. So were her vivacity and hysteria, her manic cooking and simmering resentments, her long memory and selective amnesia, her great, galloping, incandescent joys. I couldn't see anyone else who seemed even a tiny bit like Mum. (Except Edit, but then she was Hungarian, too.) I knew I had something special. I sometimes feared her, sometimes resented her, but I loved her. Most of the time. It would be a fib to say it wasn't hard work, though. Warmth, fear, adoration and bafflement went hand in hand; she'd been left behind by a spaceship, after all.

Incidentally, the Big Bang is known in Hungarian as the *Nagy Bumm*.

I'd been back to Hungary and Pécs a few times as an adult, a couple of weeks here and there that passed in an almost religious ecstasy at both the strangeness and the familiarity of it all, the world of my mother's kitchen expanded into an entire country complete with the right sounds and smells and strict adherence to calories by the truckload, but with noticeably less hysteria.

I had gazed at the Mecsek Hills curling gently beyond the rendered walls and radish-domed steeples, cloaked in a mosaic of little vineyards that pushed their way up the slopes and nudged the dark hem of forest that rang all summer long with the sound of woodpeckers. On the plain behind me, beyond the fringes of the town, lay constellations of villages where dreadlocked sheepdogs drowsed by water pumps and geese as big as children roamed dusty streets past kerchiefed clusters of spherical old women who stood outside their whitewashed houses, swapping artery-clogging recipes and minor family scandals, tut-tutting or cackling uproariously at each fresh revelation.

I had tried to picture my father, a mining engineer, all those years ago when his company was selling machinery to a state-owned coal mine near Pécs. He'd launched himself out of the slag heaps of middle England just as columns of Soviet tanks converged on Czechoslovakia to snuff out the Prague Spring. As turmoil erupted across Hungary's border, Dad found himself in this small university town two hundred kilometres south of Budapest, a mixture of Catholic exuberance, Ottoman confidence, Habsburg solidity and Calvinist restraint, a place of wine and fierce music, of towering cakes and goatskin bagpipes, of Turkish minarets and Roman tombs, of cobblestones and wisteria, of nesting storks and secret police. And here, between interrogations and against expectations, he found love in the arms of a divorcee, a mother of two. An Englishman abroad, he would loiter by the fountain in the square outside the shoe shop where my mother had just started working, alternately blushing and grinning when she noticed him. That they could barely communicate proved a bonus.

It was to Pécs that I was drawn, my mother's home town, the place where their love had had its brief blossoming, the place where my life had begun, the place from which so much effort and emotion had gone into escaping.

I headed back to Hungary once more with my wife, Bel, just a few months after we were married, arriving on a frigid February day, clunking across the Drava River on a Croatian train and inching towards Pécs across a stark, brown landscape where the only movement came from the lugubriously circling crows and the occasional deer, each one so solitary it looked as if it might be the last left on earth. I was nervous: if my beloved announced that she didn't like Hungary, it would have proved something of a stumbling block in our relationship. Thank Christ she did like it, and as the desolation of that winter's end – in truth a very mild effort by Magyar standards – unfurled into the most glorious spring either of us have ever lived through, that fondness for Hungary blossomed into love. Of course, this love was helped by the six months we subsequently spent trying to make a living in Dublin, then the gruelling year in Moscow that followed. With every week that passed in Ireland's damp and snotty climate and among Moscow's inhuman boulevards and epic layers of humanity and pollution (air you can crunch between your teeth!), Pécs took on a halcyon glow. When I was granted a week's parole from my job in Moscow, we headed west as fast as we could with our baby girl, Daisy, and went mad with the joy of a homecoming, only to find ourselves back in the bleakness of a Russian November a few days later, suffering from psychological whiplash.

Ever since then, we'd been pining for Hungary with a sort of surrogate homesickness. How beautiful it would be to take time off from my newspaper job to go back and stay for longer. We tried not mentioning it to Mum for fear of triggering either one of her why-don't-we-leave-this-forsaken-Australia-and-all-go-back-to-beautiful-little-Europe emotional avalanches, or one of her why-do-you-want-to-go-back-there avalanches, but it did slip out from time to time. And Mum tended to use an extraordinary amount of oxygen with her reaction.

The birth of our second child, Leo, gave us a little more clarity. In a couple of years time, we realised, we would be under some sort of obligation to enrol Daisy in school, and just as drastically, Leo would require a full airfare to travel anywhere. It was with such excuses that we graduated from wistfulness to plot-hatching – we would return to Hungary for six months and really get to know the place that, in a feat vaguely comparable to Tito holding Yugoslavia together, had somehow united my parents.

As we finally performed the miracle of pulling our fingers out and converting our dreamy Magyar yearnings into action, I realised I was exactly the same age as Dad was when he went to Hungary for the first time. I began to feel nervous.

Projected Yearnings

'W E ALL FOUGHT like dogs to get out of there,' Mum wailed in her kitchen when I first raised the possibility that Bel and I might move to Hungary. 'Now all our children want to do is go back. Look at Kapusi's son. Oh, it breaks her heart – and here you are, hell-bent on doing the same to me.' To properly berate me, Mum even abandoned her cabbage-chopping duties, always a sign she wasn't taking something especially well. But that first tidal wave of emotion was soon swallowed by an even fiercer wave of plans to follow us. It was inevitable. Mum was one of those émigrés who never felt whole anywhere so did what she could to make up for it by constantly yo-yoing between her adopted home and the land of her birth, feeling her greatest sense of completeness when in transit between the two. Not that I was in any position to point the finger.

When I was tiny, Hungary meant light and my grandparents' faces. During those first years in England, Mum would bundle us (and an array of kitchen utensils) up and we'd head off toward the Iron Curtain. Our commutes from the subdued greys and the sporadic, somehow damp Lancashire sunshine must have had quite an impact on my toddler brain, because for years afterwards the light was what I remembered of Pécs. A strong light, a warm light, a gold light (no doubt more golden in my head than it ever was in reality) that washed over the communist-era apartment blocks, the playgrounds and the copper dome of the Ottoman mosque-cum-church that squatted in the middle of Széchenyi Square, and turned molten the waters of the Danube as my cousin Andris and I hurled in pebbles. I have faint images of snow one year, my one and only white Christmas, but for me Hungary was always at that point late on a summer's afternoon when the heat is beginning to ease and everyone is stirring from their post-lunch torpor with thoughts of ice-cream, perhaps a little promenading – preferably in the direction of another ice-cream stand – and, with a little luck, giving me a good, solid go on the swings behind my grandparents' flat in the suburb of Uránváros, which translates as Uranium Town. Moving through this luminous world were my grandparents, Eszter and Mihály. Of course I wasn't even aware they had names other than Nagymama and Nagypapa, or Grandma and Grandpa. Nagymama usually got shortened to Nagyi, an excellent word to a three-year-old because not only did it sum up all that was best in the world, it also rhymed with *fagyi*, which means ice-cream. Such things are rarely coincidence.

So good was the title of Nagyi that my paternal grandmother, an upstanding Nottingham woman who probably never had any particular love for either my mother or her culture, adopted it herself and wore it well. Granny, she reasoned, would only make her feel old, and Nanna was beyond the pale.

One of my parents' last major acts before leaving Hungary for England in 1972 was to get pregnant with me. Thinking about them getting up to any sort of hanky-panky isn't easy, but there's no escaping it. Every time I return to the land of my almost birth, there comes the inevitable moment when I'll pass the old family home in Pécs with my Aunt Joli and her shoulders will begin trembling. 'You know, Jimmy, that is the house where your life began. Hee hee.'

It isn't just grown-ups who suffer incredulity attacks. One afternoon before we left Australia, Dad turned up with a boxful of slides and photos he'd unearthed down the back of one of his labyrinthine wardrobes, which I'm convinced leads to a sort of dust-coated Narnia. The first picture he pulled out was a black-and-white snap of him and his mining colleagues in Pécs in 1969. My three-year-old daughter, Daisy, squinted at it.

'Where's my granddad?' she asked after much scrutiny.

'That's him there,' said Bel, pointing to a fresh-faced figure in sandals. 'He was the same age Daddy is now. He was in Hungary and in love with Nagyi.'

Daisy seemed taken aback, as if she'd been told there were badgers on the moon. 'Was he?'

'Yes, he was. It's a bit like a fairytale because it doesn't seem true.'

Dad took this in his stride and started pulling out the slides.

THE LAST FEW MONTHS before we left were often spent in splendidly unproductive reveries. For me, there were still deadlines to meet, stories to finish, but the useful part of my brain, rather irresponsibly, had abandoned such matters and migrated ahead to Hungary, where it was impatiently waiting for the rest of me to catch up. So it was just as well I had Dad around to snap me out of these daydreams and reconnect me to the present day – often by means of my mobile phone rudely vibrating its way across my office desk, laden with more questions about the forthcoming odyssey.

'Yes, I believe you had some questions about my time in Pécs, bonny lad. I didn't want to disturb you again at work, but as your departure date is getting near...'

I'd already had one session with Dad and a tape recorder, during which he had shown a lot more enthusiasm for talking about mining equipment than about courting Mum. But when I asked Mum about the first time she saw Dad, she clapped her hands together.

'Oh, Jimmy,' she cried, as if it had all happened just the afternoon before. 'He was so handsome.' She pondered this for a moment, then in case I'd missed the point, added, 'Your farder was a very good-looking man.'

When I interrupted a lovingly told account of the equipment he was meant to be installing in the Pécs coal mine to ask Dad about the first time he'd seen Mum, his mouth contracted like a cat's bottom that sensed the approaching cold of the veterinarian's thermometer.

'I believe,' he said at length in a voice clearly aching to return to talk of shafts and seams and pit ponies and methane build-ups, 'that she had some dealings with the colliery I was working at.'

('Dealings!' Mum cried later. 'I worked there.')

'What do you mean by "dealings"?'

'I seem to recall that she would on occasion visit the head office.'

'Do you remember when you first saw her?'

'I *may* have seen her off in the distance.'

'And what did you think?'

Dad's dismay at this deviation was palpable. 'It wasn't part of my job.'

'Come on, Dad. She was a beautiful woman in a foreign land, a woman you were going to fall in love with and marry. Something must have flickered through your mind.'

'It wasn't part of my job.'

Nevertheless, my vague suggestion of reconvening some time for a second session had seen Dad hit the phones with fresh zeal.

'About that second interview, bonny lad . . .'

It had been interesting watching the development of Dad's relationship with the telephone. He was like a hunter and the more widespread the technology became – voicemail, mobile phones and, I recoil at the memory, pagers – the more keenly he spread his net. If I didn't pick up the phone at home, he'd try my work number. If I didn't pick up there, he might call Bel's mobile, feigning a reluctance to disturb me at work. 'You might just get him to give me a call when he has a moment . . .' and so forth. But then the façade would crumble and I'd feel the mobile buzzing in my pocket or clattering against my coffee cup, the telltale words 'private number' on the screen as plain and undodgeable as a subpoena.

'Yep,' Dad would say, dispensing with time-wasting pleasantries and getting down to business, which often consisted of asking whether it was me at the other end of the incoming call that had rung out before he had a chance to huff and puff his way down the hall to pick up the receiver. (My favourite was when he once rang me late at night during the Moscow sojourn. 'Did you just try ringing?' 'No, Dad.' 'Only I heard the phone while I was in the garden and it had all the hallmarks of a long-distance call.')

Or it was to let me know he was going to be out on the off-chance I might want to call him. But now he had the issue of that interview.

'What's the hurry?' I said one afternoon, coming out of a trance and noticing with a twinge of discomfort a barely started article on my computer screen. 'We've got three months.'

'You'll find that will go very quickly, bonny lad.'

'It's a quarter of a year.'

That didn't sway my retired father. 'I've got a lot on my plate and I want to organise my schedule.'

'For three months?'

'Yes.'

Luckily, there were some useful distractions along the way, not least of which was the cache of slides. The bold yellow containers were helpfully captioned in black felt pen with headings such as 'Pécs', 'Balaton', 'Parbold', 'Hungary', 'Wedding', 'Countryside', 'Boring' and, accompanying one of the Borings, a solitary 'Better!'

'I don't know whose handwriting it is,' said Dad, adding with an accusing tone, 'It could be László's.' I couldn't tell what irked him more – the boring or the better. Perhaps it was just the impudent little exclamation mark.

For Mum, who had completely forgotten they existed, the slides came as a bit of a jolt. In between her joy and her tears as we began looking through them together, she grumbled about Dad, her accent getting thicker as she got crosser.

'Vhy does he keep these slides hidden avay? They are not just for him, the old fool, they are for all of us. All of us!' Which was something she didn't say when she took nearly every family photo with her when she left Dad. 'Vhy doesn't he share them?'

Unusually for Mum, who would often craft such grievances into dissertations that could stretch venomously across the hours (for Mum, like Dad, the divorce was felt just as keenly as if it had happened only the previous month), the sense of upset was fleeting, outweighed by the time capsule being vividly splashed on the wall. The colours were so fresh and vibrant, they looked as if they could have been taken yesterday. There was Nagypapa looking impish, as if he'd just ridden his wobbly bike home from his vineyard, and Nagyi looking as if she were about to give him an earful. Then there was Mum with an array of hairdos that grew more carefree about the laws of gravity with each passing month, and Dad, on the odd occasion he came out from behind the camera, looking boyish and so very chuffed.

'You know, Jimmykém,' Mum confessed over the projector's elderly rattle, 'I loved your farder very much back then.' Dad made no such concession when I looked at the slides with him.

'Look how beautiful I was then. You know, they used to say I was the prettiest woman in Pécs. When I walked down the street, people used to turn their heads to look at me. Look at me now. I am an old bag – not like then.' I clicked the projector again and there was Mum on honeymoon by Lake Balaton with a green swimsuit, teetering beehive and an ice-cream.

It wasn't just Mum's hair that headed up; so did her hemlines. Her wedding dress ('I designed it myself') was a triumph, even in a country which features the shortest skirts in the known universe. Among the wedding party, my Uncle Pali peered from behind a pair of spivvy sunglasses and sported the sort of suit Michael Caine would have been comfortable wearing in the 1960s. I couldn't recognise all the faces assembled on the steps of Pécs's Reformation Church, but Mum was happy to fill in the gaps.

'Oh, look, dat is Albert,' she said, leaping from her seat and bustling over to the wall to point out Dad's best man. 'He was *very* interested in me. Wanted to dance wid me, but your farder stepped right in.' She chuckled. She had never been shy about her magnetism on the dance floor. ('All the men – they all want to dance wid me. They go crazy for me. Crazy!')

Mum was striking in most of the slides, but it wasn't until the pictures made it across the water to the English Midlands that she looked truly exotic, a tropical bird in a resolutely, stolidly untropical country.

'We had such happiness then. It was such a beautiful house,' Mum said as we looked at shots of our staid neighbourhood of dull brick and weak light in the Lancashire village of Parbold. Then there was Nagypapa looking dapper in a blazer and woollen vest in various locations around the Lake District during a short visit from

Hungary with Nagyi for my christening. There was pale-skinned baby me, glowing like a fluorescent tube between my big sister and brother, Eszter and László. There were pictures of hedgerows and pasty-skinned vicars and deeply unpleasant houses.

'Yes, such happiness,' Mum added with a theatrical sigh. 'But I cried every night for four years until we moved away.'

The first year must have been a lachrymose doozy; Dad told me a couple of years ago that when I was barely twelve months old, he was planning to do a runner with me to South Africa. I thought this to be a top-shelf revelation, but it was eclipsed barely a fortnight later when Mum mentioned over lunch with me and Eszter that she'd once been ravished by a poltergeist. ('Yes – a ghost! Look, I am shivering just sinking about it.')

Luckily, Dad's plan of escape was as successful as the half-hearted attempt he once made to help Mum defect in Bulgaria, but when I mentioned it to Mum, I thought she was going to burst one of her more vital blood vessels.

'He vanted to steal you? How dare he! The snake! The *mocskos dög*!' This is pronounced mochkosh durg, means filthy carcase and is most effective when accompanied by a fleck of spittle.

'But that was thirty years ago and he didn't go, so why does it matter?'

'He vanted to steal you.'

'You tried to do the same thing with me and Olivia,' I said, alluding to a doomed scenario that only partially unfurled after the separation, a planned two-stage abduction that was to have taken us first to the neighbouring suburb (Sutherland), thence to the neighbouring state (Queensland). This was dealt a fatal blow when a local magistrate, having admired the floridness of Mum's performance in the courthouse, handed me and Olivia over to Dad. (Eszter and László had already moved out of home.)

'Well,' she said with a magnificent shrug. 'That was different.'

'How?'

'I am your mother.'

The sight of her own mother and father cooled her sense of outrage, then tipped her straight into sorrow. 'Oh, my beautiful parents. Where have they gone?' Her mottled hands quivered toward her wet cheeks, glistening eyes locked on the perfectly preserved versions of us as they appeared in slow clicking procession on the white bricks. 'Where have we all gone?'

We sipped lemon tea to the buzz of the projector.

'When I look at these pictures of your farder, I don't feel any hate. That is all just history,' Mum said. 'I was in love with him. He was such a good-looking man. What a shame he became so stupid.'

'So,' Dad said a couple of days later, doing his best to make it sound like an afterthought. 'What did your mother make of the slides?'

I tell him most of it, omitting the stupid and the *mocskos dög* bits. 'She spent a lot of time banging on about how handsome you were and how much she was in love with you.' I suspect from the look on Dad's face that it wasn't quite the response he'd expected.

'You know, I saw him in Engadine just the other day,' Mum said later that week, referring to a nearby Sydney suburb which, in a fit of overdeveloped whimsy, shares its name with a town in Switzerland. 'He growled hello at me. Normally he just ignores me.' I could tell from her little smile as she waddled over to the kettle that she saw this as a sign of progress. Mind you, she'd just heard that László was in all probability moving to London for a few years, so it was possible she wasn't feeling herself. Or perhaps she was just having flashbacks to the days when she and Dad used to dance together.

'Fate is a funny thing,' she said as she finally sat down with a bowl of *pogácsa* scones. 'We left Hungary and went to England, then we left England and went to Australia. Now my English son is going to Hungary and the Hungarian one is going to England.' For Mum, who was on a quest to follow her children wherever they went in the world, the year was shaping up as an unusually tough one. Then she snapped out of her reverie, realising there were more practical issues to tackle. 'Why aren't you eating your *pogácsa*?'

Salami Side

I'M STILL NOT SURE if it was slightly perverse or merely appropriate that one of my last images of Australia for six months was that of Mum and Dad standing together, waving as Bel and I disappeared with the kids through the hole in the wall at Sydney airport. Well, not *together*, but in each other's vicinity. Within metres, even. They had plenty to chat about – it had been decided that they would both be travelling to visit us in Hungary, if not at the same time – but I think they managed to avoid exchanging a single word with each other. But the sight of them looking – if you squinted a bit and perhaps drank a little – almost like a married couple made some part of my brain wobble for the next God knows how many hours as we made our way north by northwest first to Singapore, then Bahrain and eventually, after what felt like a month in the sky, Frankfurt.

Of Frankfurt (suggested motto: When you're tired of life, Frankfurt will give you some fresh perspective), there's not much to report. The sun shone for a bit, we ate some sausage and then we left.

From Frankfurt, the train threaded its way across Germany through countryside that looked immaculately scrubbed beneath a burnished sky. At Regensburg we met the flooding Danube – a brown patchwork quilt of eddies and upswells – and left it again at Passau as we entered the old Habsburg Empire. Austria passed in a vague, jetlagged blur of chocolate box and strong coffee (though I clearly remember Daisy dancing to the Wiggles as we rolled out of Vienna) and we made our clattering way east toward the Hungarian border.

Until 1989, this frontier was marked by electrified barbed wire, the cutting of which Helmut Kohl later referred to as the first brick out of the Berlin Wall. As Hungarian troops went to work with boltcutters, East Germans on holidays in Hungary were able to pour through the suddenly and miraculously porous border into the West, something which gave the unravelling of the Soviet empire its final, irresistible momentum. Now all I could see over the nearby road was a trim blue sign announcing: Magyarország.

We were quickly processed by the Austrian border guards, then assailed by their Hungarian colleagues. While my memory of the Austrians is one of thin moustaches and a polite lack of interest, the Hungarians were a group of raven-haired beauties in ill-fitting, unflattering uniforms who still seemed to be grappling with the new visa regulations that come with being a member of the European Union.

Eventually, and possibly against their better instincts, they inked our passports and we rolled through towns and villages, past factories and buildings in varying stages of dereliction, little box houses that looked as though they had been rendered in lumpy cement and grand, freshly painted villas. Whichever direction we looked, there were turnip-domed churches and steel water towers that stood like alien sentinels. Fields of bare dirt alternated with patches of baize green, speckled with rich, dark chocolate-coloured constellations of molehills. Sleek hares and plump pheasants watched with mild curiosity as the train passed. On the other side of the railway line, in some places just metres from the tracks, the overfed Danube quivered threateningly at white walls of sandbags and, here and there, spilled over to claim a field or orchard or lap at someone's back stairs. It was a national emergency for the politicians to deal with while fighting through the final days of an election campaign.

Their faces were all over the buildings as we emerged from the grimy glass cathedral of Budapest's Keleti – or Eastern – Station. The socialist prime minister, Ferenc Gyurcsány (a hasty replacement after his predecessor's communist-era career in counter-intelligence became public), gazed out from red posters, looking like Harry Potter might if he gave up wizardry for life as a chartered accountant. His opponent, former prime minister and Fidesz Party leader, Viktor Orbán, the man who'd had the kahunas to tell the Russians to go home back in 1989, meanwhile appeared on posters of a retina-searing orange with a face like a constipated owl.

'They're all the same,' our cab driver opined as we drove away from the station. 'Politics has gone down the sewer in this part of the world, entirely down the sewer.' The rain began to blatter against the windscreen. 'You picked a good time to come. It's been gorgeous all day until just a couple of hours ago, then *piff poof*, it started pissing down.' He scratched his chin contemplatively. 'I tell you what, though, the Danube could do without it.'

It occurred to me that we were driving down the very road where, several years before, I'd belatedly realised I was in love with Hungary. It was the evening of St Nicholas Day and I'd just arrived from a dank Dublin December, jumping into a minibus taxi and racing through snow-powdered streets toward Budapest's Southern Station to catch the last train to Pécs. As we came down this road, I remember catching glimpses through steamed-up windows of *fin-de-siècle* excess and a slumped St Nicholas trudging along the white pavements in a blaze of scarlet. And then there was the Danube, flickering like the frames of a Super 8 film between the girders of the Chain Bridge.

The river was far less well behaved this time around and had risen high enough to swallow the roads that run along the lower embankment, all but drowning the traffic lights, marooning the string of floating restaurants that cling to the bank and sweeping logs past Margit Island and the Parliament, which rose from the Pest side like a neo-Gothic ice-cream cake.

We were duly deposited at Budapest's Déli – or Southern – Station, which manages to lift my spirits every time I see it, despite being something of a bleak, concrete armpit. I all but floated to the booth and even smiled as the potato-shaped woman sold me tickets to Pécs with just the right touch of surliness I've come to know and expect from Hungarian State Railways. Were it not for fear of hernias, I would have sung as we lugged our mountains of gear onto the perky blue intercity train. Not that everyone was ready to share our excitement about being back in Hungary. Bel found an elderly couple in our seats and she politely explained this in imperfect but understandable Magyar. The old man grimaced as he heaved himself out of the seat, grumbling to Bel that she should go enrol in Hungarian school. Which seemed a bit rich coming from a man who couldn't read his own ticket.

With Déli's blighted expanse receding, we caught one last glimpse of the bloated, brown Danube as we rolled south. We sat with noses pressed to the window, probably with that slightly drugged and dizzy look of born-again Christians as we plunged ever deeper into this parallel universe where my father had danced and my parents had loved, passing lakes that glistened like mercury in the low sun and reedy wetlands where herons stalked gauntly through the shallows. Some of the first storks of the season flapped overhead in a low procession of black and white feathers and red beaks, patrolling for frogs or returning to nests that had sat empty through the freezing winter while their owners sojourned in the warmth of northern Africa. The nests perched like massive Russian fur hats on the pole-top platforms specially designed to dissuade the storks from setting up in potentially more disastrous locations, such as chimney tops.

We cried out at the sight of our first horse-drawn cart trundling along the ragged roads, not to mention the geese and chickens that spilled from the yards of ramshackle houses and the deer wandering across the fields or through copses of trees still bare but for the sleeves of moss on their boughs.

The trip to Pécs involves travelling due south – from nearly the very top of the country to nearly the very bottom – apart from the last quarter of an hour when the train turns ninety degrees to the east, swinging around the end of the Mecsek Hills at the small town of Szentlőrinc. From there, it's just a matter of minutes – deliciously, agonisingly slow minutes – until the first houses begin to speckle the hillsides, then the patchwork of vineyards unfolds, then the sight of the television tower, a spindly silhouette thrusting from the top of Misina Peak that marks Pécs as surely as an X on a treasure map. Then just as surely, the not so spindly shape of my Aunt Joli quivering on the platform with her load of shopping bags, ready to pounce and explode with five years worth of pent-up kisses.

'Hello, hello,' she called, throwing her arms around Bel and me in turn. 'Thank God you have arrived safely.' Then, with a cry of 'my beautifuls', she fell upon the children, kissing them ferociously. Watching her in action, I noticed how much she was looking like her younger sister. Roughly as short and round as each other, Mum and Joli were two dumplings boiled in the same batch.

With frequent inquiries as to the state of our health, the length of the trip, how keenly Leo was taking the breast, the overall happiness of the family back in Australia, the undoubtedly hideous expense of everything in Germany and Budapest and so forth, Joli ushered us toward the row of taxis that stood outside the grimy palace of the main station building.

'It would be better if we got a Volán taxi,' she said, lowering her voice to a penetrating whisper. 'They are honest, but some of the other companies will rob you blind. They have no shame at all – this is how it has become in Hungary. You have to be careful all the time! And you want to make sure you look after your money.'

The cab drivers stood about with cigarettes, wearing expressions of resigned suffering that softened at the sight of Leo and Daisy.

'Such beautiful children,' our driver said in between heaving our luggage into the back. 'What a wonderful thing it is to have little ones in your life.'

Bel and I agreed that this was the case. With Joli industriously rustling through her collection of Tesco bags and giving us a running commentary about what she'd bought us (tea, biscuits, packet soup, crackers, a tube of extra spicy goulash paste and so on), we set off on the short drive into the middle of Pécs. We passed through the defence layer of communist-era apartment blocks and I noticed they'd been given new, colourful coats of paint that made them look almost pleasant. And then we were in the Belváros, the Inner Town, zipping beneath pastel rendered walls, green porcelain fountains and the copper dome of the Djami, the converted mosque in the very middle of town, a relic from the Ottoman times now fitted with a huge pipe organ for the benefit of Jehovah rather than Allah. I glanced back and caught Bel's eye.

'Oh, my love,' she said. 'It's like coming home.'

Equipped with Joli's judiciously selected rations, we were to spend our first week just off Széchenyi Square in a rented apartment in a house owned by a family called Gulyás, which means goulash. (Their close relatives just a few blocks away sport the family name of Pénz, or money. It was as if two of Mum's driving concerns in life had been given human form.) Their rambling old house – complete with a courtyard shaded by fruit trees and populated by a fluctuating and indeterminate population of pets – stood not far from the old city wall, where the narrow streets spread out in a maze of cobblestones and wild chestnut trees. Apart from the kitchen with its chessboard floor and some pressed wildflowers from an uncle in Australia, the whole house was fitted out like a boudoir with deep reds and rich browns and the sort of armchairs that look as though they should contain gentlemen with waxed moustaches, spats and cigarette holders. The whole show was run by Gabi, a vivacious woman with the most powerfully rolled r's in Hungary, an ability to hear the pulling of a cork from the other side of a thick wall, and a cheerfully loose grip on the minutiae of day-to-day life.

Sample conversation

G: I thought you weren't arriving until Thursday.
US: Today is Thursday.
G: Really? Oh, well I thought you were arriving on a different day.

Gabi was not really the silent type and, depleted as we were by the journey, it was a buffeting experience to listen to her and Joli firing away in stereo until the words began to jangle and blur together in our bleary brains.

When they eventually left, Leo fell asleep with a gurgle and a fart, and Daisy marked the colonisation of a new room in her traditional way, jumping up and down on the bed and singing a short version of Handel's 'Hallelujah Chorus', a habit I'm afraid to say she may have picked up from her father. Bel and I lay down with our arms around each other, exhausted but ecstatic. As Daisy hallelujahed herself out, seven o'clock announced itself with a tinkling music box ditty that erupted from the town hall clocktower across the square. As it floated into its final bars, it was joined by a single bell tolling in doleful counterpoint. The music box petered out, but the doleful bell was joined by an insistently pealing one, only for the doleful one to fall by the wayside and be replaced by a clanging.

For good measure, what sounded like an organ with helium pumped through its pipes joined in, and then the doleful bell (or perhaps another one) started up again, followed by a light and joyful ringing from another direction altogether. Not even the Trabant that came rumbling down the street, smelling like a diesel tanker that's crashed into a potato warehouse, could drown it out. I thought about the American missionaries I'd met here five years before, and the look of anguish they wore as it dawned on them that post-communist Eastern Europe wasn't quite the godless wasteland their pastors back home had led them to believe. German speakers still call Pécs Fünfkirchen, or Five Churches, in honour of its pre-Magyar name of Quinque Basilicae. (Before then, the Romans knew it as Sopianae, a name which has the honour of living on as a local cigarette brand.)

Eventually, we were down to one bell and a solitary dog barking on the off beat. Then it was just the dog.

A little later, I wandered down to sit on the steps beneath the Djami's ogee arches, listening to the footstomps and claps and cries from the folk dance class on the first floor of the Nagy Lajos high school. The violins sent their notes careening and bouncing off the stone walls, the lugubrious sawing of the bass lumbering after them. Above me, the half moon shone down on the Ottomans' copper dome and cast its shadows across the façade of the Nádor Hotel, the place where my parents had first properly met nearly forty years before.

For He is an Englishman

Mum, being Mum, noticed the car first. At a time when the privileged few Hungarians who had survived the long waiting lists and had cars were either driving East German Wartburgs or Trabants, the shiny white Vauxhall stood out like a peacock in a flock of pigeons. It was parked every day across the road from the main building of the coal mine at Istvánakna where Mum was working, a glossy piece of the West that had somehow wound up in the hills behind Pécs. Unlike the Trabis, it appeared to be made of actual metal.

Filing past it with her colleagues, Mum would announce, 'Girls, one of these days I'm going to get a ride in that beautiful car.'

'You? How? You'll never even set foot in it.'

Mum, of course, knew who owned it. A team of Englishmen had turned up a while ago to do some work at the state-owned mine, but the one who had caught her eye was the one with the Vauxhall keys, the tall, dark-haired one.

'He was a good-looking guy,' Mum said, her hands floating up from her lap as she spoke, whirling around like a pair of butterflies in a tornado. 'I would smile and say hello whenever we walked past each other. I don't remember if he said anything, but he would turn as red as a traffic light.' She roared with laughter. 'Oh my God, so red. Just like a stop light. Like his skin was burning. I liked him straight away.'

It wouldn't be Dad who first asked her out. Tongue-tied and blushing, he was beaten to the punch by his colleague, Ronny.

'He was a little man with a nice smile. He was the one who had the courage to ask me out,' Mum said, adding reflectively, 'I was twenty-seven. I was still so pretty then.'

The language barrier tumbled beneath a barrage of sign language, and when it was all done, Ronny had invited Mum to dinner at the Nádor. Just a little do with the boys, maybe a couple of local girls. Dad was going, too.

It was the summer of 1969, the year after Dad was first sent to communist Hungary, which, like all communist countries, was distinguished by not actually having communism. A soggy, slipshod sort of socialism, yes, but not communism. Across the border in the Soviet Union, Khrushchev had gotten himself in all sorts of trouble just a few years before by promising such wild things as the achievement by 1980 of actual communism, as devised and/or interpreted by the three beards – Marx, Engels and Lenin. The comrades thought this most rash and ditched Khrushchev for the preternaturally dull Brezhnev. Brezhnev mightn't have been above invading his client states with tanks, but at least he never banged his shoe against any microphones at the UN. Not that I suspect any of this was particularly weighing on Dad's mind at the time. He was thirty-four, single and still getting a kick out of working in export, a job that sent him from England all around the world, from Japan and America to Australia and South Africa, and now the People's Republic of Hungary.

One of his missions this time was to install machinery in the Istvánakna colliery. In communications with Dad's employers in

England, Istvánakna's directors took a careful look at the facts and decided an approach other than the literal truth might be necessary.

'Our mine is top-notch,' is what they ultimately told the English, when what they really should have said was, 'Our mine is not good. Neither our language nor yours contains words capable of conveying just how good it is not. No one and nothing should even come near it, unless they happen to be an exceptionally big meteorite.' Or something vaguely along those lines.

The English swallowed the first version and Dad was sent east just as the Russians were busily heading in the opposite direction to show the next-door neighbours how effective Soviet tanks still were. (It was only twelve years since Stalin's heirs had to almost flatten Budapest when the natives got out of hand; now they were having to go to Prague to do the very same thing. You could almost imagine Brezhnev in the Kremlin sighing with exasperation at the pigheaded ingratitude of the socialist colonies.)

In Pécs Dad set up camp at the Nádor Hotel, which had survived János Köszl's inadvertent attempt to launch the nearby town hall into space. Like every self-respecting Westerner travelling behind the Iron Curtain, Dad was sure his room was bugged, so he made a point each night of turning to the vase of flowers on the bedside table and declaring, 'I've been a good boy today.'

It was in this frame of mind that he headed to Istvánakna, where he soon discovered just how wide a berth the facts had been given. (The day I asked Dad about it was one of the exceedingly rare occasions I heard him use the word 'shithouse'.) But it did give him the major benefit of time. He was only meant to be in Pécs for a few weeks, but the true state of Istvánakna ballooned this to seven months, more than enough time for Hungary to cast its spell on him. One night at the neighbouring Palatinus Hotel – I write this with a due sense of awe – he even set foot on a dance floor, a course of action that may gently be described as uncharacteristic.

The Nádor and the Palatinus might not have been quite the same bywords for hedonism and grand times they had been at the turn of the century, but they were still the places to gravitate to whether you were a foreigner wanting to let your hair down or a Hungarian wanting to live it up. Or indeed if you were a local looking to bag yourself a Westerner; even in 1969, Hungary wasn't one of the Soviet bloc countries where a chat with a foreigner guaranteed an awkward chat with the police.

Even with his rudimentary sign language, Ronny had made it perfectly clear which night Mum should turn up at the Nádor. In her Uranium Town flat, she dolled herself up to the nth degree and headed into town ('Oh, I dressed up, that's for sure. I had a bit of the devil in me that night'), where she found the Englishmen amid the Nádor's blaze of light and music.

'It was such a beautiful place, the Nádor. Such a shame they closed it, the stupids. It is so strange to walk past these days and see it standing in darkness.'

The Nádor has been closed for years now, nobody seems sure how many. It stands in a prime spot in Pécs, but now it is just an elegant façade on an empty shell, bickered over uselessly while rats run free in its unbroken shadows.

'I feel terrible seeing it wasted that way. But then, it was a magical place. And when the band began to play . . .' Mum glanced up toward some undefined point above us and let her hands slowly slide apart in mid-air with fingers unfurling to indicate an almost indescribable, vanished glory. Give Mum lights, music and men, and she's away.

Something happened to Dad, too. That night, he got past his blushes and became an operator, language barrier or no.

'As soon as Ronny had to go to the toilet for the first time, *zsup*! Your farder jumped straight into the seat next to me. He couldn't speak any Hungarian, and I couldn't speak any English, but he was very good at sign language. He carefully explained that Ronny had a wedding ring – he showed me that with his fingers, such elegant fingers for a miner – and then he held up his hands to show me that he did not.'

With this vital tactical manoeuvre accomplished, the group finished dinner and moved next door to the Palatinus to dance.

Dad isn't exactly a trove of information about his dazzling debut on the Palatinus floor or his impressions of Mum ('Outward going, cheerful. Happy to be seen with a handsome, intelligent man') as she shook her booty that night. But Mum gleefully recalls that she was on the receiving end of the attentions of not one but *three* Englishmen – a veritable jackpot. The other was Dad's service engineer Albert ('Good bloke. Totally diligent, totally loyal, good at his job,' says Dad at his most effusive), but he had to make way for my father, who outranked him. The Brits take the management structure thing very seriously.

'Well,' Mum said, 'I know it is very difficult to imagine it now, but your farder could dance.'

I agreed that it was indeed difficult to imagine. As part of a random exercise, I found it easier to picture a wombat at the controls of a Boeing 747.

'He was so keen on me, he threw in every dance move he knew. It must have cleaned him out because he never danced after that, but that night, he put on all the moves. And he made sure no one else danced with me, that's for sure.'

If Mum was going to keep talking like this, I was going to need some extra oxygen. My father, showing all *the moves*?

'I tell you what it was about your farder. He was kind, he was handsome and he was a gentleman, a real gentleman. Pff, it's not like Pécs was full of those. But the other thing about your farder was that for me, he was another world, a whole new different world.'

This was a surprising echo of my father. Dad has always felt drawn to those who aren't his kind, and in conversations and letters always dutifully notes a person's ethnicity as a way of praising them. ('I had coffee with Lise, who is half-Dutch, half-Indonesian, then later I ran into Steve who, as you may recall, is of *Serb* origin.' And so on.) Mum, with her jet-coloured coiffure, dark, glittering eyes, tanned skin, smattering of German and almost non-existent English, wouldn't have seemed very much like the girls back home. Plus she could dance as if the floor was burning, and Dad would have regarded this with the same sense of wonder felt by New Guinean highlanders when they first clap eyes on an aeroplane. And if the dress she was wearing was anywhere near as short as the one she would wear on her wedding day two years later, not a lot would have been left to the workings of the imagination. That she was a divorcee with two children already on her scorecard could only have added to the spice.

It was just before his thirty-fifth birthday and, after a string of relationships that had never gone all that far, Dad had met the woman he was going to marry.

For Mum it was the beginning of a chance to make up for the failure of her first marriage, and perhaps even the beginning of a way to the West, an escape route out of socialist Europe.

With next to no language in common, they slipped into a fuzzy, mutually uncomprehending love.

The Owl versus the Wizard

THE FIRST ROUND of the election was due to take place that weekend, just a couple of days after we arrived. On the Friday night, the main opposition party, Fidesz, staged a rock concert under an inflatable arch on Széchenyi Square. The whole Inner Town had been pulsating since late afternoon with 1980s stadium rock sounds fatly layered with synthesisers, thumpetty drums and long, soaring guitar solos. For this alone, I reasoned, Fidesz deserved to go down. But the incumbent prime minister, Ferenc Gyurcsány, had recently videoed himself dancing around his office to the Pointer Sisters' song 'Jump (For Your Love)', an act of homage, apparently, to the prime minister played by Hugh Grant in the movie *Love Actually*. I figured this at the very least placed him even with his opponents.

Despite the music, I wandered down. Among the Hungarian tricolours, European Union flags were fluttering from the buildings in such quantities, they looked like an insurance policy against the Russians returning. In the square, the crowd, which had already been bouncing up and down, licking ice-creams and waving orange balloons for a couple of hours, was being introduced to the members of the band. The singer who came out was a boulder-bellied man of surprisingly advanced years in leather waistcoat, tight jeans, regulation orange Fidesz T-shirt, bald head and a moustache that flowed into a set of muttonchops that looked as white, fluffy and almost as big as a pair of Pomeranians.

'Hungary!' Muttonchop shouted to the crowd while oversized Hungarian flags were helpfully waved around him. 'Europe!' On the fringes, tipsy youngsters passed beer bottles and a few snogging couples twiddled each other's rears so frantically, it was as if they were communicating in morse code. (The whole arse-grabbing thing is almost a national pastime. It looks like couples are constantly doing mutual buttock inventories. 'One, two – all present and accounted for. Oops, better start again.')

A nearby newspaper stand was plastered with a poster for a magazine whose cover had Gyurcsány and Orbán as Jedi knights, light sabres drawn beneath the imperial-looking dome of the parliament chamber. 'With whom is the Force?' it asked. In the surrounding streets, someone had stencilled their thoughts onto the walls. I'd found the police out in the rain the night before, grumbling and using a mobile phone to photograph the fiend's handiwork: Gyurcsány's and Orbán's faces side by side, accompanied by a message for voters: 'It's all the same which one you vote for, YOU'RE STILL WORKING FOR US.' (It's better in Hungarian, because it rhymes.) Some of the local Fidesz candidates' posters, meanwhile, had been enigmatically defaced with tiny stickers that simply stated 'Bicycle thief'.

'If this is how you want it,' Muttonchop sang, his larynx sounding as though it might explode at any moment. 'If this is how you want it . . .'

Churlishly, I wanted to answer, 'Not really', but then at 10 pm sharp, the concert wrapped up. There was no way a right of centre party whose motto was 'Work. Home. Family.' was going to let the show run late. A couple of metres away, a young woman in an orange

T-shirt was receiving advice from a friend: 'Of course your parrot's not coming back. It's a fucking bird.'

The pollsters were predicting Fidesz – which had run the country for a single term only to get ditched at the first opportunity – would not win. But if they did, there was the exciting prospect that István Mikola would become deputy prime minister. At a campaign rally in Pécs just before we arrived, Mikola had given birth to the quote of the campaign when he declared young, single people to be a 'self-destructive horde', who not only wore earrings and listened to techno, but were in dire need of having their yearnings for freedom restricted. This from the party started by liberal, anti-socialist, ratbag students.

Tonight's concert featured no techno.

Back at the Gulyás household, as Gabi's husband, Laci, got busy sweeping the apricot blossom petals that lay like snow in the courtyard, her brother Lolo arrived wearing an expression of impotent sourness, like a motorist who has to stand around watching while a parking inspector completes his ticket.

'Who's going to win the election?' I asked, because in Hungary you're not really meant to talk about the weather.

Lolo's expression became that of a man watching the parking inspector and his colleagues setting fire to his car.

'The communists,' he said. Because Hungarian gives every syllable a thorough airing, Lolo was able to punch out the word with more vehemence than he would have been able to in English. 'I really hope I'm wrong, but they've been busy appealing to all the pensioners and we've got plenty of those in this country. We got rid of the socialists in '89, cut them off entirely. And now here we are.' His fingers twitched around his pockets, searching for cigarettes that weren't there. There was a thumping from the floor and I noticed the family rabbit (name: Ralph) scratching himself with great vigour behind an armchair. 'It's bad enough that we're getting them back, but the fact that we're actually choosing them . . .' He trailed off for a moment. 'Anyway, we'll all know in twenty-four hours.'

'Lolo just gets fed up,' Gabi chuckled later. 'Pécs is a socialist town; they always vote red here.' She hastened to add that her family had never been communist leaning, oh no. They preferred the liberal Christian Democrat sort of thing.

Sadly for Lolo, twenty-four hours brought no greater clarity. The accursed commies pulled a few more votes than Fidesz, but not enough for victory. And of course the smaller parties had stirred up some of democracy's murk. The election was heading to a second round and the major political parties began shamelessly buttering up the minor ones with all manner of sweet talk about making beautiful coalitions together.

The stencil bandits struck again on the wall below the bishop's palace, this time accompanying Orbán's and Gyurcsány's faces with the message: 'DON'T VOTE FOR ANYONE.' Far less visibly, the Green Party resorted to tiny, plaintive stickers that begged: 'Help get us into parliament', while plugging the party as the ideal choice 'for those who don't vote for anyone because there isn't anyone to vote for'.

Against my better instincts, I picked up a copy of the *Budapest Times* for a shorthand guide to the main parties. Columnist, professional gossip distributor and rusted-on Budapest resident Erik D'Amato sounded like the sort of bloke who could have long and productive chats with Lolo. In his 'Weekly Stink' column, he opined that the Hungarian Socialist Party ought to abandon its customary red in favour of white to better reflect 'the party's long tradition of betraying Hungary to whatever foreign power may happen to be strolling by'.

Of Fidesz he wrote: 'If enacted, the party's program would do to the Hungarian economy what a kilo of pure cocaine would do to a bed-ridden grandmother. While not as crusty or bigoted as some believe or fear, party leaders have recently been heard denouncing young people for wearing nose-rings and listening to techno. Get a half-bottle of decent *pálinka* into a die-hard Fidesz head and you're bound to hear something interesting about the Jews.'

FOR MUM, my father was husband number two in a series of three. László and Eszter's father was, of course, the first. László Kruller remarried faster than Mum did, but he kept things local and wed a local girl called Rózsa, with whom he stayed for the rest of his life. Together, they had a son and called him Attila, a name which remains wildly popular in Hungary. Attila's original namesake, the Hun of raping, pillaging and conquering fame, like all his fellow Huns was not Hungarian. But there has been, in the past, a certain amount of conflation and Hungarians thought – and were happy to believe – that they were cut from the same genetic cloth as Attila's rampaging hordes. After all, when the Magyars first arrived on the European scene, they were a little unruly themselves. At least to the extent that a new prayer sprang up across the continent, the gist of which was: 'Dear God, please spare us from the arrows of the Hungarians.' It was a time of conquering and ransacking, revolutionising cavalry warfare and making a tidy sum out of being mercenaries. Hungarian historians sometimes refer to this as the 'Age of Adventures', a period generally regarded as more fun than the blighted centuries that were to follow. So it can be imagined that Hungarians weren't quite as excited as they might have been when it was decided that they weren't related to the warlike Huns at all, but to the dour and gloomy Finns. And not just the Finns, but the Estonians as well, not to mention some basically peaceful tribes wrapped in animal skins and eking out an existence in western Siberia.

The name Attila has hung on all the same, a raised finger to the historians and those bloody irritating ethnographers. Our Attila –

László and Eszter's half-brother – wore his name well (László never tired of introducing him as Attila the Hun . . . garian) and handled the barbecue with a true Attila's careful attention to raw flesh and fire. And with a name like Attila, he wasn't going to be ruffled by an election; what Attila could truly be interested in the peaceful transfer of power?

It was the day of the second round elections when Bel and I (riding in a taxi with a driver who had a brother in Brisbane and a string of ever more probing questions on the frequency of shark and/or crocodile attacks) turned up at his house near Pécs in the village-cum-suburb of Nagykozár. 'The only village in Hungary that hides its church,' Attila had explained.

The house was a canary yellow number he'd designed and built with the help of his mates and it erupted with Attila's family. His wife, Zsuzsa, flew from the front door like a small blonde cannonball, trailed by a burst of children. A few days before, when I'd called to tell her we'd arrived in Hungary, Zsuzsa gave off a squeal that almost made my mobile phone ignite. She'd been in Australia with Attila just a short time ago and she was all but vibrating with excitement that we were all together again in Hungary. Particularly as it meant she could continue her mission to kiss Leo's fuzzy little blond head bald. With her owlishly round glasses and her toothy smile, she had something of a cheery nocturnal animal about her, lavishing doses of worship on Leo while expressing her hope that we might stay in Hungary for at least a few years.

Daisy hid behind my legs with a three-year-old's shyness until the three kids, Dani, Dalma (a miniature of her mother) and Laci (a rare Magyar redhead), coaxed her out to play. I asked Attila if he was planning to vote and he chuckled and made some uncommitted noise about attending to the workings of democracy later. His pressing concern was that there was enough meat on the table (there was – picture the set of *Babe* after a napalm attack) and enough beer in the fridge (there was – enough to drown any survivors of the *Babe* napalming).

We sat at a table in the garden by the vegetable patch and the tiny swimming pool, where Attila had been trying without success to replicate the pool filters he'd meticulously studied in Australia. He was a builder and good with his hands, and his failure with this latest venture was troubling him.

'I tell people that in Australia, I saw whole shops that sell nothing but swimming pool equipment,' he mentioned over a hunk of pork. 'It amazes people here, believe me.'

Partly to prove that we could still move despite the dimensions of lunch, we set off through the exploding magnolias and blazing white apricot trees for a slow lap of Nagykozár. Attila and Zsuzsa made some mention of wanting to vote, but no polling booth was ever approached and getting ice-cream for the kids took over as the priority. Kerchiefed old women peered down from the long, shaded verandas of whitewashed peasant houses, or scurried small and bright along footpaths, past tulip-sprouting gardens and hemmed-in dogs that barked at passers-by with a singular lack of conviction.

At the most decrepit farmhouse, Daisy and I watched transfixed as a pair of turkeys abandoned their schedule to strut across the dusty yard and express their objection to our presence. A devoted fan of my gobble-gobble noises during renditions of 'Old MacDonald', Daisy thought the turkeys were magnificent. As they puffed up their feathers, their gobbles grew ever shriller and they scraped their glossy black wing feathers in the dirt as they approached the gate, eyes glaring at us from those extravagant, knobbly arrangements of red skin that make every turkey's head look like a scrotal version of Dali's melting watches.

Further up the hill, we passed Nagykozár's cemetery and I learned that in Hungary, the favoured and more economically responsible course of action when your spouse leaves this earth is to get his'n'hers tombstones done together, rather than all that mucking about with waiting for mortality to do its bit. Looking around the cemetery, it seemed that it was nearly always the husband who went first, often by quite a few years. Sometimes just his name was put on the tombstone, sometimes a photo as well, along with a few chiselled sentiments ('Beloved husband, father and grandfather' etc) and his arrival and departure dates. Move across the tombstone a bit and there's the woman's name, along with the photo, the same stale description ('Beloved wife, mother and grandmother' and so on) and the birth date. All that's missing is the year of death (largely on the grounds that she's still breathing), but that space has strategically been left blank for when the time comes.

'Just imagine it,' Attila said. 'Every time she comes here to lay flowers, she's staring at her own grave. I can't say I like it all that much; it's a terrible tradition.'

Zsuzsa agreed then looked at me and gave me a pat on the belly.

'Still got room in there for some cake?' she asked.

'I've never heard James say no,' Bel said.

'Weren't you going to vote?'

'Ah,' Attila chuckled with a dismissive wave of the hand. 'Pfff.'

To Lolo's disgust but lack of surprise, the socialists won in the end. If only he'd known there'd be anti-government riots by the end of the year, he might have managed a smile.

The International Language

Love caught Dad unawares. 'I have no situation with which to compare it. I'd never reached that stage in a relationship before. I think six months was my limit. And that was exceptional, too. I tended to lose interest and it would show, and that would be that.'

Perhaps I shouldn't be surprised my parents fell in love when they did – Dad was already in the habit of talking to vases, so nothing he did should have surprised anyone. And besides, the summer of 1969 was a time when humans were defying expectations: Dad set foot on a dance floor and Neil Armstrong set foot on the moon. Not that Dad got to watch as Armstrong planted his tentative boot in the lunar dust; he was stuck in a waiting room while the Istvánakna directors huddled around a television on the other side of a locked door, watching with dismay as Uncle Sam overtook the eternal and fraternal comrades in the space race with that one small step.

In photos taken around that time, my sister Eszter looks so girlish and yet so precocious, even though she was yet to escape the tyranny of the bowl haircuts that Mum so remorselessly gave her. Almost every picture shows an impish, knowing face peering out from beneath a severe helmet of hair. László was scarcely more than a year younger, but he looks infinitely more childlike, invariably captured on film with either a smear of chocolate on his face or a booger perched inside a nostril with unsettling prominence. His name was usually shortened to Laci (pronounced Lotsy) or the ever so slightly Anglicised Lac, which comes out sounding like Lats.

Dad maintains it was never an issue for him that his exotic girlfriend had a seven-year-old daughter and a six-year-old son. As Mum and Dad's courtship progressed, Eszt and Lac began joining them on excursions. The first one was to Orfű, an artificial lake in one of the lovelier valleys in the Mecsek Hills. The road there is a convoluted, twisting one, and Eszter, being used to neither cars nor bends, responded by vomiting all over the inside of the Vauxhall. Laci was fine until later, when he fell in the lake. Love went on.

Somewhere between romance and puke and man's conquest of space, Dad was still obliged to meet the myriad bureaucratic requirements for staying on in the Hungarian People's Republic. The main one was visa renewal, a task which usually required a few hours, some routine questions from a visibly bored Hungarian official and the soft, inevitable thud of rubber stamp against passport paper. The routine changed only once. Dad was kept in a waiting room for the best part of a day, staring at a sign ordering 'Visit Hungary' in German. Eventually, a door creaked open and instead of one of the usual selection of uninterested Magyars, the true power of Hungary emerged – a Soviet officer in a dull olive uniform. He motioned for Dad to step inside.

'Do take a seat, Mr Jeffrey.' It was all so terribly, surprisingly urbane, almost charming. Except for some of the words. 'I would be happy if you would answer a few questions for me. What I would like you to tell us is this: why you are really here in Hungary.'

Dad felt prepared after his many chats with hotel vases. 'Because,' he said, 'you invited me here to commission equipment at Istvánakna colliery.'

The Russian seemed greatly taken with this answer and enthusiastically recorded it in Cyrillic letters before moving on to the next question.

'Who do you see?'

Sitting beneath Lenin's plaster of Paris gaze, Dad decided it might be prudent to play it straight and listed the names and titles of a host of mine officers and managers whom he dealt with in his official business. Everything was duly noted with a furiously scratching pen.

'And tell me, Mr Jeffrey, where else do you go in Hungary?'

The Russian was soon listing the names of mines, while possibly suppressing a shudder at the paucity of Dad's social life. Or maybe he was impressed by his apparently single-minded devotion to socialist labour. If only he'd known Dad would soon be planning to whisk away three of the Empire's subjects to the West.

'Who do you see at these mines?'

More names, more scratching.

'Thank you, Mr Jeffrey. Now I would like to go through all this again with you.'

Days later, Dad ran into one of the Hungarian mine staff on Széchenyi Square. The man was looking cheery. 'A good report on you has gone through to Budapest,' he announced, adding a little more furtively that he knew this because his brother was in the police.

Dad never was sure whether it was his chat with the Russian or the vases that got him over the line.

Paperwork moved at different speeds in Hungary. Approval to stay in the country was one thing, approval to marry one of the natives quite another. This became an issue when Dad, rather daringly, popped the question and Mum, just as daringly, said yes.

Dad told me it all happened in the Vauxhall – which would have pleased Mum – somewhere on the road south from Budapest to Pécs. He pulled out a ring he'd chosen back in Derbyshire with the help of his mother ('I wasn't an expert in these matters') and asked Mum if she'd do him the tremendous honour and so forth of becoming his wife.

I asked Dad if he stopped the car.

'I don't remember,' he replied after some thought. 'I suppose logically I would have.'

'No,' Mum said firmly. 'That is not what happened. I gave your farder an ultimatum. I told him, when you come back from England, I want to see an engagement ring or it is finished. Finished! Goodnight Charlie. So I went up to Budapest, to Ferihegy airport, to wait for him the next time he came back from England.' Long drag on the cigarette. 'He came out, all happy, friendly, full of smiles, and I say to him, so, where is the ring? Huh, where is it then? His smile disappeared and he told me he had forgotten it. I told him that is bullshit. Bullshit!' Mum said bullshit in English; somehow its Hungarian equivalent, *bika szar*, just doesn't ring true. 'I bet it was his mother. The old lady wasn't thrilled her only son wanted to marry a Hungarian divorcee, especially one from a poor family.' Another long drag. '"You said you would bring me a ring, and you come here with empty hands." That's what I said to him. So I told him to go away, it was finished, I would not see him any more.'

Eventually it was decided that Dad could have a second chance, but it would be for the best if he brought a ring next time around.

'So he borrowed one of my mother's rings so he would get the right size, and eventually he went back to England. Again, I went up to Pest and waited for him. Again, he came off the plane, grinning like a monkey that's just found all the bananas. But this time, he pulled out a little box. Oh yes, I said to him, that's a very nice box – what's in it? And he opened it up and there inside was the most beautiful diamond ring. My God! Diamonds! We never saw my mother's ring again, but what can you do. She asked me, what about my ring? When can I have that back? Who knows. But those diamonds, *jaj*, they were lovely.' Mum was fond of *jaj*, a useful exclamation that could convey everything from wonder and joy to awe and extreme dismay. She lowered the glowing tip of the cigarette and twisted it against the bottom of the ashtray, before reaching down for another. She wasn't smoking regular cigarettes any more; she was buying pre-rolled paper tubes, stuffing tobacco in one end and a filter in the other. 'A beautiful ring,' she sighed with a thin wisp of blue. 'I still have it.'

They celebrated in some Budapest club that night, one of those fine establishments that provides for its guests an elegant backdrop of slowly disrobing young women. Mum snorted smoke at the memory.

'Your farder was too embarrassed to look. He held his hand up to the side of his face and looked down. *Jaj*, it was too much for him.'

The authorities in Pécs eventually gave the go-ahead for my parents to get married. While some of the local miners ribbed Dad about foreigners snaffling all the best local women, his mother and sister, Elizabeth, flew out from England for the big day. Then the authorities turned around and told Dad that it turned out he didn't have all the necessary permits and sundry other bits of paperwork. It would be another month at least before he could get hitched. Dad didn't take the news especially well, but soon learned that raging against something as big and inert as the bureaucratic labyrinth of the People's Republic was energy wasted.

'It's no use complaining, Mr Jeffrey. These laws were in place long before you came here.'

My grandmother and aunt played tourist for a few days then headed back to Derbyshire, never to return.

A month later, Dad was better schooled in what to do. He was taken to the office of the mayor, who greeted him jovially.

'Ah, Mr Jeffrey, I have something in my drawer for you.' The mayor pulled out the official marriage approval and Dad thanked him the proper way, accidentally leaving behind a bottle of black label Scotch.

It was a rainy, windy midsummer day when my parents were finally married. Dad awoke in the Nádor Hotel with a clear head ('I didn't have a stag night as far as I recall. It wasn't the sort of thing I was interested in. I thought stag nights were a pretty silly pastime.') and put on his best suit.

He collected Mum in her minimalist wedding dress and they drove off in the Vauxhall to the town hall for the officially recognised part of their wedding, and then down to the Reformation Church that rises near the train station like a brown and white missile. The ceremony was conducted by Father Lajos, a possibly tone-deaf minister with a dark bouffant, moustache and black, pleated Calvinist garb that left him looking a cross between Batman and an accordion. (I would be the only one of Mum's children who didn't get baptised by him, scoring instead a pale-to-the-point-of-translucency Anglican vicar at a church perched on a windswept Lancashire hill.)

'God Himself,' Father Lajos declared, 'has sent this man across Europe to marry this lady.' And it was done. With the dual blessing of Lenin and the Lord, Mum and Dad were wed.

(Father Lajos is still there, albeit with the black departed from the bouffant. Bel and I sat mesmerised through one of his sermons in which, after christening our goddaughter Evelin, he put a group of youngsters through confirmation with some vital life advice: 'And as you walk through parks, do not bring shame to your parents by tipping over bins or writing on the benches . . .')

My parents' memories of the rest of the day are vague. The wedding party eventually trooped off to Uranium Town where they shoehorned themselves inside my grandparents' tiny flat. Nagyi was able to indulge her passion for feeding the masses, presiding over a cauldron of chicken soup. That would have been just the entrée, doled out in mighty portions that would have looked like steaming lakes almost big enough to be divided into separate time zones. No one can remember what she served for mains – something cooked with the aid of dollops of pig fat and a mesmerising dose of paprika, no doubt – but if anyone suggested they were full after the massive soup, she would have given them short shrift and an extra large helping, just to teach them a lesson. 'I won't have you wasting away here in my home. Eat!' And while she directed the action, Nagypapa would have been smiling gently to himself. He couldn't speak with his new son-in-law, but he was already growing fond of him.

Swine Buffs

'AND IT'S A LOVELY day here in Budapest. The sun is shining straight through the ladies' skirts. God be praised!' There is something cheeringly un-PC about Hungarian radio. With half an ear listening to the two DJs as they merrily buffooned their way through the morning, I swung open the wooden shutters and noted that the sun's rays had made it all the way south to Pécs as well.

I eventually set out after lunch, unsuccessfully resisting the urge to sing as I wandered streets that cut their slender way between cherry trees and buildings that looked as though they'd either just been delivered fresh from the patisserie or accidentally left to go stale in the sunshine, crumbling icing on the pavements. I passed between the Children's Home and the County Jail (or Punishment Institute, as they prefer to term it these days), a fat Vienna slice of a Habsburg edifice with stout grilles over its otherwise ornate windows. Some days, conversation of varying degrees of saltiness flew through the air between the two buildings. Other days it was just someone shouting out over and over again trying to get somebody's attention. Today, a woman was standing on the street, leaning against the wall of the Children's Home with two boys, one in his late teens, the other maybe twelve.

'Who's calling me a whore?' she called up to one of the cell windows.

'No one's calling you that, my heart,' answered a good-humoured voice from the darkness behind the bars.

'I'm not a whore. I just took his money.'

There was an outbreak of giggling from the Children's Home. The man continued, but by then I was too far up the street to make out what he was saying, though I heard her reply.

'It's okay,' she said in a comforting tone. 'No one saw anything. And besides, you were hungry.'

I passed through the city wall and started up Tettye utca (or street), passing a place that, rather eclectically, doubled as a car tyre shop and a beauty parlour for dogs. ('Gumi Szervisz & Kutya Kozmetika', the sign proclaimed.) Among the steeply sloping streets remained a few semi-fossilised street signs with the old spelling of *utcza*, more than a century after the Hungarian Academy of Sciences officially decreed the 'z' obsolete. A playground was bursting with families and flowers and prams and ice-creams and soccer balls and floppy-tongued dogs and tuft-eared squirrels and magnolias as big as cats' heads, grandly deploying their pink and white petals. There was also a lot of merry shrieking; this may have had something to do with the fact that Hungarian councils have not yet been terrified by thoughts of lawsuits into making their playgrounds as safe and exciting as a Volvo. Above me stood the ruins of a bishop's palace, now a popular venue for concerts and weddings. (Daisy would watch enraptured one weekend as a bride emerged from the crumbling walls, convinced she was watching a princess in a castle. As she learned fragments of Hungary's rough and tumble history, she deduced that women got married in castles, only for their husbands to be killed by invading armies, who would then proceed to kidnap the bride. 'I will protect the princesses from the armies by making thicker curtains for their castles,' Daisy announced after much thought.)

Past the squealing children and the ruins, a trio of old women encrusted a park bench and tut-tutted about the workings of the world.

'And I said to young Erzsi, why do you stay with him?'

'Me, too,' another nodded.

'Not for the money, that's for sure.'

Then I was in the woods among carpets of daisies and violets and great salvos of erupting shoots and detonating buds, freed from the dead weight of winter. Sleek, dun-coloured skinks slipped liquidly among the rocks and mossy stumps. Birds tinkled like music boxes and every now and then a bumblebee, sporting a dandelion-yellow sash around its ample, fuzz-cloaked girth, droned past my ear like an airborne Trabant, floating over fungus-frilled logs and ravishing the flowers.

I skirted the zoo and its assortment of fairy-floss scoffing children and moulting camels, threading my way down through the moneyed villas of the Mecsek to the Kikelet Hotel. The terrace was empty, leaving me alone with views across the spires and domes of Pécs's Inner Town, and the more distant communist-era suburbs of Uranium Town and Kertváros (Garden Town), which stood in great marches of prefabricated concrete and looked like spare parts for the Death Star. Beyond them spread a string of lakes glistening in the afternoon sun, and hills rippled toward nearby Croatia. A trio of waistcoated waiters was loitering and gossiping at reception. A roundish one with owl-like eyes broke from the group and ushered me to a table in the sunshine, where I privately reflected on the fact that what I'd just done counted as exercise. There was only one thing for it.

'A pint of beer, please.'

'We only have it in bottles, unfortunately.'

'A bottle would be perfectly fine.'

'Very good. Would you like a foreign beer, or a Hungarian one?'

I said Hungarian. Mild surprise flickered across his face, but he quickly recomposed himself and stiffened professionally.

I ducked off to the lav, and when I returned the table had been set with a crisp and immaculately white cloth, a glass and a tall, brown bottle. When the waiter brought out the bill later, he asked if I'd liked the beer. My yes produced the ghost of a smile on his lips.

Thunder rumbled across the plain ahead of a murky curtain of rain that crept across the villages and yellowing fields of canola, edging closer to one of the most pointless buildings in Hungary.

We drove past it the following morning on our way to meet the real estate agent who'd taken on the job of finding us a home. Bel was unable to suppress a chuckle at the sight of its blue, white and black mass unsympathetically rising above its cowering neighbours like a colossal licorice allsort.

'I was wondering if it might have just been the exaggeration of memory, but no, it's every bit as hideous as I remember it,' Bel said.

'I see you're familiar with our great architectural masterpiece,' the taxi driver observed sardonically. It was built in the late 1980s in a big hurry with the mystifying aim of helping Pécs – the city of museums, universities, wine and culture – wrest the honour of being home to regional Hungary's biggest building. Mind-bogglingly out of scale with the rest of Pécs – even some of the more gruesome bits added by the Communist regime – the licorice block contains more than two hundred apartments that house about eight hundred people, or at least did until those responsible realised that in their haste they had built a giant death trap that might collapse at any moment. All the residents were hastily evacuated and the building has since stood empty, lightless and, apart from the hundreds of appreciative pigeons, lifeless. Bel and I used to gaze at its bleak silhouette on moonlit nights; it felt weird standing in the thick of a living city and staring at such a thoroughly dead building. But it's still the biggest in regional Hungary.

'There really is a lot of stupidity in the way things are run here – it's all political,' the driver said. 'Now they can't make up their minds whether they're going to tear the bloody thing down or turn it into accommodation for students.'

We met the real estate agent in a hillside suburb. She teetered out of her sports car with improbable nails and a pair of flimsy-looking heels and showed us through a house that not only came with a grand piano and views over a valley and the forested slopes of the Mecsek, it even had a fire pit in the back garden, complete with a metal hook for hanging a goulash cauldron.

'It's lovely,' Bel said. 'But it would take us forever to get into town from here.'

'You can get a bus into Uranium Town, then change for another into town,' the agent suggested.

'With Daze and Leo, that will definitely take forever.'

So we looked at a flat that cost more than the house. 'There's something just a bit too . . . German about it,' Bel concluded. We hit the jackpot with the third place, an apartment in the Inner Town with a living room as big as an oval and a view that stretched from the carved face of Apollo on the converted cinema next door to the thrusting roof of the National Theatre, capped by a sculpted figure that Daisy insisted on dubbing the Dancing Man, despite its impressive bust.

We'd barely moved in when Bel's childhood friend Ruth arrived on a flying visit. Hoping to help Ruth overcome her disappointment that the rest of the world seemed so unexotic after Tokyo, which she'd just visited for the first time, Bel took her to the theatre under the Dancing Man for a performance of Strauss's *Die Fledermaus*. Critically, I volunteered to stay home with the kids.

Some moments in life are marked by what you just missed seeing. I still lose sleep over a moment in the Galapagos Islands when I looked away just seconds before a fat marine iguana that had been perched on a blowhole got blasted into the air and dumped into the sea. A moment that nearly matched it in terms of emotional catastrophe was when Bel came running up from the theatre during an interval that evening.

'You should have been there,' she panted. 'Oh how I wish you'd been there.' She went on to explain that during one of the dancing scenes, there was a loud rip from one of the male dancers and some tittering from the front few rows.

'I thought he'd farted, but he'd actually ripped his pants,' Bel said in between attempts to catch her breath. 'And he didn't have any undies on. He just kept on dancing with his bollocks on display the whole time.' Then she was racing down the stairs again, ever keen to perform her duty as a patron of the arts. It suddenly seemed appropriate that the Hungarian word for theatre is *színház*, which sounds like sin house. When she and Ruth returned late in the night, their critical assessment of the final act was concise.

'There were no more flying bollocks,' Bel said as they trooped through the kitchen.

'Major disappointment,' Ruth said. 'We could have done with an encore. It was just big, hairy sack right there in front of us in the spotlight. The applause at the end was stupendous.' She didn't seem to mind not being in Tokyo so much now.

'And the diva had no idea about the bollocks,' Bel said. 'The crowd went mad and she thought it was for her.'

Of course they went mad; Hungarians applaud flesh in all its forms. My favourite line in Lonely Planet's guide to Hungary was, until it was eventually edited out, an overheard snippet of a waiter berating some hapless backpacker thus: 'If you don't want meat, go to Romania!'

Last time we were in Hungary, we were visited by a string of friends who'd moved to London and turned vegetarian, partly for ethical reasons, partly because they were living in a country where meat was both comically expensive and potentially lethal. In Hungary, though, vegetarianism was something you resorted to because you'd either just had a world war and that had completely buggered things up, or the Russians had taken all the meat, which completely buggered things up. But voluntarily turning your back on it?

Occasionally, away from the restaurants that would cling to the happy belief that something like a carp – with its eyes, mouth, brain, backbone and fully developed nervous system – was a form of vegetable, we would find places with more likely offerings. After double-checking whether, say, the bean soup was safe for vegetarians and eliciting a wounded reply from the waiter in the process, we would order away, only for the bean soup to yield a significant segment of pig at the first prod of the spoon to surface like a purple submarine.

'But that is just for flavour,' the waiter would explain when summoned. 'Your friends don't actually have to eat it.'

It had become simpler in the five years since, but only up to a point. As we walked down to the market and took in the fragrant curtains of salami, the pigs' heads staring blankly from atop piles of trotters, the sizzle of blood sausages being lowered into hissing slicks of swine fat and the dull thwack of live carp and perch being subdued for the shopping bag, Bel and I figured Hungary would probably remain relatively tofu-free for a while yet. The Iron Curtain might have vanished, but the Pork Curtain was safely intact.

Saturday was when the market was at its busiest, and it was also the day of matriarchal rule. We passed a sign where *füstölt sertés láb* (smoked pigs' feet) had appositely been shortened to 'f.láb', skirted the so-called tourist salami, the tubs of pig fat and the Mangalica sausage (the end of the road for pigs with coats as woolly as sheep's) and emerged into a throng of old women. Whichever way we looked – across the mounds of garlic and tomatoes, wild mushrooms picked in the Mecsek Hills and carrots still flecked with dirt – bobbed a sea of headscarves. Round and wrinkled dolls in aprons and kerchiefs, few of whom would have come up to my shoulders, chatted away through mouths no longer fully populated with teeth, the light glinting off spectacle lenses scarcely any thinner or smaller than a 1950s television screen. Wherever I glanced, I saw reminders of my grandmother and I had to fight the urge to leap across produce-laden trestle tables to kiss the plump and ruddy cheeks. This was probably just as well, as I'm sure most of the matriarchs would have decked me.

The only one I didn't want to smooch was an almost mummified-looking crone selling flowers. Clutching a freshly purchased bunch of white and purple blooms, I asked her what it was I'd just bought. She rolled her eyes back into her kerchiefed head, bared a few well-spaced yellow teeth and, in the pained voice of one who felt she made nowhere near enough money to have to make conversation with idiots, answered, 'Lilacs'. The man next to her shook his head slightly, muttered 'My God,' and shuffled off for a smoke.

Then we ran into Joli, and she immediately pressed a lipstick-red paprika on us.

'Never mind the marks on the outside,' she urged while stuffing it into our already swollen bag. 'It's Spanish paprika and it tastes wonderful. Buy them from the blonde woman over there – yes, the one with the kerchief and glasses. She's got the cheapest stuff in the whole market. Oh, let me look at Leo. *Jaj, jaj!* He's so beautiful. He has it better than all of us, doesn't he? Full belly and fast asleep, *hu ha*. Hello, Daisy. Yes, my angel, you're beautiful, too. Yes, yes, so very cute. Do you like shopping here? So much better than going to Interspar. Everything's cheaper, everything's fresher (Annabel, don't leave your purse sticking out like that; this place is full of thieves) and it's more interesting wandering around here and looking at all the people than being stuck under that fluorescent light. (It's such a big, red one, Annabel; it's an invitation to the pickpockets.) I hear you're going to the car market tomorrow, though I don't know where you're going to drive. You say the Great Plain, but most of that's still under water. Oh, the poor people. And what happens when the flood recedes? All those potatoes drowned in the earth. God knows where we're going to get our food from. Be very, very careful at the car market. There are thieves everywhere so guard your money. Don't buy anything Russian or Romanian, make sure the engine works and have a look on the information board to see whether or not you're buying stolen property. Yes! It happens *all* the time. Those rascals just steal the cars and, *piff poof*, they sell them to innocent people like you at the market – and you end up with nothing. *Nothing!* And don't go to Attila's afterwards. It's no good for us if you only turn up for lunch at two o'clock – we can't start eating until you turn up. Okay then, I'd better be going. Make sure you don't leave Daisy behind at the market when you go. Are you all eating properly? All right, I kiss you all and we'll meet tomorrow. Oh, and Jimmy, I know you still want to go walking about in that forest; just don't forget what I told you about the gypsies. Bye bye, bye bye, yes, I love you Daisy, bye bye. Hello.' Then she went.

Gerald Durrell once wrote about the silence when great music ends. This was similar. Conversations with Joli – or, rather, from Joli – often left you with an urge to start clapping the moment you regained your senses. But it was too late; she had already vanished into the teeming kerchiefs and the noise of the market slowly filled our ears once more. Somewhere in the background, I heard the wet thwack of another carp being readied for the shopping bag.

•

I FOUND A CAFÉ near our flat on the lately pedestrianised shopping strip of Király utca, or King Street, that distinguished itself from the bulk of Pécs's coffeehouses by serving nice coffee, a development that managed to be welcome and alarming in equal measure. A decent latte surely meant the end of Pécs, as we knew it, was approaching. The café was also a prime people-watching spot, as I discovered the first time I went there. As I sat at my outdoor table, sipping my coffee, my eardrums pummelled by the bells in the nearby church and the chatter of clumps of students filing into the neighbouring seminary-cum-high-school, a man in a decomposing relic of a jumper walked past with a fossilised television set strapped into a tiny pushchair, carefully navigating his way around a group of shouting gypsies. Another gypsy, in a denim jacket and sporting a slot-like crease on his left temple that made him look like a money box, approached a nearby table and began to ask for something. He was barely seconds into his spiel when a tiny, tracksuited woman, possibly his wife, grabbed him by the shoulder and started berating him with great zeal.

'How many times do I have to tell you not to bother these people? Huh? How many times?'

His whole body slackened as if all his tendons had been cut and he muttered something as they walked away, but she was having none of it and kept roaring as they moved off toward Színház Square. 'Just remember what I told you at the train station. My God.'

Some days, the café seemed to exert a magnetic effect on derelicts, drifters and other human flotsam. They came to stand and briefly stare, lips slowly moving and releasing half-formed sounds and embryonic words, before stumbling on their way. Others would loiter for a bit of a chat. One morning, a man with a face like a bearded saddle stood nearby, anchoring himself to a lamp post with one hand and smiling indulgently while Daisy blethered on in her sing-song voice about how her dollies had scratched their knees and gotten sick, and how she'd made them better.

'Oh, she's so pretty, so cute. *Jaj, de szép, de aranyos,*' he beamed. *Aranyos* literally means gold-like. 'How I wish I'd had a daughter. Oh, it tears my heart that I never had one.' And with that he let go of the lamp post and floated off toward where the pavers of Király utca finally turned to bitumen and dissipated into the suburbs.

Sometimes things would take a surprisingly formal turn. That same afternoon, another tramp materialised, his face ingrained with dirt. A pair of brown, calloused hands pushed a trolley piled with sheets of cardboard, a jumble of boxes and a batch of carefully tied plastic bags.

'Excuse me, sir,' he boomed. 'But would you be so kind as to tell me . . .' he raised a glass shaker to the sunlight, '. . . what is in this?'

'Sugar,' I said.

'Sugar? *This?*' He stared at the shaker, lines spreading across his grimy forehead.

'Raw sugar.'

'Interesting,' he nodded slowly, appraising the beige crystals. 'Very interesting. May I taste it, please?'

I wondered if I should at that point mention that this wasn't my café, but decided against it. 'Go ahead,' I said and he poured some into his hand, admired it for a moment then licked it up. Apparently pleased with the result, he moved on to the white.

'I believe this is sugar also. I would be happy if you were to permit me to taste it, too.'

The old ladies sitting at the next table with their espressos and bubbling mineral waters had until this moment been rigid with apprehension and, judging by their faces, a touch of distaste, as if a dissolute relative had turned up uninvited at a family christening and slurped water from the font. But now they relaxed as they found themselves able to settle into a familiar role.

'Taste it,' they urged him. 'Eat it, go on, eat it, eat it.'

'Thank you kindly,' he murmured, then swiped the little white heap with his tongue. 'It does wonders for my throat.' And with a bow of the head, he reattached himself to his trolley and trundled off.

Sometimes these encounters were entirely without words. One afternoon just outside Pécs, I took Leo on an excursion from the restaurant where we'd ordered lunch – to give everyone a break from his latest bout of noisy disgruntlement. We ambled along the road from the wine village of Villány-kövesd to its sister village of Villány which, sadly, is not pronounced the Villainy. The road that ran between the two rumbled and creaked with tractors hauling redundant farming equipment, Skodas of varying vintages, Trabants that all looked the same no matter when they were built, the odd BMW thumping with techno, old women in sensible leggings on bicycles and a slow, sporadic procession of carts pulled by horses negotiating the bitumen with their heads bowed and a clatter of hooves.

Leo and I turned up the road to the hamlet of Kisjákabfalva. Behind us, the afternoon light spread across tight ranks of grapevines stretching steeply up the hillside to the tiny press houses and beyond to a copse of trees perched at the top like a bedraggled toupee. Ahead, the forest enclosed the narrow road in bottle green. Constellations of brilliant white daisies and purple ranks of nettle blossom spilled from the ditches in a tide of colour, washing through the woods where soft beams of buttery light slanted through the trunks and the still thickening canopy.

Leo lay in my arms staring all about him, offering coos and the odd contented gurgle as the birds tinkled and piped. As we walked, a figure floated silently from a forest trail onto the road ahead of us. But for a faded khaki jacket and trousers so ancient they were more fray than fabric, he looked strangely like Rasputin, a long, dark, tapering fang of beard thrusting down from a face studded with eyes shining as coolly as a pair of Venuses in the dusk sky.

They met mine in a moment of silence and surprise that reminded me of coming face to face with a deer as it crosses a forest path. Then Rasputin melted back into the woods and a tractor came rumbling and snorting past, neatly breaking the spell.

'Agoo,' Leo observed at length and we headed back toward the restaurant where the others were waiting with a feast of well-cooked flesh.

BACK IN AUSTRALIA, my parents were gearing up for their Hungarian odysseys in their own very different ways.

'Your farder is speaking to me,' Mum shouted down the phone, keeping it loud on the off-chance the line went down and she had to make herself heard from Australia. 'Yes, it's true. A miracle! He is calling me whenever he hears from you. He wants to make reports to me like a policeman.'

I made the mistake of telling her that Dad was getting cold feet about the trip, even though he already had a ticket. Mum took this as a challenge.

'I talked to your farder. I told him a thing or two,' she informed me during our next call (through a mouthful of what later proved to be cheese jaffle). My heart sank. 'I told him, don't be silly.' In Hungarian, this sounds like shoe-shoe. 'Don't you think about not going. Who else is going to ask you? This is your last chance! *Ja*, I told him good.'

If anything was going to prompt Dad to build a bonfire in the backyard and toss his passport and suitcase onto it, it was instructions from Mum. I hoped she didn't call him when she was in the midst of a cheese jaffle.

'What did he say?' I heard the words limp out of my mouth.

'Nothing. He just muttered something. I didn't understand what he said. It was a growl like an old dog's.'

Well, that had done it.

But when I talked to Dad again, he was sounding chipper about the trip. There was no question any more; perhaps he just wanted to avoid a sequel to his conversation with Mum.

Mum, meanwhile, was bursting to come. A combination of homesickness and pangs for her absent grandchildren had possessed her with a junkie's single-mindedness. There was a slight but exciting danger her visit would overlap with Dad's.

To the Goose Fatmobile

Despite the legend of the Vauxhall, there were so many reasons to not drive in Hungary. Petrol, in true European style, is expensive, almost to the point where it would make more economical sense to run your car on cognac, while public transport is cheap and, for the large part, pretty good. Give or take. Then there are the roads which, to a large extent, suck. Give or take. They're cracked and rutted and in some places feature so many holes it's hard not to wonder whether or not they doubled as firing ranges for the Hungarian army in the very recent past. ('Sounds like one part of Hungary hasn't changed since my time then,' Dad commented on the phone. 'I once had some new tyres sent over from England, had them fitted to the Vauxhall and set off for Balaton with some colleagues to celebrate. We punctured three on the way.')

In between dodging potholes (some of which you could fall into and possibly not be seen again for days), your reflexes are further honed by an obstacle course of horse-drawn carts, lumbering tractors, the occasional drunken cyclist, and a host of miscellaneous and not readily identifiable farming vehicles.

As a bonus, the roads seem to have been meticulously designed to not drain when the heavens open up, so driving in anything more than a light shower involves an awful lot of spray, terror and a heightened awareness of just how powerless you are over your own destiny, which is also how survivors describe going over Niagara Falls in a barrel.

This is perhaps one reason why German tourists get stuck in the Australian outback and Hungarians don't. Germans are used to good roads, but for Hungarians, even the Tanami Desert would be child's play compared to, say, Route 66 to Kaposvár in a thunderstorm.

But the main reason to not drive in Hungary is that Hungarian motorists are maniacs. Not maniacs in the overtly macho way of Italians or the ramshackle and apparently-unaware-of-the-concept-of-death way of Russians, but they are maniacs nonetheless, driving the way you'd expect of the populace of a country routinely in the top five for suicide statistics. Even quite sensible Magyars can be transformed by the feel of a steering wheel in their hands, almost as if possessed by some ancestral memory of horse reins and longbows. Worse yet, some surge into the traffic and proceed to drive as if they've just been watching *Top Gun* and are keen to try out some of the moves without having to go to all the effort of joining an air force. They tailgate so closely that the space between the bumper bars is scarcely wider than a theoretical particle, then turn wildly from outside lanes as an afterthought, oncoming bus or no. And speed limits are viewed as nothing less than a personal insult that can only be properly responded to by becoming the first person to break the sound barrier in, say, a Fiat Bravo.

Added to this exciting cocktail is the passion for overtaking on blind bends and crests, which means that wherever you drive there's always a possibility that you're going to be suddenly faced with two cars side by side coming straight at you. Apparent motto: Don't change lanes till you see the whites of their eyes. (This is what happened to Pécs's mayor, László Toller, as he headed home one bright June afternoon. His chauffeur swerved to dodge the oncoming vehicles and ended up flipping the one he was driving, mortally injuring himself and leaving his boss with major and permanent brain damage. The following afternoon, with ink on the newspaper stories about the accident barely dry, everyone around Pécs was driving as per usual.)

I used to think Croatians were worse – there's something about the image of big trucks overtaking buses just before hairpin bends on two-lane roads cut into near vertical mountainsides that can't be purged from your brain no matter how hard you try – but I eventually realised that it's topography and not mentality that gives Croats the edge. It's only because Hungary suffers something of a shortage in the hill, mountain and perilous ravine department that the Hungarians don't slaughter themselves on the road in bigger numbers. But you know they would if they could.

I remember the exact moment my terror of Hungarian driving began – it was the first time I got in a car with my cousin Andris, Joli's son. I should have paid more attention to the peculiar gleam in his eye as he turned the key in the ignition; it was a borrowed car and I just put it down to natural excitement. There was nothing natural about what went through my head during the next couple of hours as we hurtled into the Mecsek, swooped around the edge of Lake Orfű like a space probe using the gravity of a planet to slingshot itself deeper into space, then, once the headlights were pointed roughly in the direction of Lake Balaton, engaged warp drive. Andris kept up a terse running commentary for my benefit as we accelerated toward hairpin bends and overtook various vehicles without anything as namby-pamby as a clear line of sight to help us. I could have reached out and traced my final words on the dusty flanks of any number of trucks as we zoomed past them with roughly six inches clearance.

I doubt Balaton ever looked as beautiful to anyone as it did to me a little later that afternoon as I climbed from the car, surprised to find I hadn't left any fingernails embedded in the passenger seat. But there was time for that yet; we still had the drive home. This came with the added excitement of darkness, torrential rain, thunder, lightning and a tape of country music that Andris had discovered in the glovebox. As a concession to the conditions, Andris dropped his speed by about five kilometres an hour and we sliced and fishtailed across southern Transdanubia to twanging guitars and the sort of thunder that made me suspect the end of the entire world – and not just my own life – was nigh. The whole time, frogs of surprising dimensions leaped about in the downpour in ecstasy, their spindly limbs spotlit in our headlights as they arced through the air. What twats, they probably thought to themselves as they watched us pass.

The rain did finally ease at Kaposvár and we paused so Andris could have a cigarette. As I contemplated taking up smoking myself, Andris mentioned that he'd done his national service nearby, stationed at a barracks built at a careful distance from the Soviet barracks. Fraternal and eternal comrades they may have been, but the Magyars and the Russkies apparently had a terrible habit of picking fights with each other.

Before he'd gone off to serve his time, Andris made the mistake of sharing with Joli his plan to visit us in Australia, then hide out in the desert to avoid joining the army. There was an emergency council convened between the Hungarian and Australian chapters of the family and it was decided that Andris wouldn't be going to Australia any time soon.

In the end, he said, the eighteen months in uniform passed quickly, if not quite quickly enough. If he's sore about anything, it's that he didn't get to Australia.

These days, there's no national service and no Soviet troops. Just before they left in their great, eastbound convoys, the comrades smashed everything at their barracks – right down to the last handbasin – as a final thank you to their less than willing hosts.

As we drove on, Andris pointed out a black mass of trees where anti-NATO radar stations had been tucked away. This distracted me momentarily from thoughts of imminent death, but then Andris hit his stride again. It should be noted that his driving has calmed down since he became a family man and bought his own car, but at the time, as I finally stood trembling faintly beneath the streetlights of Uranium Town, I decided I'd had my fill of Magyar driving forever.

Ten years down the track, Bel and I decided we wanted a car with Hungarian numberplates, anyway. Reasoning that getting on and off buses with two kids would become a drag, we recruited Attila (proud owner of two cars) and headed out past the remains of what had been, until an accidental inferno, Pécs's top disco to descend into the fevered throng of the *autovásár*, or car market.

Zsuzsa and Dalma came too, smiling politely as we examined the selection of Soviet bloc relics that fell within our tiny price range, before discreetly fleeing for a bout of shoe shopping. Looking back now, I'm still not entirely sure what attracted us to the Skoda Favorit. Attila introduced us to one that had caught his fancy among a sea of used Opels, Ladas, Fiats and Volkswagens so optimistically priced, I got the feeling Hungarians had yet to completely recover from the days when buying a car meant joining a waiting list longer than the average natural lifespan of some dog breeds, a situation that was endured with the help of jokes like this:

> Your Trabant will be ready for you in seven years.
> *Will that be morning or afternoon?*
> Afternoon. Why?
> *The plumber's coming in the morning.*

(It wasn't just cars. Back in the days when Hungary suffered the distinction of having the second lowest number of telephones per capita in Europe after Albania, waiting lists were so extraordinarily long that an MP in the then Communist parliament drolly suggested that phone applications be made inheritable.)

The Skoda Favorit was one of the last Skodas to have been built in Czechoslovakia before Volkswagen took over the company, and Czechoslovakia ceased to exist. ('Oh, a *Skoda* Skoda,' one mechanic later remarked as he cast his bemused gaze over our acquisition.) It had an engine with roughly the same dimensions and power as a largeish rabbit. Perhaps it was a largeish rabbit – it seemed to go faster whenever there were dogs about – but I was never brave enough to look that closely. If I were in any way mechanically inclined, I suspect I would have sucked in my breath as the bonnet was lifted, and possibly even called for smelling salts before I swooned to the ground. Instead, I stood next to Attila, bent over the array of shuddering, rattling belts and wheels and did my level, unconvincing best to look like a Bloke Who Understands Cars.

'Look, it goes, it stops,' Attila giggled. 'It even goes backwards. It should get you through the next few months while you're here.'

Whatever air of command economy gimcrackery the Skoda exuded was easily eclipsed by the beige and powder blue ranks of East German Trabants and their marginally less primitive relatives, the Wartburg. If you squinted hard enough it had what could be perceived as a certain perkiness, and it was painted in a yellowish hue that made goose fat leap irresistibly to mind. In a good way. There are surely worse reasons to buy a car, Bel and I reassured each other as we handed over a pile of forints to a young man with a gold chain, a head more closely cropped than a tennis ball and the honesty to laugh when Attila asked whether he might be interested in buying it back when we left Hungary.

'If you have any problems or get stuck anywhere, just call me,' Attila said cheerily once the paperwork was sorted.

Not counting a short-lived fiasco involving major jetlag and a hire car in Zagreb, I'd only ever driven on the right-hand side of the road once before. That was behind the wheel of a fossilised Dacia – the Romanian approximation of a Renault – in the depths of rural Transylvania. The Dacia had a long gearstick that vanished into the mushiest gearbox I've ever encountered, including a reverse gear that I spent an entertaining ten minutes trying to find during an attempted three-point turn that blocked a back road and left a few locals keen to teach me some of their native tongue. Once that was taken care of and the chorus of sardonic cheers faded, I was overcome by (a) the exhilaration of driving on the other side of the road, and (b) the terror that at any moment I would careen into a horse or one of the sprawling bands of gypsies wandering the bendy road to Sighisoara.

Driving in Hungary seemed relatively straightforward in comparison, I thought as I negotiated my first roundabout and set of potholes without running into anything. Then having successfully managed to change gears several times in a row rather than accidentally winding down the window instead, I felt like I was getting on top of things. Bel, who once spent a couple of months driving around America, watched my progress with some amusement.

We hadn't been driving long when we had to make our first call to Attila. The fan, which was set up in a way I'd never seen in a car before, stopped working and the only way to keep the engine from overheating was to drive fast enough to keep up the airflow over the radiator. Not an easy task in Pécs.

'I know this guy,' Attila said. 'It will be a lot better if we go see him. Take the Skoda to most places and they'll start charging money from the moment they see your face. You'll be paying them while they sit and scratch and ponder the world, or go off to have a cigarette. Every cigarette and every scratch ends up being counted as "labour" on your bill. Let me talk to Bandi; we'll go see him.'

Bandi's home and workshop were in the village of Nagyárpád. Even though it was in reality a tiny satellite suburb just a handful of metres beyond Pécs city limits, Nagyárpád had something of a rural atmosphere. Brightly painted wells stood in gardens teeming with vegetables and hens, storks nested on platforms high above the road, dusty crucifixes rose in front of houses encrusted with satellite dishes, and just beyond Bandi's elderly house, fields were being worked by women in headscarves.

Flanked by a Caucasian wolfhound and a wirehaired dachshund, Bandi wore the expression of a man who, after years of firmly believing he has seen the worst life has to offer, is surprised to discover he was wrong. As he set to work on the Skoda with a sigh, Attila and I stood about, talking family. I kept noticing all the physical similarities he shared with László – the shape of the head, the set of the eyes, the way they stood – courtesy of their dead father.

'How should I refer to you then?' I said. 'Cousin?'

'No, that wouldn't be quite right,' Attila said, scratching his head momentarily, then brightening. 'What about half-brother? It's almost true.'

'Half-brother,' I pondered aloud. What it lacked in accuracy it made up for by having a certain ring. 'Why not?'

'Done.'

As we stood there with a half-brother and sister – László and Eszter – but no actual genes in common, I asked Attila when it was he found out he wasn't an only child.

'You know,' Attila said simply, 'I was looking through these piles of photos and I found one of me inside my pram, being pushed by two older kids – a boy and a girl. I went to Mum and asked who they were, and she said, Eszter and Laci. I said to her, who are Eszter and Laci? And she told me, they're your sister and brother.'

As we talked, I could see the scowl on Bandi's face waxing and waning. He was the very picture of a man locked in the eternal struggle between diplomacy and truth.

'Skodas, Skodas, Skodas,' he muttered. 'I think we can say they weren't the greatest car ever put on this planet.' Among its many shortcomings, it would be revealed that the Skoda Favorit was a loose copy of the Lada Samara, which is another way of saying it may as well have been modelled on a coconut. This news wasn't especially helpful to Attila, who'd just bought a Samara as a second car. But Attila being Attila laughed it off and got back to tribal matters.

'I eventually forgot about them for a while, but later in life I started thinking that maybe I should try to track Eszter and Laci down. I thought, they can't have just vanished off the face of the earth. Then one day my Uncle Jancsi comes down, walks straight up to my father and says, "You'll never guess who just rang." And my father says, "Who?" And Jancsi says, "Laci and Eszter. And they're calling back in an hour." So my father very calmly got up, put his jacket on and went off with my uncle.'

The dogs, which had hitherto been content to lope about in the dust, decided the moment was right to stage a mock battle. With the mismatch in sizes, it was like watching a ferret attack a bear, but the wolfhound had the good manners to go down to the dachshund in a volley of half-hearted snarls and telltale tail-wagging.

I only knew the story from our side of the family fence – the short court case my father fought and won for the right to take Eszter and Lac out of Hungary, then Mum filling their heads with stories that helped persuade them to not contact their father for nearly two decades.

'You know, my father was always a good father to me,' Attila continued. 'He was always hugging me, talking with me, joking with me, planning outings for us. We'd always be out on the weekends fishing or picking mushrooms in the forest. But the way his mentality worked, he would have decided, well, Eszter and Laci have gone, so that's that. And he closed off that part of his brain and never talked about them again.'

There was a clang from under the bonnet and some reflective cursing.

'I can honestly say that I only saw my father cry twice. The first time was when I left Hungary to go to Poland, the other time was when Eszter and Laci called.'

Before we could pursue this line any further, Bandi emerged with the guilty party – the heat sensor from the radiator – gripped between a greasy thumb and forefinger.

'The thing is . . . The thing is . . .' he said, hunting for just the right word to express how he felt both as a mechanic and as a human being. 'The thing is,' he said, holding the sensor aloft in the sun's harsh glare, 'is that this is shit.'

Bandi quickly figured out that shit – or *szar* – was in my Hungarian vocabulary and I got to hear him use it a lot during my subsequent visits to Nagyárpád. *Szar* might not be as short and sharp as shit, but it sounds like it's more likely to stick. Sometimes he'd throw in the German, too, as older Hungarians are wont to do when speaking with foreigners.

'This here – see this where the wires are loose? – this is also shit.' Once Bandi saw that I understood the Skoda was shit and had made my peace with the situation, he relaxed and was all too happy to explain things and put the word through all its permutations. Shit. Shittier. Shittiest. Then of course we had comparative studies: Czech shit, Russian shit, Romanian shit. You can't, as they say in some circles, polish a turd, but you might just be able to sustain a false sense of hope for slightly longer with a Czech one than with, say, a Romanian one. In Hungary, this passes for optimism.

Bandi kept a sign on the wall indicating that the lighting of matches and the smoking of pipes was forbidden (*tilos*), but he happily toiled away under the bonnet puffing on a cigarette, tapping away the ash with an oil-smeared finger. On the floor squatted a Soviet short-wave radio with roughly the same dimensions as a modest apartment block, its monolithic face covered in the names of cities written out in Cyrillic letters – Novosibirsk, Petrozavodsk, Omsk, Rostov-on-Don, Brussels (ah, the power of the EU), Minsk, Kiev and Leningrad. Moscow alone warranted red letters. MOCKBA!

'I thought a Russian radio would make a nice decoration. A bit like some of their cars,' Bandi commented.

From the foam-insulated ceiling hung a disco ball, a cheerful incongruity that had somehow managed to dodge the layer of workshop grime that coated everything else. The radio was pumping out that song by Enigma that features singing monks. Bandi got busy draining the oil and cursing the air filter and pondering the erratic workings of the water pump while Gregorian chants washed over the piles of tools and parts and the obligatory collection of pornographic posters – candid, even by mechanic standards – that illuminated the walls as thoroughly as a medieval manuscript.

'You know what?' Attila said. 'I should go see my mother and ask her for the photos. I know she's got them in a box or somewhere; you should see them.' Of course, he turned up a whole stash of them. I looked at them weeks later and found myself jarred by the experience. There was something about seeing Eszt and Lac looking so small and so obviously chuffed with their father. Within a year of the last pictures being taken, my sister and brother had vanished from his life. Not that any of that was of any particular consequence to Bandi. He emerged from his cavern of oil and breasts, wiping grease from his hands.

'There,' he announced. 'I've made it less shit.'

Intergalactic

'The thing about Hungarians and that weird language of theirs is that it all begins to make sense when you understand this.' He was drunk and Danish, but his brain was being interrupted by a moment of lucidity. 'All you have to understand is that they all came to earth in a giant spaceship. Once you have that thought clear in your brain, the rest of it all fits into place. The people, the language and . . . and all the other stuff. It's the only explanation.' He burped thoughtfully while his fellow Danes considered his theory.

It's true that for all their fondness for boulevards, string quartets and the rest of it, Hungarians do have a certain something that makes them stick out on the continent, and it isn't just that their tongue isn't even a member of the Indo-European group.

There's the tradition of putting the surname before the Christian name, thus rendering, say, Ilona Kiss as the altogether more appealing Kiss Ilona. Then there's the slightly disconcerting use of 'Hello' as a farewell, something that Beatles scholars may choose to term the 'I Say Goodbye, You Say Hello' Syndrome. This has been a fairly recent addition to Hungarian speech – Mum, who left in 1972, was surprised by it – and was one I just couldn't get my head around.

No matter how much I forced myself, that 'Hello' as I walked out the door came out strangled and peculiar. Daisy had no such problems, and we wondered what effect this would have when we eventually returned to Australia.

Bel and I discovered another little back-to-front quirk when we went to see folk music superstar Márta Sebestyén singing at Pécs's Piusz Church. Knowing how barmy Hungarians tended to go for her, we booked tickets in advance and arrived to find the church fast filling with a capacity crowd. The front two rows were plastered with 'reserved' signs, so we edged as close as we could, pressing through a wall of clamouring flesh. The thing was, Sebestyén actually sang from behind us, standing next to the pipe organ that was accompanying her. No one turned, not even those who'd so proudly taken their rightful and reserved places in the front two rows.

'This is amazing,' Bel whispered in between craning her neck to see the source of that clear, powerful and yet somehow delicate voice. 'Bugger this, I'm going to get a better seat.' And up she got and moved forward a few metres to sit on the altar steps. This radical course of action triggered an avalanche of reproachful whispering behind me. I scurried over to join Bel on the cold marble, and although it chilled our backsides, we could finally see Sebestyén. We could also see all the faces of the audience staring at us, apart from a few older members who were sleeping peacefully while a cameraman filmed them.

A more stunning and far more agreeable Magyar reversal of order was the time one of the nation's most elderly and revered living writers chose to pose nude on the cover of *Penthouse* (Hungarian edition only). With his mad, long, grey frizz and his octogenarian skin more wrinkled than an elephant's scrotum, György Faludy – poet, former enemy of the state and author of such works as *My Happy Days in Hell* – peered gleefully from the cover like a lecherous Gandalf ('I'll show you an enchanted ring!'). The editors of *Penthouse* thoughtfully used Faludy's much, much younger and equally naked girlfriend – the poet Fanny Kovács – as a fig leaf (since no one really needed to know exactly how many wrinkles Faludy had), but coming from what is coyly known as the adult entertainment industry, it was a move as wonderfully eccentric as it was surprising. At least that's what I told Bel when I walked through the door with a copy. She took one look at the cover and was smitten. I wasn't allowed to get a haircut for a while after that.

So, yes, there is the odd thing, but a spaceship? It wasn't a radically new line of thinking. Hints were dropped when England's aura of football invincibility was battered twice by Hungary's 'golden team' – first 6–3 at Wembley in 1953, then 7–1 in Budapest the following year. After the 7–1 demolition, England's centre half Syd Owen was moved to describe the experience as being 'like playing people from outer space'.

The Italian–American physicist Enrico Fermi was asked if he believed in the existence of extraterrestrial life. 'Yes,' he reportedly replied. 'And they are already here among us. They are called Hungarians.' Fermi was in the process of helping to invent the atom bomb at the time, so make of it what you will. He may have been pleased that his theory still had currency half a century later, even on a little Danish merchant ship moored in the Neva River.

I'd been walking the streets of St Petersburg with my Finnish friend Outi, partly in a display of Finno-Ugric solidarity, partly out of a desire to find a bar and get whammed. For that is what one did in Russia. Somehow we'd finished up on this ship; alcohol may have played a role. It was getting late and the bridges of the Neva would soon be opening up, leaving everyone stuck on whichever island they happened to be on. There'd be lines of cars that hadn't made it before the cut-off point, drivers dozing behind their steering wheels while streetwalkers wandered up and down, looking for trade among the stranded.

We drank and listened to the Dane until Outi, tiring of the man's growing fondness for his own voice, made a comment which could possibly have been construed as denigrating Denmark.

'Fucking Finns!' the Dane snarled. 'You're not even proper Scandinavians.' The debate continued along its short but bumpy course until Outi walked around the table and, with a gentle smile, emptied a bottle of beer over the Dane's head. It was at this point that we were asked to leave. This worked out well, as we were able to hail a cab before the bridges went up. As we drove away beneath that pearly, all-night twilight, I had to admit there was a chance the Dane was right – accept the flying saucer theory and everything else makes sense. Especially the language. And my mother.

PUBERTY WAS A particularly turbulent time for me. My balls dropped, my voice broke, my hair curled and I began speaking Hungarian.

The first two events on the program were expected (though no less traumatic for it), but my hair's act of rebellion was not. Hitherto as bereft of curves as a Volvo, it began at first to ripple, then wrinkle, then slowly but inexorably tighten into silly little ringlets. It wouldn't have been so bad if it had all happened evenly, but instead it curled a section at a time, making my head look even more like a work-in-progress than usual and testing the creative powers of the school bullies. As my blond afro developed, I looked at my parents that little bit more carefully – Dad with his dark, straight hair and Mum with her almost black, low-key wavy look she'd adopted after she finally abandoned her beehives – and began contemplating the possibility that a blond, curly-headed milkman had been servicing Pécs back in 1972. Mum laughed (a *little* too hard, perhaps?) when I suggested this, then very soberly informed me there were no milkmen in 1970s Hungary.

'Your hair comes from my side of the family,' she added with an air of finality.

The matter of speaking Hungarian, on the other hand, merely felt overdue. Mum, after all, had been talking Magyar to us all our lives. Very early on in Lancashire, as her pregnant belly expanded with me and as Lac and Eszt waded bravely into the English language in their Parbold school, she made the decision that she would teach me – then Olivia a few years later – her native tongue as well. This wasn't necessarily a foregone conclusion. Put in a similar position, many of Mum's fellow Hungarians, like émigré communities everywhere, would decide to abandon the language and speak to their kids only in English, convinced this would be the only way they would assimilate and thrive in their new environment. And others agreed. Mum says her mother-in-law was constantly in her ear about how the children didn't need Hungarian as they were living in England, and that getting two languages at once would only confuse them.

Later in life, during visits to the Hungarian Club in far western Sydney – known unaffectionately as *Szúnyog Sziget*, or Mosquito Island – and at various Hungarian gatherings, János and Edit's carving-knife spectacular included, I would regularly meet children who barely knew more than a word of their parents' language. It was a pity for them, not just because attitudes later changed and it was decided that growing up with more than one language was actually a big advantage – it cut them off from their relatives who'd stayed in Hungary. Grandparents desperate to dote on their grandkids would be left smiling uselessly on the other side of an all but impenetrable linguistic fog.

From the moment Olivia and I were born, Mum spoke – and occasionally bellowed – to us in Hungarian. Of course we didn't fully appreciate at the time that she was giving us the keys to a language that sits in the middle of Europe as a great, glaring anomaly, a resolutely non Indo-European tongue that crept into the heart of the continent from the western fringe of Asia and survived. Miraculous when you consider how many languages and cultures have washed back and forth across Europe only to evaporate with barely a trace. No, our considerations were a little more basic than that. Such as how much *fa kanál* – or wooden spoon – sounded like fucken 'ell, and how appropriate this was given the way Mum used to shout it as she chased us round and round the kitchen when we'd been up to no good and threatened to smack us with it.

The *fa kanál* was an early lesson in the realities of life, a two-faced instrument of both retribution and reward, a tool that could be coated in embryonic chocolate cake and in need of a good licking from whichever one of us kids was fast enough to respond to Mum's call, or equally might be applied to the seat of our pants when we'd, say, trailed mud into the house or tested the laws of gravity using nothing but the dozen eggs in the fridge and the front veranda.

*Fa kanál*s aside, Magyar wrapped us in its staccato rhythms and cadences, its rolled r's and stretched vowels, and we understood it as easily and comfortably as English. It never felt unusual or exotic, it just was. But while we understood Mum, we answered her in English and it wasn't until much later that we began to answer in Hungarian as well. (I started seeing the same with Daisy, who seemed to understand a little more Hungarian with every week we were in Pécs. The big breakthrough came the afternoon a friend asked her, '*Hol van az apukád?*' or 'Where's your daddy?' Without skipping a beat, she said in English, 'Oh, he's just gone outside.')

Looking back now, I only wish I'd had some formal schooling in it, or had been forced to read the language while someone stood behind me with a big stick or, better yet, an electric cattle prod. My Hungarian has struggled to ever really rise beyond the level of what we learned around the kitchen table, and while I feel comfortable in day-to-day conversation, I'm tantalisingly close to, but unable to ever reach, a level that would let me talk like a normal adult. My competency is best described as functioning shambolic. But it's better than nothing.

Having grown up with Hungarian in my ears, it's hard for me to say what it sounds like, rather like trying to describe the sound of English. I asked my relatives about the latter, and they said it struck them as sounding a lot like Dutch. As for Hungarian, I turn to Patrick Leigh Fermor, traveller and writer, who described Magyar as having a fast, incisive resonance, a different inflection to any other European language and 'a wild and most unfamiliar ring'.

That unfamiliar ring could have all but vanished. Early in the nineteenth century, at a time when Latin was the language of parliament and German was widely spoken in Budapest, there was every likelihood that the ancient Magyar would succumb to its more powerful linguistic neighbour, left to float ever more faintly in the shadow of a Germanic tongue, like Irish does.

It took the efforts of some particularly pigheaded poets, writers and scholars to stop this from happening, raising a mountain of new words from Hungarian roots to make the language adapt to the modern world. And it has survived, largely and happily free of words that might give hints and make things easier for foreigners. There are no chemists, or *apotekas*, in Hungary, but there are *gyógyszertár*. Likewise 'restaurant', a word recognisable in its minor variations across the continent, has in Hungary become *étterem*.

Couple that with all those tricky vowels, some confoundedly difficult grammar, no separate words for 'he' and 'she' (something that often dogs Hungarians when they learn English) and you have a language that has established for itself a reputation as being an extremely tough nut to crack. This is something Hungarians take a degree of pride in, in between using it as an excuse for their own lack of proficiency in foreign languages and for being the least bilingual country in Europe. (Best not to mention that the Finns, who speak a distantly related language, don't seem to have any particular trouble with languages.)

When Bel and I were preparing to travel to Hungary together for the first time, a friend and former Eastern European correspondent warned Bel of the folly of tackling Magyar: 'Many friends of mine, correspondents, intelligent people, tried and got nowhere with it.' This only ensured that Bel enrolled in Hungarian classes almost the day we arrived. Her guide through the Ugric maze was a young literature teacher called Zsolt, who cycled over from Uranium Town each week to put Bel through her paces, and then stuck around to drink wine and talk books and poetry, drink some more wine and then somehow ride back home to Uranium Town. With his wife, Lilla, an expert in Finnish, Zsolt was well placed to concede the possibility that the Hungarian language's reputation has managed to ever so slightly outstrip reality.

There was some disgruntlement (or at least within the minuscule universe of Budapest's English language newspapers) when the US State Department ranked Hungarian as merely semi-tough to learn. Based on how long it takes an average student at its Foreign Service Institute to reach proficiency in a language, the State Department put Magyar in Category 2. This makes it harder than Spanish and French, and about as hard as Russian and Thai, but a piece of creamy cake next to Arabic, Cantonese and Japanese.

Well.

'Expats of all language skills angrily dismissed the results,' the *Budapest Times* declared on its regularly and bewitchingly trivial front page, probably with tongue firmly planted in cheek. '"I find it unbelievable that Hungarian isn't listed as harder," said translator John Purvis, 37, who believes the ranking belittles his diligence in learning to speak the language ... Self-confessed language dunce Alexander O'Connell also could not believe the results. Despite marrying a Hungarian, raising two Hungarian kids and living in the country for almost four years, the 36-year-old consultant can barely string two words together. He blames the language: "You just can't tell when one word ends and another one starts. It gets better with time, but it's still a problem."

As for me, I don't really know. I just love the sound of it. It feels like home.

If I were a Bumblebee

As spring wore on, the last patches of brown vanished from the hills and the Mecsek swelled behind the town in a great wave of luminous greens and delicate yellows. I pulled on my boots early one morning and set out from home before the sun came up. Király utca was empty except for a couple of green-uniformed street-sweepers quietly swapping jokes as they worked their way along the pavers, and a few pigeons sleepily courting each other by the still fountains in front of the theatre. Somewhere in the distance I heard the grumble of a bus, but otherwise it was just the sound of my boots against the footpath as I walked along Széchenyi Square, gazing up at the Djami and its Mecca-facing front wall. Its copper dome, as round and greeny blue as a duck's egg, was topped with a cross positioned emphatically above a defeated crescent moon. When the Turks originally took Pécs in the sixteenth century, they went to the effort of destroying the church that stood in the middle of the square and used its stone to build a mosque. When the Turks were finally sent packing over a hundred and fifty years later, the Catholic Church expended less energy and simply redecorated the mosque in a manner they thought might be more pleasing to Jesus. And, just as importantly, to the Pope.

Nearby, János Hunyadi, the one-time scourge of the Ottomans, glowered in bronze from the saddle of his charger, probably still ticked off that his successors had let their guard down and allowed those turbaned infidels in. Or perhaps he was just disgruntled about the new-fangled belltower that had been installed at the back of the Djami, which, following a schedule nobody deigned to understand, rose out of the ground like some ecclesiastical missile and pealed noisily to heaven from a tripod of wobbly steel before sinking back into the ground again.

I passed through the city wall – which had done so little to keep the Turks out all those centuries ago – and crossed over to the bus stop, exchanging bleary greetings with a henna-haired woman. The stop was near where the road tunnelled its way beneath Kalvária Hill. (Mum once tried to convince us that the tunnel was the handiwork of the ancient Romans back in the days when Pécs had been the settlement of Sopianae. 'Jeez, Mum, those Romans must have been pretty handy with the ferro-concrete,' Lac had chuckled at the time. The tunnel was actually built after Mum moved out of Hungary, but in this part of the world it's easy to get confused. As Mum regularly notes, 'This place *breathes* history.' She doesn't necessarily know what happened at any given spot, but she knows a lot has gone on.)

But for a lone puff of cumulus, the pink dawn sky was empty. The 34 bus, on the other hand, was packed with staff, visitors and the odd patient heading up the hill to the sanatorium. The driver, who looked as though he might have last slept some time in the late 1980s, cranked up the radio and we made our way up the serpentine road to the sound of Robbie Williams.

I was the only one to hop off at the Mandulás camping stop, the last one before the sanatorium. The sanatorium is an outpost of the

Baranya County Hospital and was built with the notion of giving patients a place to recuperate amidst birdsong and fresh forest air. It was only much later that someone actually conducted any studies and worked out that in certain wind conditions the bulk of Pécs's pollution is funnelled straight up the hillside to the sanatorium's front door. The invalids who loiter out the front with their dressing gowns and gaspers and dangling drip-bags probably figure that whatever it is they're sucking through their cigarette filters, it's not a whole lot worse than what's blowing in the wind.

As the raspy farting of the bus faded in the direction of the ill-placed sanatorium, I was left with the dawn chorus blasting invisibly from the wall of trees, joined in earnest by a solitary cockerel in a nearby yard.

Barely metres into the woods, a sudden crash made my heart almost crack my ribs. A pair of deer went careening away in the green gloom, only to stop and let rip with a strangely baboon-like bark that echoed through the trees. The last time I heard a noise anything like it I was lying in a tent in South Africa, realising that there are far more unsettling sounds in the savannah night than the ponderous roaring of lions. The call was answered by another deer somewhere off to my left, followed by more crashes as they scattered in different directions. There was a brief silence, then the birds got back to business.

The path snaked its way up to Misina Peak toward the TV tower, which was mercifully obscured by leaves for much of the way. Below, a marmalade light was spreading across the old town and beyond, lending even the monstrosities of Uranium Town and Garden Town a fleeting loveliness. Ahead, everything – with the exception of a badger carcase decaying by the roadside – was vibrating with life. The whole forest seemed to be trembling to the sounds of song thrushes, chaffinches, blackbirds and woodpeckers, a liquid warbling washing over staccato twittering, short but passionate melodies in major keys and furious, jackhammering rhythms from the woodpeckers.

(Once upon a time, Mum and Joli would warn me and Bel away from walking in these woods, convinced that they were filled with ruffians who liked nothing better than stretching piano wire across the trails at throat level and decapitating hikers. I was never sure how fast Mum and Joli thought we did our bushwalking, but I'm confident we never came close to decapitation speed. Any mention that we had yet to see any piano wire whatsoever would bring knowing looks. 'They are finding new ways to rob people, *ja ja*', and so on.)

As I followed a pale path of limestone gravel along the saddle between two peaks, the tops of the trees ignited with the first light of day. The apricot glow slowly crept down the trunks and warmed the leaves, and I noticed a gentle buzzing high above that grew louder as the sun's rays stirred the bees to life in the blossom-choked canopy. As the sun edged higher, fingers of light slowly stretched between the oaks and birches across a pungent carpet of *medvehagyma*, or bear onion. Bear onion rules the forest floor almost unchallenged for a handful of weeks in the spring, sending up clusters of flowers that explode like white fireworks above a bed of broad green leaves and flood the entire forest with an unmistakably oniony whiff. The scent is unmissable, even when driving through the Mecsek at warp speed with the windows up. I've walked in these hills often – after thunderstorms when puddles brim with frogs and the occasional interloping newt; in the naked, solemn browns of early spring and the crisp whites of winter (while Joli, clad in fur coat and purple beret nimbly sidestepped kids on sleds as they hurtled down the snowy paths); and in the full furnace heat of summer when the deep green light of the beech forest is as reviving as a dip in a lake – but I still think bear onion season is the Mecsek at its fecund, fragrant, fertile prime.

Apart from the bear onion, harvested by locals for making soups and salads and wrapping around meat, the understorey was still thin, compared to what it would become. Most of the forest's energy seemed to be channelled into the extraordinary profusion of flowers that loaded the air with a syrupy commotion of scents. At János Lookout – a stone tower with views across the Mecsek and the villa and vineyard-peppered valleys of western Pécs – I bumped into a fellow walker, who seemed as surprised as I was to run into another person. From there, the path began its zig-zagging descent toward the lakes of Orfű. The oaks and black pines gave way to beech, their slender and almost silk-smooth grey trunks rising gracefully into a canopy that looked as distant and solid and vaulted as a cathedral ceiling. The path led to a clearing with a *kulcsház*, or keyhouse – a bare-bones lodging for bushwalkers – and a spring, which despite its less than encouraging name of Büdöskút, or Stinky Spring, flowed with clear, sweet water that chilled my fingers as I drank.

I passed some loggers working a small coupe. They paused and nodded, the slightest of smiles creasing their ruddy, weather-worn faces as they wished me a good morning. A little further down the track, I almost tripped over what I at first took to be a snake. Then I noticed its earholes – something no snake has – and realised it was a legless lizard trying to warm its body in the early sun. It was as long as my forearm, as thick as my finger and so sluggish with cold, it did little when I picked it up other than slowly flicker its round, grey tongue. But as I took photos, the heat from my hand did the trick and it began to slowly writhe before finally losing patience, opening up its cloaca and emptying its bowels down said forearm. Despite being a journalist by trade, I can take a hint and I put it back down. The reptile wasted no time in slipping away into the leaf litter. The snails I found a little further on were far more co-operative for the camera as they slowly glided across the dew-sequinned grass. Some were pale brown, others the size and almost the colour of golf balls.

As I edged closer to Orfű, the birds began to fade and be replaced by a barrage of roosters. I eventually emerged into the streets near the bus stop, where a small group of solidly built locals waiting with their shopping bags for the bus over the hills to Pécs stopped talking for a few moments to stare at me with troubled expressions. 'What could this dishevelled blond thing be doing coming out of the woods this early?' their faces seemed to say. 'Why is he so skinny? And why is his forearm covered in lizard crap?'

I left them to their thoughts and walked along streets of pretty villas offering accommodation in Hungarian and German and headed towards the lakes of Orfű. I passed one spot – the first of many – where years before I'd been convinced I would die with Andris. Somewhere around here, Eszter once redecorated the inside of the Vauxhall and Lac fell in the lake. I was lost in a reverie for a minute, maybe longer, until I was nearly run down by an Ikarus bus.

Instruments of Satan

For someone admired, feared and reviled as a modern composer, Béla Bartók spent an awful lot of time immersed in folk music. Two decades before the rise of fascism finally drove him across the Atlantic, he gathered together his friend and fellow composer Zoltán Kodály, some patient horses and the finest gramophone recording equipment money could buy (or at least whatever they could lay their hands on) and set off to explore Hungary – and for good measure some places that had until the Treaty of Trianon just a few years before been part of Hungary – through the music of its villages. Their journey through this traditional culture – a culture that would slowly die during the twentieth century until a revival welled up out of Transylvania in the 1970s – had a deep and lasting effect on both men that resonated through their music. As Kodály would later say of his friend, 'What did he find . . . ? An unknown world, a Hungarianness thought long vanished in full flower.'

As a casual lover of Hungarian music, I wanted to be touched by it too, to feel it with something other than just my eardrums. That meant playing it. Despite all the possibilities, I looked past the shepherd's flutes, the three-stringed basses, the zithers (even though my grandmother had played one) and the rickety, hammered cimbaloms. I also shunned the violin, despite folk musicians so often choosing to rakishly play at a ninety-degree angle, their noses and sometimes even their lips resting against that sensuously curved bottom.

From the very beginning of the affair, I only had ears for the *duda* – the Hungarian bagpipe.

It may be both fascinating and terrifying to learn that the *Oxford Dictionary of Music* lists dozens of different kinds of bagpipe. Most people are happy believing the whole noisy story begins and ends with Scotland, not realising that it's a big and varied family that spreads all the way from Ireland to northern Africa, to Russia and the fringes of the Middle East. It softens the blow to learn that none of the others is as loud as its Scottish relatives, nor does it oblige its players to wear sporrans. From the convoluted uilleann pipes of Ireland to the superbly named *dudelsack* of Germany to the huge *zampogna* of southern Italy (which looks like a pygmy hippo–giant octopus hybrid being given a Heimlich manoeuvre), the world of bagpipery is like an eccentric cult, comprising to a large extent members with excellent lungs and questionable livers.

As a serial abuser of three different types of bagpipes (my neighbours have all found various ways to mask their enthusiasm), I was excited to learn that Hungary has its own breed. Like many of the bagpipes found through Central and Eastern Europe, the Hungarian pipe – or *duda* – is made largely from goat and tends to look as if it has only just been slaughtered, and occasionally sounds like it's still putting up a fight. Obviously I had to get my hands on one, but the *duda* is a tradition that has only just been pulled back from extinction. I'd talked to some pipers along the way, including one I knew only as Tesko, a lanky bearded man with wild eyes, a laconic mouth and a reputation among the folk music crowd for throwing legendary parties that take care of roughly a third of Hungary's annual wine output.

The first time we met, he talked me through his set of pipes, stroking the fur on the bag the whole time. 'I knew this one when she was alive,' he casually intoned. 'Nice little goat she was, too. But she makes a better bagpipe.' (Incidentally, it turned out that Tesko had just come back from touring Australia with a band I had very nearly gone to see. Mrs Tesko, on the other hand, hadn't gone. The Australian government, in its wisdom, had denied her a visa and this was clearly a sore topic judging by the way she unloaded her emotions on the first Australian she met, which was me.)

Like the other *duda* players I'd talked to, there was no way Tesko was going to be persuaded to part with his instrument. I had to find a maker, and there weren't many of those. Luckily, the almost nauseatingly talented Andor Végh stepped into the picture before I did something drastic and potentially suicidal, like trying to steal Tesko's *duda*.

I first met Andor at a wine bar on the hill behind the basilica. It was the perfect place to sit on long summer evenings, sipping *cirfandli* from the local vineyards as the moon floated low across the sky behind the cathederal's four stone towers. It was also a haunt favoured by the folk music crowd. Never the most welcoming bunch to outsiders, they treated Bel and me, at best, as a mild curiosity, no matter how many times we went to watch them swirling in their fussily patterned dresses or slapping their long leather boots. Even after several months, some of them would still react to a greeting from us as if we had tried to stick a tongue in their ear.

The exception to this was the bagpipe players, a breed who always seem overcome with a sort of bewildered joy whenever they encounter someone else who has of their own free will joined the cult. As the Australian uilleann piper and pipemaker Ian Mackenzie told me the first time we met: 'I always love meeting other pipers. They're never quite right in the head.'

By this measure, Andor would be approaching a level of advanced derangement.

Driving out to his home in the nearby village of Bóly, which lay just off the Mohács road (a two-lane mosaic of ruts and potholes that the Skoda's suspension translated a little too faithfully), I pulled over and phoned for instructions, only to spot a silhouetted figure down the road, one hand pressing a mobile to his ear and the other waving merrily.

Minutes later, Andor was ushering me inside the whitewashed house – doing his best to deflect the affections of a moth-eaten vizsla dog – and into a room filled with more bagpipes than I've ever seen in my life. It was like a catalogue of all the demon pipes of southeastern Europe, laid out in a spread of carved goats' heads and horn-tipped chanters with wax picks on chains dangling from their ends like silver fangs. There were drones of walnut, pear and plumwood inlaid with intricate lattices of pewter. Goatskin bags lay in flaccid mounds, wrinkled and windless and as pale yellow as parchment. But as soon as Andor plugged his bellows into one and started pumping his elbow, the torso swelled and took on an air that was part comedy, part menace.

Along with the Hungarian *dudas*, there were Croatian *dudes*, Serbo-Croat *gajdes*, pale *diples* from the ragged cliffs and limestone islands of Dalmatia and dark ones from the shadowy valleys of Hercegovina, plus an Istrian bagpipe that looked like a marrow with plumbing. The most unnerving of them all – both aurally and aesthetically – were without doubt the *diples*. Instead of drone pipes, each *diple* had a pair of wild boar tusks tied into the legholes in the goatskin bag. When inflated, the instrument looked like a giant tick hunting for something to sink its fangs into.

'Even for me, the sound of the *diple* is an acquired taste,' Andor admitted with a grin as he took the blowpipe between his teeth and started puffing. His fingers slipped into a blur on the short double chanter and the sound that came out would have worked well as elevator music in one of Saddam's palaces, preferably in one of the lifts leading down to the torture level.

'And here's a completely different tune,' Andor announced as he drew breath, before unleashing a second salvo of jagged notes barely discernible from the first. 'I had to make a *diple* in a hurry for a concert I was playing at,' he explained afterwards as he deflated the bag to a state of harmlessness and laid the *diple* on the bed. 'As I got ready to start, I said to the audience, "There are people who enjoy listening to this sort of music all day long."' A gentle smile momentarily bent his lips. 'It was interesting watching their faces.'

The different sets of pipes were like animal species, some ranging across the plains and many villages, while others were confined to a few valleys or a couple of handkerchief-sized counties. Andor stood bent over the map, feverishly explaining bagpipe distribution like a naturalist talking about his favourite creature.

'This *gajde* was played through these parts of old Hungary, but it was just the Croats who played them, whereas the *duda* was right across here –' His hand swept across the Great Plain and the fringes of Transylvania. 'And here in southern Transdanubia, and here in the north in Nógrád county and the uplands.'

Presently, his mother came in. 'Oh, what a disaster. It's quite chaotic in here, isn't it?' she said with an apologetic giggle.

I explained that such a spread of bagpipes was paradise to me. Mrs Végh studied my face as if checking for signs of a stroke. Bagpipe devotees are used to this sort of thing.

'And where did you learn to speak Hungarian so well?' This was the usual sort of sweet flattery; I felt like the linguistic version of the dog that can walk on its hind legs. It wasn't that I could speak

Hungarian well but that I could speak it at all – or just as unusually, wanted to speak it – that attracted attention. I went through my usual spiel about Mum, and was rewarded with a steaming, oil-black thimbleful of coffee on a silver tray.

After the refreshment break, Andor took me out the back to his workshop where my own *duda* was to take shape. Goatskins lay curing in tubs of salt and alum ('The longer they stay in that, the yellower they get.') Rough-hewn hunks of timber were heaped in mounds around a lathe near piles of reamers and boxes of chanters with wax-rimmed fingerholes.

It was, if the assortment of local legends was anything to go by, a world of supernatural danger I was entering. If I took up the *duda*, chances were I'd meet the devil at a crossroads one day, or worse, wake him from his slumbers inside the goatskin bag. And if it wasn't the devil, then it would be witches – witches who would teach me to play by sending a wasp down my throat, or witches who would lure me to their den and entice me to play for them on one of their own bagpipes, dancing into the night and showering me with gold coins, whereupon I'd wake up in the fork of a tree with pocketfuls of broken tiles and a dead dog under my arm. Or so it was said.

'The question is,' Andor finally asked, 'whether you'd prefer your bagpipe with or without a goat's head.' Given all the local legends that essentially laid the credit/blame for the bagpipe's invention at the feet of Satan himself (or occasionally his little horned helpers), there was no question at all – a goat's head it would be. Sometimes, you just have to take the risk.

Terminal Condition

It was late in the spring when Dad finally put aside his apprehensions and packed his bags for Europe. He was going to England for a fortnight to visit relatives before heading to Hungary, so I went to meet him in Frankfurt, to join him for the last leg to Manchester.

This involved close to three hours on the dawn train from Pécs in a carriage stuffed with schoolchildren who were so high-spirited they could have caused aural bleeding. Then almost the moment I joined the Frankfurt train in Budapest, I got stuck helplessly eavesdropping on a conversation, partly on the grounds that it completely dominated the carriage.

One of the conversational parties was an Austrian who spoke in a high, excitable voice, like a Mitteleuropean Archbishop Desmond Tutu. 'Thet is a reMARKable thought. Then, who would you SINK was the most imPORtant political personage of the twentieth century, eef NOT Weenston CHURchill?'

The other was a young man who sounded like something I sometimes feared I was becoming myself – a not-quite-Hungarian who gets more overheated about Magyar issues than the Magyars do. As the train quietly zipped along through northwestern Hungary toward Austria, he started speaking in a clipped, public-school English accent that slipped into a Central European mélange one vowel at a time. The thing about Mr Clipped was how proud he was of his lineage, judging by the number of times he used the word 'forefathers'. It transpired that his father was a Hungarian who'd fled the homeland for Britain after the 1956 revolution, and his mother was Austrian. He was soon onto his aristocratic background and reciting his full family name, a task which required the best part of a minute. There'd been property confiscated by the communists, but now returned and due to one day be inherited by Mr Clipped himself. It was clear he didn't regard Gyurcsány or the Hungarian Socialist Party, or MSzP, as anything more than a bunch of vile commies and it was a source of bewilderment to him that the stupid, uncomprehending Hungarian nation could have voted the traitors back in. The fault, he deduced, had to lie with the proles in the poorer counties. Unlike, say, the voters in more monied areas such as Sopron, where his girlfriend evidently hailed from.

'My girlfriend said to me, "You know, Jozsef, I'm very proud of Sopron." And I said, you know, "Why are you so proud of Sopron, Klára?" And she said, "Because they voted 60 per cent for Fidesz." And I kissed her.'

Curiously, the subject of Jews came up and Mr Clipped sounded like one of Erik D'Amato's Fidesz supporters without the *pálinka*.

'Whether you love them or hate them, it doesn't matter – we have to live with them,' he declared, before going on to sound a conciliatory note. 'Still, we're all people, we're all the same, aren't we?' There followed stories about the staunchly communist aunt who'd stayed in Hungary and now lived in a big house in Budapest's poshest suburb, then a passionate dissertation on the foolishness of

Transylvanian Hungarians who kept themselves culturally isolated by refusing to learn Romanian and engage with Romania, preferring instead to somehow imagine that they still belonged to a world that, to most intents and purposes, was wiped out in 1920.

And then, as the train sighed its way into Vienna's Westbahnhof station, it was back to those hints of aristocracy. It had been going on without pause for two-and-a-half hours and my attention was slipping.

'And I don't have to explain myself to these people, and do you know why? It's because I don't care about them. They *mean* nothing to me. Absolutely nothing. What. So. Ever. Anyway, it's back to work in Wien, *c'est la vie*.'

'And WHEN will you be reTURNing to Hungary?'

'On the weekend,' said Mr Clipped, shouldering his bag with a jolly laugh before raising his voice and adding, 'Thank God.'

The train fell into a strange silence after that.

SEVERAL HOURS LATER, I stiffly made my way across the road from Frankfurt's Hauptbahnhof to the hotel I'd stayed at with Bel and the kids just six weeks before, confident that I'd be okay without a booking; the concierge soon set me straight on that count. His eyebrows lifted like the wings of a bird about to take flight as he peered at me across the rims of his spectacles. He looked like an owl that had swallowed a slug and only just realised its mistake.

'No, I'm afraid we have no rooms,' he said at last. 'I think you will find Frankfurt is full tonight.'

It was a line I heard repeatedly as I trudged from one hotel to another. I got so desperate, I even started asking at youth hostels, the whole time trying to wipe my brain clean of memories from ten years ago, especially ones involving being woken in the small hours by drunken Dutch boys who, between hiccups and the odd bout of projectile vomiting, imparted information on the quality of the beer being served downstairs.

'You mean you have not booked?' asked one hostel keeper, looking like an owl that had swallowed two slugs. 'I wish you luck, my friend. Frankfurt is full tonight.'

It had been all so easy in April when the hotels were giving away beer to attract guests, a marketing strategy that would have pleased those Dutch boys. Now the city was warming up for the World Cup and Frankfurt was buzzing with trade fairs and conferences and a schmuck like me was faced with the option of either joining the hobos outside the main train station, or trying my luck at an upmarket hotel and handing over the equivalent of two months' rent. It had to be said, the hobos looked kind of friendly. Or at least the ones with bottles did.

A sheepish despondency descended upon me; surely I could have managed slightly better than this. I didn't even want to be in Frankfurt. It's the sort of place I'd only really want to be in if I needed to feel better about the idea of death or, as was the case now, wait for my father. It was then I started contemplating the Third Way. I'd never spent a night in an airport before – the whole idea holds as much appeal as a burst abscess – but as I sat on the airport train, I reminded myself that you've got to start somewhere.

The airport train was in itself a revelation, or at least it was to me, a regular user of what is whimsically referred to as an airport train in Sydney. The Frankfurt version was clean, fast, comfortable and, in the most radical move of all, had space specifically designed for storing luggage. For all these wonders, one was only expected to shell out 3.35 euros, compared to the megafare they ask for in Sydney.

With my head still spinning, I floated into Frankfurt airport, feeling a slight twinge as I passed the entrance to the Sheraton.

Large posters emphasising the barely imaginable comfiness of the hotel's space age beds had an almost calculated cruelty about them as I entered the realm of harried faces, swarming baggage trolleys and hard seating. I headed straight to a bar for an overpriced beer to help shorten the night, and a dire soup that only ended up prolonging it.

To escape the noise, I made the mistake of retreating to a toilet cubicle with a magazine, but the loo was dominated by burly Germans who declaimed such witticisms as 'Ah, Luft!' in stentorian voices as they broke wind at the urinal. I returned to the bar and waited.

As the crowds thinned out and the check-in counters shut down one after the other, I took a breath, girded my loins and, like a man who's just been given a choice of execution methods, headed out to examine the sleeping options. This pleased the waitress, who had been dropping hints of an increasingly truculent nature that she'd like me to settle up.

Apart from the music (Sting, Robbie Williams and Boney M on punishingly high rotation) and a call for passengers for the last flight of the night (to Armenia, I think), the quiet in this cavernous space was almost unsettling. Now and then there was the soft whir of a security guard trundling past on a bicycle or the distant, bat-like squeak of luggage trolley wheel. Luminous soccer balls advertising the World Cup festooned the ceiling and bright lights shone on nearly every surface. With almost no one left to soak up the photons, the glare had a merciless, almost outback quality to it.

My first attempt to set up camp in the shade beneath an escalator was brought to a polite end by a security guard. Wandering on, I noted that most of the seating was fitted with the sort of metal armrests they put on park benches to keep homeless people from sleeping on them. This was presumably why Frankfurt's hobos hung out at the train station instead.

As I sat down and made myself uncomfortable, I saw I wasn't the only schmuck in town. I started to notice people slowly traipsing back and forth across the glossy wasteland with dark patches under their eyes and the slack jaws of the undead. Others tried to rig up footrests with their trolleys or arrange their bags into vaguely bed-like arrangements; laptops were a popular if ultimately unpleasant choice of pillow. Everyone looked either resigned, depressed or recently exhumed, apart from a small group of Poles passing around a bottle of something clear and evidently cheering.

As the first hour passed with thoughts of the growing chiropractor bill, I eased myself to the floor, curled up and started wishing that Dell made softer laptops and that the Germans made warmer airport floors. Within half an hour, I surrendered and joined the ranks of the Terminal 2 zombies, propped up against a luggage trolley and shuffling and squeaking my way up and down. I even tried outside for the fresh air – or as fresh as it was likely to be at one of the world's busiest airports – but beaten by drizzle and wafts of kerosene, I passed back through the sliding doors, wondering whether this was all worth the two days I was going to spend in England before hightailing it back to Hungary.

It was then that I noticed some of my fellow schmucks doing something remarkable – they were *sleeping*. My exhausted brain managed a feeble somersault at the sight. They had carefully threaded their way around the anti-hobo armrests like garter snakes and, miracle of miracles, made it to the land of nod. Almost hysterical with gratitude, I hurled myself at an empty row of seats, followed their example and almost immediately passed out. Roughly twenty minutes later, I was wakened by the sound of passengers shuffling off the Sydney flight, my father among them.

'Bloody hell, bonny lad,' Dad said, looking me up and down. 'You look like you could do with a coffee.' This from a man who'd spent the best part of the past twenty-one hours sitting bolt upright with a string of bad movies and his knees pinned against the seat in front.

A couple of hours later we were in the air, but not before Dad had passed the time quizzing airport staff about the extra security measures ('Good grief. Is it really necessary for me to take my belt off too? What's going to hold my pants up? Well, I'll take it off if you're interested in seeing my underpants.'), oblivious to the grumbling queue of passengers banking up behind him.

It was interesting to watch Dad in action. After three decades in Australia, his English accent was as broad as ever. When I was at school, he used to answer the phone by reciting the number ('Hello, nine fahv two wan' etc) and my friends would call up just to hear him do it. Nevertheless, he was a proud Australian with the paperwork to prove it. With that pride came the apparent right to harp on about the bloody Poms, the whingeing Poms, the crap-at-cricket Poms, the voting-for-Margaret-Thatcher Poms, the failing-to-properly-index-his-British-pension Poms, and the non-washing-and-possibly-quite-allergic-to-soap Poms. (This was balanced by fervour for all things Scottish and Celtic, but that's a different matter.) But as we sat in the tiny British Airways plane high above the continent, chugging beers in an attempt to take the edge off our sleep-deprivation-induced delirium, he got whingier the closer we got to England.

'What are those flight attendants blethering about? You'd think they'd make it their priority to serve the passengers. What could they be talking about all this time? Oh, no, don't mind us. No, no, not us. We're just the paying customers. Bloody stupid. Ah, here they come at last. That's right, in your own sweet time. Blethering females. What? Oh, bloody marvellous, isn't it, Jim? You ask for something on the menu and they don't have it. You could put Daisy in charge of running an airline and she'd do a better job.'

I commented that he sounded just like one of those whingeing Poms he was so fond of banging on about. He paused and lifted one of his eyebrows, which had of late become quite shaggy. 'You watch your tone there, bonny lad.'

The Dutch coast passed in a long haze of straight beach, followed by the bruise-coloured North Sea then a vast, dark blanket of cloud, somewhere beneath which lay England.

'What do you think to that, then?' Dad said, before putting on a Yorkshire accent and lapsing into one of his favourite Michael Palin sketches. 'It were always raining in Denley Moor. And when it weren't raining, it were precipitating . . .' It wasn't until we began the descent that we caught any glimpses of the land.

From the air, the suburbs of Manchester spread like globs of stale porridge beneath clouds the colour of cigarette ash. Here and there, the porridge gave way to a rain-lashed shade of putty, only to become exhausted by the effort and lapse back into porridge. It was as if the full light spectrum was yet to be discovered in this part of England. After Hungary's sunshine and poppies and vineyards, I felt like I'd been whacked in the face with a dead haddock. As the plane sank towards the greyness, I kept hearing Mum's voice in my popping ears: 'I cried every night for four years!'

'Enjoying it, bonny lad?' Dad chortled. One of the things he enjoyed most in life were reminders that the decision to move the family from the Sodden Isles to sun-fried Australia had been nothing short of marvellous. Back in Sydney, no visit to the harbour with Dad was ever complete until he'd asked me – with the downward-curving smile he usually wore when he was amusing himself – if I thought it was a good idea we'd left Wigan.

A short time later, we passed through streets of houses that looked as if they were covered in a sheen of sweat, then rose up into the stone walls and emerald fields of the Pennines. Prim little pubs and sheep so white and fluffy they looked as if they had just been laundered flashed in the windows. Dad looked ecstatic. I tried to picture him arriving back in this world with Mum and Eszt and Lac, but only the blurriest images took shape in my mind.

The Incredible Shrinking Country

WHAT COULD BE the most beautiful word in the Hungarian language? There are always lists suggested. The word for pearl – *gyöngy* – is all but impossible to write out for an English speaker, other than to say that it sounds nothing like it looks. It's nudged by the tip of the tongue from that silken space behind the top teeth with the gentlest of d's softened yet further with a drop of j, the vestiges of its edge bevelled away by the most fleeting of y's before yielding the floor to a sensuous but indescribable ö that gently arcs down onto a satin n that melts straight back into one of those j-flavoured soft d's and the faintest ghost of a y. All so circular and lustrous, but without gloss – like a pearl itself. *Csók*, on the other hand, has the heat, the intensity and the lingering locking of lips of the kiss that it describes. Then there's *gulyás*, or goulash, a word with a beauty of its very own. On other days, with the right perversity of mood, *vihar* – storm – and the remorselessly staccato *retenetes* – terrible – take on an irresistible, delicious appeal. Just roll the r, sh the s, and fire the syllables like bullets: rrre-te-ne-tesh.

At the ugly end of the spectrum, Trianon is a regular favourite.

The Treaty of Trianon is to Hungarians what the Treaty of Versailles is to Germans. Both were drawn up in Paris in the aftermath of the Great War as punishment for those who lost; both helped clear the path toward World War II. Or, more specifically, Versailles helped make the rise of Hitler possible; Trianon provided him with a few more lunatics.

For Hungary, Trianon meant the loss of people and the loss of land, more than they'd ever imagined possible. It meant the end of any remaining delusions that Hungary – the thousand-year-old kingdom that had survived the Tatars, the Turks, but not quite the Habsburgs – was still one of Europe's players. Trianon was the beginning of smallness.

I knew next to nothing about any of this until my first trip back to Hungary as an adult in 1995 when my cousin Andris – bullheaded, scowling Andris – presented me with a pre-Trianon map. 'Here,' he said, 'see what we once were.' Andris' simmering awareness of Hungary's achievements and losses, and his equally simmering awareness of the rest of the world's ignorance, ensured moments like this were semi-regular. The first time he met Bel, he demanded she tell him what she knew of Hungary and its many inventions (the ballpoint pen, carburettor, Rubik's cube, hydrogen bomb [shared credit] and so on), discoveries (vitamin C, how to make skirts less than three inches long) and Nobel prizes (mainly to Jewish Hungarians who did their best work after bailing out of Hungary, but that's a detail). Come to think of it, I may have done the same thing to Bel, but I'm pretty sure it wasn't on the first date.

Now that communism has faded, taking with it any obligations of solidarity with the Warsaw Pact neighbours, Hungarians have become more open about Trianon and many have taken to buying bumper stickers showing the old Hungary, the three times bigger Hungary. Not that I've noticed Andris resorting to one.

The unfamiliar shape was a source of puzzlement to non-Hungarian friends who came to visit; they were familiar with the dimensions of the country – like a jelly bean's but only slightly bigger – but this other Hungary was a mystery. To my eyes at least, it looked irresistibly like a *duda*. The more often I saw the map – in shop windows, on provocative T-shirts, stencilled onto bus shelters and even carved out of wood to form one of the world's few truly nationalistic salad trays – the more clearly I saw the tiny wooden goat head dangling from the front of an inflated goatskin bag. Others showed the present-day Hungary helpfully positioned within the bigger set of borders. All of them were reminders that there's one basic lesson history keeps handing out – if you go to war, don't lose.

Hungary had variously embraced the Habsburgs, tried to shake them off, gone to war against them (only for the Emperor to cheat and call on the Tsar, who unsportingly obliged with two hundred thousand troops) and eventually reached a compromise with them that left Hungary as one half (a junior half, truth be told) in a dual monarchy, one half in an empire that bore the names of both countries. So when the heir to the throne of that Austro-Hungarian Empire was assassinated in the clumsily annexed Sarajevo and Europe dissolved into war, Hungary could hardly stand by. Far from it. As in so many countries across the globe, the citizens cheered like children at a carnival as their young men marched off to the newest and most advanced interpretation of hell the human race had yet conceived.

By the time it was over, when the last of the trenches had been emptied and the last of the mustard gas had faded from those fields of mud and blood, the side that won looked at Hungary – junior partner on the side that didn't – with dim, unforgiving eyes. It was time to pull out the maps and the razors.

Cartographically speaking, the pre-Trianon Kingdom of Hungary looked, for the great majority who are not of a bagpipular disposition, like a heart (anatomically correct rather than a Valentine's) covering a great swathe of central Europe, filling the Carpathian Basin and covering Transylvania, Slovakia, plenty of Croatia and Serbia, and even a chunk of Ukraine. From the heart, one major blood vessel reached all the way down to Fiume (now Rijeka) on the Adriatic coast, from where steamers with names like the *Pannonia* and the *Transylvania* would set out for faraway New York. After Trianon, the truncated and suddenly landlocked Hungary looked more like a small, lonely kidney.

A multi-ethnic kingdom with a dizzying multitude of languages, an inexplicably ham-fisted approach to non-Magyar minorities and vast sweeps of territory dominated by other races that wanted out, Hungary was ripe for plucking. Foreign armies and armed bands marched in unimpeded with the approval of the Entente powers to grab the bits they wanted. The Czechoslovaks went to town in the north, the Yugoslavs in the south and the Romanians worked their way right up to Budapest. The Romanian army mightn't have been much chop as an ally to the Entente powers during the war, but it made up for its earlier shortcomings in spades, swooping on Hungary like battalions of repo men on crack. (Pécs escaped Romania's attentions, falling instead under Serbian control until 1921.) To cap it off, Hungary chose this particular moment in history to have its first stab at communism. Less than two years after the Bolshevik revolution in Russia that had given almost everyone else the willies, the birth of the Republic of Councils – the Soviet Republic of Hungary – was declared in Budapest.

Led by a provincial journalist called Béla Kun, it lasted for one hundred and thirty days – 'marked,' wrote historian John Lukács, 'by imbecility, inefficiency and terror' – and could not have been more badly timed. Hungary had lasted, more or less, for a thousand years, but now, as the victorious allies gathered to mete out punishment, its number was up.

Germany, as has regularly been noted, did not fare well under the conditions laid down by the Treaty of Versailles. A wounded corporal called Hitler would have plenty to say about that at a later date. Austria, which had the blowtorch of the Saint-Germain-en-Laye Treaty applied to it, didn't come out of the Paris peace talks a whole lot better. But for some reason – one which no one has yet entirely worked out, except in moments of deepest drunkenness – when the time came to frame the Treaty of Trianon and bollock Hungary, the delegates went for gold.

Writing in his diary, the British diplomat Harold Nicolson described that May day in Paris: 'There (in that heavy tapestried room, under the simper of Marie de Medicis, with the windows open upon the garden and the sound of water sprinkling from a fountain and from a lawn hose) the fate of the Austro-Hungarian Empire is finally settled. Hungary is partitioned by these five distinguished gentlemen – indolently, irresponsibly partitioned – while the water sprinkles on the lilac outside, while the experts watch expertly.'

Just over a year later, the peace treaty with the shrivelled Hungary was finally signed in Paris – on 4 June 1920 – and the conditions of Trianon officially took effect. Halfway across the continent, church bells tolled and black flags flew. Hungary had lost two-thirds of its territory and three million Magyars had woken up in foreign countries. It wouldn't be the last time either in a part of the world especially prone to the moveable feast of borders. (There is the joke about the man who was born in the Austro-Hungarian Empire, spent his childhood in Hungary, studied in Czechoslovakia, was married in Hungary, worked in the Soviet Union and eventually retired in Ukraine – without ever leaving his home town of Ungvár. 'In this part of the world,' Péter Esterházy wrote wryly, 'this is how you become a cosmopolitan.')

In Europe, it was only the regularly invaded and partitioned Poles – a Slavic race that Hungarians speak of in much warmer terms than they generally reserve for their neighbours – who could truly appreciate the scale of this cartographical bonsai.

As bad as it all was, nothing else hurt the way the loss of Transylvania did. Croatia was autonomous anyway and Slovakia, it had ruefully been noted, was full of Slovaks. (Though it would have been nice to hang on to Bratislava, or Pozsony, as the Hungarians called it, which was Hungary's second city, and perhaps a few other bits.) The Voivodina part of Serbia and that sliver of Ukraine caused a bit of a twinge (goodbye, Ungvár), and it was something of a surreal insult that Austria, which had done so much to kick-start the war and had been judged an aggressor state, was *rewarded* with its own slice of Hungary. Not a big slice – a shade over four thousand square kilometres – but still.

Vienna almost picked up Sopron into the bargain, but for some miraculous reason, the citizens of Sopron – alone among all the cities of Hungary that the victors were slicing off and divvying up – were allowed to vote in a plebiscite. They elected to stay in Hungary, though the coming decades would have given them ample opportunity to regret it. (It seems Austria won in the end, all the same. 'There are hardly any Hungarians left in Sopron these days,' a Budapest friend once commented. 'Just about the only people there now are Austrians and dentists.')

Transylvania, the *tünderkert* or fairy garden of Hungarian legend, was something else altogether, but it's best not to call it Transylvania when talking to Hungarians. A few years back I mentioned that I was going to Romania to travel through Transylvania – Transylvania of the looming peaks and the shadowy, haunted valleys – and visit the cities of Cluj-Napoca and Sighisoara. Travel plans that involve Romania can still cause nose-wrinkling in some quarters here (or, in the case of Joli, heart palpitations: 'They will rob you the moment you cross the border!'), but that wasn't what caused me my biggest problem. The sharpness of the rebuke that followed taught me to call the towns by their Hungarian names – Cluj was Kolozsvár, Sighisoara was Segesvár and so on. It felt a bit quaint, like referring to Sri Lanka as Ceylon or preferring, as my father seems to, Constantinople to Istanbul. But it kept people happy and allowed me to join in that lingering sense of collective protest and/or denial about the loss of Transylvania to those no-good Romanians.

Even more important than getting the towns right was to forget the name Transylvania ever existed and call the region by its proper name – Erdély. Pronounced Air-day with a strong, rolled r, Erdély, like Transylvania, means land beyond the forest, and when said by Hungarians carries with it a wistful dreaminess as it is released, almost reluctantly, to float free from the tongue.

When Hungary was torn asunder by the Turks, Hungarian nobles helped the Habsburgs, who were rarely blind to a good opportunity, pounce on the Ottoman-free western third of the old Kingdom, leaving Transylvania as the semi-defiant last bastion of the Hungarian nation, a vassal state that the Ottoman pashas never entirely tightened their grip on. It was the Transylvanian János Hunyadi who'd kept the Turks out in the first place and the Transylvanian Prince Rákoczi who rose up with his peasant army to throw off Habsburg rule. (Not that any of it was straightforward – Hunyadi was probably a Magyarised Romanian and Rákoczi, in true Hungarian style, provided another glorious failure for national celebration.) As the sway of foreign powers waxed and waned in Budapest, Transylvania was the repository of all that was most truly Hungarian, and if Budapest was Hungary's head, Erdély was the heart.

The piece of Hungary that Romania managed to wrest for itself was actually bigger than what remained of Hungary. Just to rub it in that little bit harder, the Romanians also managed to nab a string of cities (Arad, Nagyvárad/Oradea, Temesvár/Timisoara and others) that were never even considered to be a part of historical Transylvania and now lie just out of reach on the other side of that resented frontier. It's amazing they didn't ask for Budapest as well and be done with it.

There is always the danger of emotion and, God forbid, nationalism clouding these matters, but it's hard not to read the historical record and conclude that Hungary, alone and friendless at the Paris peace talks, was well and truly fleeced. Both sides to this day have much that is true and much that is, at best, historically dubious in their claims, but in the end it was Romania that got all the real estate.

'Why do you want to go there?' Joli wailed. 'How many times do I have to remind you? First they'll rob you, then they'll cut your throat! *Retenetes*!'

Yes, Romania has long, strong links to a lot of Transylvania; yes, they ultimately outnumbered the Hungarians; and yes, they probably (sorry Mum, the devil is making me write this) had the strongest claims to the majority of it. But *all of it*? That's what irks more than anything else. It irked so much that the next time the world went collectively insane and had itself a war, Hungary signed up on the side of Hitler, and for a while even had parts of Transylvania back in its possession. But the celebrations were louder in Budapest than they were in Transylvania, where many of the Hungarian locals, including the fading ranks of the Magyar aristocracy, preferred the idea of an autonomous Transylvania to one tied to either the old capital or the new. But who was listening to them?

The rest of the war and the decades of Soviet domination that came as a reward helped Hungary to reflect on the wisdom of this decision.

These days, even Hungarians who still feel strongly about Transylvania generally restrict themselves to provocative maps, grumbling, the odd alcohol-fuelled rant, some impotent bumper stickers and a bit of national melancholy each year when the anniversary falls. There's sadness – a soft, futile sort of sadness – but precious little anger. Then there's the benign influence of the EU. 'Soon, Romania will be a member, too,' I was told late one night by a pair of young folk musicians. 'We will watch as the border vanishes and Trianon just won't matter any more.'

And besides, they're close enough to the Balkans to see what happens when you take these things further.

Now and Then

Dad had kept threatening in his usual jokey way to bring the weather with him from England. I'd left him in sodden Derbyshire almost two weeks before and joyfully returned to the Hungarian spring, but now, as the rain smeared the windows of the bus out to Budapest's Ferihegy airport, it's possible I may have cursed him once or twice. Matters probably weren't helped by the perky text my Aunt Elizabeth had sent from Derbyshire to let me know that after a fortnight of almost constant rain, the sun had reappeared nearly the moment Dad's plane left British airspace. In Hungary meanwhile, it felt as if God had gone back on his promise to Noah and decided a second deluge might be in order after all.

It wasn't normal rain, either. It was the extra cold variety that feels like it might have just been melted by an emperor penguin's toes and dripped from the edge of a glacier, possibly with bits of ice still in it. Not only does it sting when it hits your skin, it manages to find its way with laser-guided accuracy through the tiny gap between your shirt and the back of your neck, landing between your shoulder blades like an electric shock. Recalling the energy I'd expended during my brief stay in England griping about the weather and banging on about how much nicer it was in the sun-kissed paprika paradise, I felt a twinge of embarrassment.

Not that any of this mattered a jot to Dad. His plane from London landed ten minutes early, only for the passengers to be held up while the airport staff struggled to remember whose job it was that night to turn on the baggage carousel. I think this was helpful to Dad as it reminded him of Hungary in 1968.

In the arrivals area, even the generally patient locals were starting to get a bit toey. 'The whore plane has been on the ground for half an hour,' one man growled into his mobile. 'And I still haven't seen any passengers. Fuck it.'

It was late at night and the few shops that do their bit to enliven Terminal 2B (or not to be, as it was by this stage) were closed, apart from a bar that had most of its security shutters down and two staff hovering with bored expressions near the remaining drinkers. Nearby, bunches of flowers revolved on a display stand inside a refrigerated vending machine. I was grateful it was Frankfurt airport I'd had to spend a night in and not Budapest.

To pass the time, I began unfolding the free maps of Budapest that sat in piles on the rental car company counters and compared them to see which had the largest number of ads for strip joints and escort agencies. Business seemed to be booming, if a little fraught with angst. 'Warning!' announced the ad for Royal Palace, an establishment that billed itself as 'More than night club . . .'

'Taxi drivers,' it continued in haphazard English, 'ask for money after each passengers from the bars and clubs, 50–70 euros in Budapest. It is paid by you in the entry fee. So we seriously ask you not to take any taxi. We will take you, so the ride and the entry are free of charge.' Rival club Aphrodite wasn't showing the same anxieties, instead promising top cuisine and something called an 'eritic show'. Even a money exchange was trying to get in on the act, promising customers that they'd experience 'good atmosphere, friendly cashier and chef' while they converted their currency into forints. It all seemed far removed from Pécs; I could feel myself turning into a provincial hick who only makes trips to the capital reluctantly and with a sense of suspicion.

'Forty minutes now and still no passengers,' said the man with the mobile, sounding as if he might do something rash.

Then the doors hissed open and out popped Dad in his bright red jumper and trusty blazer. On the occasions he hadn't been driving, Dad's arrivals in Hungary used to be at the dowdy and barely glorified shed that had since been renovated and pressed into service as the terminal for budget airlines – *fapados,* or wooden benchers, as Hungarians call them. As we hugged, he seemed taken aback by all the light and gloss and revolving carnations.

'Is this Ferihegy?' he asked, glancing warily at the flower-vending machine. 'Are you sure?'

A minute later, we were standing on the pavement waiting for a taxi, watching the rain drip from the upper level and Dad felt he was back on moistly familiar ground.

'It were always raining in Denley Moor. And when it weren't raining, it were precipitating . . .'

Budapest airport had a curious set-up with taxis. Only one company – at that time it was the ominously named Tourist Taxi – was allowed to queue in the ranks and solicit passengers. Naturally, any taxi company granted this fortunate monopoly tended to make the most of it by charging fares that required a limber imagination and a degree in astronomy to understand. It was a touchy topic that kept the letters page editors busy at Budapest's expat newspapers. But thanks to a magnanimous loophole, people were allowed to order regular taxis by phone and they would come from a little patch of wasteland just outside the airport's territory, scuttling in like cockroaches sprung in the middle of the kitchen floor when the light goes on.

We were soon on our way through the sluicing rain to the apartment where we were to spend the night before catching the train to Pécs. Dad gazed about with wide eyes while the driver hunched sullenly over the wheel.

'I can't say I'm recognising any of this,' Dad said, peering out into the murk.

'I'm not surprised, Dad. It's after midnight and it's pissing rain. Everything's practically invisible.'

'All so very unfamiliar.' He was rolling his r's; whenever Dad got tired, pedantic or simply wanted to emphasise a point, a Scottish brogue would creep like mist into his voice. Inherited from his father, he would claim, although it struck us as something he only inherited some time in his sixties.

'Where did you say we were going?' the driver asked.

I told him the fifth district – the heart of Pest – just near the Parliament. The news didn't seem to please him. We passed through the city's outer layer of service stations and giant supermarkets and a sense of faded grandeur began to infuse the buildings as we neared the centre of town.

'When I used to fly to Ferihegy in the past,' Dad said, 'we'd get off the plane and onto a bus. Everyone on the plane would be so frantic to get off the plane and pile onto the bus, the daft buggers. I'd just wait and get on the bus last, then of course I'd be the first one off.' Dad allowed himself a little chuckle at the memory.

Word went out on the taxi radio that a fellow driver had been stabbed in the thigh and robbed by his passengers somewhere across town. Our driver's mood fell further, as did his concentration. Our destination, despite being just behind the biggest and most distinctive building in the entire country, was proving elusive. We started travelling in circles in the downpour, our driver grumbling with ever greater vigour because he was transporting us at the fixed airport transfer rate; he'd kept the meter on to see how much money he was missing out on and he muttered something dark every time he glanced down. Unexpectedly, our street sign flashed wetly in the headlights.

'Here we are!' I yelped, with perhaps a little more emotion than was strictly called for.

The taxi came to a halt and the driver cocked an eyebrow at me. 'Exactly here?'

'Exactly here,' I lied.

Dad and I lugged his bags through the rain down the last couple of blocks to the front door of the apartment building where I'd rented a room for us, and into the darkened courtyard where we waited for the lift as it crept earthwards with the urgency of a stalactite.

'Welcome to Hungary,' I said as the lift arrived with a not entirely reassuring thunk.

'Thank you, bonny lad.' Even in the dark I could see he was happy.

It was Dad's first night in Hungary in three decades. It was also my first time sharing such a small room with him in quite some time. As we lay in that rented room, the glow of the elderly, insomniac landlady's TV flickered through the frosted glass of the living room door and onto the hallway's papered walls in a spasmodic kaleidoscope of silver. I half thought of joining her – there would have been the certainty of cake and tea with a slice of lemon – but instead I chose the path of valour and whiled away the dark hours in that cramped space listening with awe to how richly my father's repertoire of snores had developed during the past couple of years.

Most of the old favourites were there – the Snort 'n' Gulp, the Elephant Rumble, the Freight Train, the Freight Train in a Long Tunnel, the Freight Train in a Long Tunnel and Hitting a Landmine, the Chain-Smoking Rhino, the Window Rattler and the House Imploder. But there had been fresh additions to the playlist, including an almost magical snore that seemed to tell the short but poignant story of a pig happily rooting about in the rich, wet grass by the edge of a lake, before unexpectedly tumbling in, squealing with panic and, despite desperate attempts to paddle to safety, drowning. When the hapless porker came up for air for possibly the last time, I decided to put it out of its misery and threw my pillow at Dad.

'Wha– what is it, bonny lad?' he called out with a startled snuffle, and started snoring again.

As the darkness slowly drained out of the sky, the melancholy thought occurred to me that I might well be inheriting my father's thunderous skills. If that happened and Bel smothered me during the night, I knew the judge would look on her kindly. Then I glanced at Dad's bedside table and quietly cursed myself. I'd been planning to stick a vase of flowers there so he could have told it, for old times' sake, that he'd been a good boy today.

I sank into a brief but dream-filled sleep of contented pigs and tiny men in trenchcoats lowering themselves into bunches of chrysanthemums, while somewhere in the background Mum's voice was bellowing: 'Not chrysanthemums, you idiot! And not even numbers! They are for funerals. Funerals!' Then, under her breath, 'Such a stupid.'

By morning the sun had returned, flooding the courtyard with light and shining on the ice-cream cake dome and spires of the Parliament across the sweep of Kossuth Square. It filled the sky in a great flowering of medieval, renaissance, baroque and neo-gothic exuberance (yes, all of them), an unabashed declaration of grandeur built when the city was at its madly swirling peak, just decades before its almost total destruction and eventual subjugation. When Dad had last been here, that same dome – the no-holds-barred creation of Imre Steindl, who died with slipshod timing just weeks before it was put into use in 1902 – had been topped by a red star, much like the ones that sat balefully atop the towers of the Kremlin in a constellation of ruby. The distant, yet not quite distant enough Kremlin.

Dad was going to have to spend time untangling the resurrected city we were standing in from the one he knew. His Budapest, the Budapest of the late 1960s, was part beautiful but faded capital of an evaporated kingdom, part outlying mission station of a monolithic ideology and smothered in the names of its apostles. Soldiers adorned with the red stars and wheat-wreathed hammers and sickles of an occupying army strutted boulevards, streets and squares bearing the names of Lenin, Marx and Béla Kun. They passed beneath the lantern jaws and stern brows of socialist realist statues spanning the artistic spectrum from semi-successful to catastrophic. The discredited Stalin had been dead for fifteen years and his carved likenesses gone for twelve, but there'd been plenty of other upholders of the faith hulking in bronze and granite on pedestals across the city. Dad's first lodgings were even at a hotel in the Buda hills called the Vörös Csillag, or Red Star. One thing communism couldn't be accused of having was an overly rich stock of imagery.

'I was told by the company secretary that I was being sent to Eastern Europe because I was the company Bolshevist,' Dad said with the smile and soft twinkle that meant he was telling me something he was particularly proud of. 'I got that reputation because even though I was in management, I sometimes sided with the union. Sometimes I'd say, hang on just one minute, the union actually has a point here. Imagine the shock, the horror! Most fellers who were made mine directors at the time would start putting on posh accents and voting for the Tories.' Dad made a derisive noise to indicate that the chances of him ever undergoing such a metamorphosis were slim. 'When I went to America in the late '60s, I was told, "If you're a goddamn commie, you can get the goddamn hell out of here."' The memory of that impudent immigration officer in the Land of the Free clearly still rankled. 'Then here I was, surrounded by them.'

As we walked alongside Kossuth Square, a yellow tram went rumbling past and I feared from the look on Dad's face that he'd just been inspired for the coming night's snore-a-thon. Across the street, a flame flickered at the bottom of a black monolith commemorating the 1956 uprising. Beside us stretched a wall that had been strafed with bullets during one of the Red Army's more successful exercises in bloodletting.

A lot of the old statues had either disappeared or been relocated to an open-air museum on the outskirts of Budapest (where among other things you could buy Stalin-shaped candles), but new ones had sprung up in their place.

'You weren't even allowed to mention his name when I was here,' Dad said as we came to a statue of a bespectacled, moustachioed man on a small footbridge, glancing back over his shoulder at the Parliament, brolly hanging from his arm. 'You quite possibly would have been arrested.'

It was Imre Nagy, the prime minister during that electrifying autumn when Hungary, inspired by turmoil in Poland and Khrushchev's denunciation of Stalin, revolted against Moscow's rule. For a moment, as secret policemen were hanged from lamp posts and Russian tanks burned in the streets, it seemed as if the country might break free and follow its heart into Western Europe. Of course, it was never going to happen. Not then. Khrushchev, who had spoken out against Stalin's brutality in a 'secret' speech planned for wide-scale distribution, responded by sending two thousand tanks, while the West busied itself with the Suez crisis. Nagy was eventually betrayed by an old comrade, given a show trial and hanged. (Decades later as the sclerotic regime shuffled quietly toward its doom, Nagy was officially rehabilitated and his remains dug up for a grand, cathartic reburial. It was only as they exhumed him that it was discovered his executioners had gone to the effort to insult him one last time and buried him face down.)

'Excuse me, but would you mind taking a photo of us?' A camera was thrust into my hands by a smiling pair of young Austrian women who scampered onto the bridge and draped themselves around Nagy as if he were some fusty but fondly regarded old schoolteacher.

'Do you know who that is?' I asked, trying to swallow a faint sense of queasiness, trying to remind myself that I wasn't really Hungarian and shouldn't be getting sniffy.

'Um,' one of them said, straining to read the name plaque. 'Yeah, that guy.'

Reasonable answer, I thought, pressing the button. And besides, there were plenty of Hungarians who, while agreeing with the sentiment, thought the statue to be complete rubbish. 'Idealising to the point of falsification,' fumed András Török – writer, one-time dissident and former state secretary for culture. 'The martyr prime minister was a typical stocky, overweight Hungarian peasant type, quite unlike this melancholic café type.' (Later, as we watched the shamelessly censored footage of Nagy's 1958 show trial, we could see what Török meant.)

Feeling the need to become café types ourselves and work on becoming, if not stocky, then at least a little overweight, we pushed on, certain we could hear the siren song of *dóbos torta*, Gerbeaud slice and sour cherry strudel above the pealing of church bells. We strolled purposefully along the river bank, the brown Danube washing frenetically against the quays beneath us. Gaudy riverboats floated in shining procession beneath Budapest's many bridges, slipping effortlessly past barges that stolidly chugged along with all the colour and glamour of black puddings. Across the water, Buda rose sharply in a stately swelling of spire and palace-crowned hill, while behind us, trams as gay as buttercups clattered their way over the Margaret Bridge. As we walked, Dad was quietly adjusting to a Budapest with advertising, billboards and signs plugging something other than the values of heroic socialist labour.

'Oh God, them as well,' Dad grimaced as he caught sight of the Golden Arches. This from a man who frequents his local McDonald's on an almost daily basis. ('Yes, but that's different, bonny lad. I just go to drink their coffee – I get free refills with my senior's card – and do the *Herald* crossword. And I have a chat with the other regulars; it's café society, Engadine style.')

Then there was the traffic. Unbroken columns of cars crept along the UNESCO-protected (and therefore unalterable) Danube embankments, gaining reinforcements at the bridges as more vehicles inched off in deliriously slowly unfurling plaits of steel. And peak hour was a long way off.

'That's definitely changed. There was hardly any traffic at all back then. God's truth, look at them all.' He cast a dismayed eye at the chains of brake lights stretching into the hazy distance. 'And it's not just the volume of traffic, but the sheer diversity.' Strong r's on the last words; he was becoming a Highlander again. At home, Dad was a compulsive harasser of the local council over traffic issues, and the sight of it here was firing him up into one of his Celtic states. 'No, there was scarcely any traffic at all, and what little there was was mainly Wartburgs and Trabants and Ladas. Now look at it, grief! Everyone trapped in their little metal boxes, everyone in a great hurry and getting nowhere.' Then his tone turned conciliatory. 'At least there don't seem to be a lot of four-wheel drives.'

There was little doubt about his position on four-wheel drives; as the words were pushed with evident distaste through his lips, he sounded like William Wallace getting ready to impale some Sassenach stooge on his broadsword. The only time Dad usually displayed any broadsword-ish inclinations was when the subject of Mum came up. At least we were on completely neutral ground here; Budapest was not Mum's city and Mum was most emphatically not a Budapest type. (Was she a type at all? Hmm, different discussion.)

We walked through sunlit, pastel squares and streets slicing through blocks of low, ornate buildings that had an almost creamy richness to them. Light sparkled in the water tinkling in fountains, and in one warm corner an elderly busker dozed contentedly over the metal strings of his zither. Later in the day, gypsy bands would descend upon the restaurants with their cimbaloms and violins, flooding the air with syrupy music and only just stopping short of impaling diners' eardrums on their sawing bows. We came to a café (near a sculpture of a man and a behatted skeleton holding each other's heads) and Dad explained that this was one arena where Hungarians not actually caught up in the vast, sprawling communist apparatus – or at least working for it on a freelance basis as informers – would engage in a little passive resistance.

'You'd go into a café or a restaurant and notice that it was almost completely empty,' Dad said. 'Except for maybe a couple of Russian soldiers, who'd be given a table up the back by the toilets. And the Russians seemed to just accept this as their lot and take their seats. I don't think they were under any illusions about their popularity with the locals.'

That was the thing about the Hungary Dad first came to in 1968; compared to the neighbours, it was communist-lite. For the Soviet empire, 1956 had been both a scare and an unmitigated public relations catastrophe. Coming so soon after the beginnings of an apparent thaw, the remorselessness with which the uprising was snuffed out showed that, really, nothing had changed. All around the world, so many communists who had clung to their faith, in the face of so much, finally tore up their membership cards and turned their backs on Marx's monster forever. So rather than suffer that sort of embarrassment again, Moscow went easy on Hungary after that. And look how well behaved they were! (Unlike those bloody ingrate Czechoslovaks, who were then having the stew beaten out of them across the border – Brezhnev wanting to show the world his balls were as big as Khrushchev's.)

In 1968, János Kádár was twelve years into an extraordinary 32-year rule that ended barely a year before the Soviet empire did. He'd survived the regime's fickle favour, including bouts of imprisonment and torture at the hands of his colleagues during the darkest years of the communist terror in the 1950s. He'd even survived being a pariah – the traitor who turned on his erstwhile friend Imre Nagy and allowed himself to be installed as the Kremlin's new and more obedient poodle – to become the socialist world's most popular leader. He subverted Stalin's motto, 'He who is not for us is against us', to the altogether more agreeable 'He who is not against us is for us'. The year Dad arrived, Kádár was introducing economic reforms that allowed capitalism to haphazardly creep into the system a molecule at a time, easing the country toward the relative comforts of what became known as goulash communism (available to all good comrades willing to work their arses off for the privilege). Hungarians had a lot more freedom in many aspects of their lives – including the freedom to travel – compared to those living in the fortress of the Soviet Union or Stasi-infested East Germany. Meanwhile, next door, Nicolae Ceausescu was only a few years away from cementing his rule – a dictatorship that was equal parts viciousness, florid hypocrisy and elephantine narcissism – and turning Romania into the virtual prison it would remain until 1989. Things were far from perfect in Hungary and there was much that was deplorable, but Hungarians knew they had it better than most of the neighbours. With enough patience, they could buy a car or a house, and didn't have to worry too much about a knock on the door in the dead of the night. Hence the ironic epithet of the happiest barracks in the concentration camp of the communist world. Happiness is, of course, relative. ('Relative, relative, relative,' I can hear Mum dissent. 'All we wanted to do was get out of there.') As the historian Miklós Molnár wrote, 'A Trabant or a house was no substitute for freedom; it only made non-freedom more tolerable and the soft banality that had replaced hard-line dictatorship less suffocating.'

When the regime finally came to an end in 1989, it did so with little fuss. It was a negotiated revolution with no bang and precious little whimper, leaving the world's media to slake its thirst for drama and blood in other corners of Moscow's swiftly unravelling empire. But back in 1968, as he lay in the Red Star talking to a vase, Dad had little doubt who was calling the shots.

'Yes! It was your mother!' he said brightly as we finally sat down to cake and coffee. 'No, of course I'm just joking.' A mouthful of cake, then a reconsideration. 'Not that your mother was a complete novice when it came to dictatorial behaviour.'

'You didn't know that then.'

'That's true.' The tumultuous event that was the meeting of my parents would have to wait until the following year and the summer of 1969.

Looking back now, I'm not sure whether it was perversity or something else that compelled me to drag Dad, on his first day back in Hungary in over thirty years, to somewhere as emotionally lacerating as the House of Terror. Located at 60 Andrássy Road – once Hungary's most feared address and spoken of the same way Russians speak of the Lubyanka – this museum exists within the walls of the building that served as the headquarters, dungeon and torture centre for both the Hungarian Nazis (the Arrow Cross) during the final year of World War II, then, in one of those fine examples of totalitarian symmetry, the communist secret police.

I'd been there for the first time just a couple of weeks before, taking photos in the moody entrance hall until I was stopped by a young man with a shaved head and a serious black suit.

'You are taking photos,' he observed, not unreasonably.

'Yes.'

'This is not permitted,' he said, motioning as though to grab my camera.

'But there's no sign saying I can't.'

'It is forbidden.'

'Where does it say that?'

'It is forbidden. Delete the photos now please.'

'Where does it say it's forbidden?'

'Delete them NOW.'

Given the nature of the museum, I wondered whether this severe young man was aware of the irony. Or perhaps, I mused, deleting the photos under careful supervision, he was there to foster an authoritarian theme-park atmosphere. It turned out there was a sign around the corner near the cash register, but he was more in tune with the unquestioning obedience schtick.

It was much friendlier the second time around. The cashier eyed Dad up and down then said to me with a wink, 'I'm thinking he's older than sixty-five. He doesn't have to pay.'

'Well, it's very helpful to be let in for free,' Dad said afterwards, 'but don't think I feel flattered. Over sixty-five, indeed.'

'You're seventy-one.'

'That, bonny lad, is beside the point.'

We found ourselves standing beneath the cannon of a Soviet tank, behind which a wall of mugshots of just some of the two regimes' victims stretched to the ceiling some three storeys above us. Then a poignant quote by Imre Kovács across a wall: 'Last night I dreamed the Germans left and no one came to take their place.' But of course, they did. The so-called brown terror of the Nazis and their eager local disciples merged almost seamlessly into the red one that followed. The fevered wish of the Arrow Cross for fire and damnation to fall upon the heads of the Jews blossomed into the communist loathing of an even wider range of people, and much of it was focused in this very building. Bugging equipment and informers helped along a process rounded out with truncheons and electric shocks and interrogation chambers where those not deemed sufficiently forthcoming were beaten to death. Despite the obvious influences of Hitler then Stalin, most of what went on was Hungarian against Hungarian.

Elsewhere, the noose awaited, as did fates arguably worse than such an arbitrary death. Beyond the rotting prison cells of Hungary, the living death of the gulag system stretched all the way from the Soviet frontier across Siberia to the Russian Far East and the Pacific coast. (One night we asked Bel's language teacher, Zsolt, if he'd ever been to the House of Terror. No, he didn't have to, he replied. At the end of the war, his grandparents had been dragged away by the Russians and dumped into the gulag on the strength of their German surname. They'd survived and eventually come home – with stories. No, Zsolt said, a visit to the House of Terror would be superfluous.)

Among the collected tools of the regime, from the most bludgeoning poster to the basest cudgel, video screens on the walls spilled the testimonies of those, like Zsolt's grandparents, who'd been fed into the machine and survived.

Dad grew quieter and quieter as we moved through one floor of ghastliness after another, and I found myself longing for the sunshine and the reassuring buzz of the traffic.

Flicking through the guest book, I noticed, among the more bewildered commentary of Western visitors ('We had no idea this was happening in your country!'), some voices of dissent.

'As scandalous as Hungarian history is,' wrote one Hungarian in a furiously jabbing pen, 'this house is just as scandalous. Ninety-five per cent of this house is devoted to the red terror when the brown terror in this country killed more people.'

(There was also a white terror between the wars under the right-wing Horthy regime; Hungary really tried its damnedest last century to get a whole terror rainbow happening.)

We stepped back out into the innocence of the present, into a grand streetscape that spoke of the time before painting and poetry gave way to the deadweight rule of the psychotic and the prosaic. We stood in the breeze, letting the blood move back into our faces and watching the cars glide beneath the gilded façades of Andrássy Road toward the distant column of Heroes Square.

DAD'S FIRST FEW TRIPS to 1960s Hungary had been scouting trips, flying visits from England to check the lie of the land and to start coming to terms with a socialist state's leviathan bureaucracy. Coming from England, Dad was not entirely unprepared.

Of the first visit, Dad remembers little ('other than a general sense of excitement'), but the second was a different matter. The Prague Spring, or rather the ending of it, was in full swing and Dad's flight into Budapest was delayed by a day after the Hungarian border was temporarily sealed. When he finally got in, he thought the most interesting, if not necessarily wisest, course of action was to join a German associate with the excellent name of Willy Birkemeier and travel the short distance north to the town of Esztergom, which perched with its enormous, heavily columned basilica just across the Danube from Czechoslovakia. They found the place awash with Red Army soldiers, Hungarian militia and a lot of guns. Peering across to the far side of the river, the two men saw 'COME HELP US!' painted plaintively on the concrete bank. Whether it was out of some sense of mischief-making or a genuine curiosity about the local take on events, Dad asked a passing militiaman what was going on.

'He had a rather startled look on his face, as I recall,' Dad said. 'And he said to us, "The West Germans are invading Hungary through Czechoslovakia, and the Soviet Union is coming to the rescue." Of course we knew this was complete bullshit, but he looked like he believed it.' It was barely two decades since Hungary had last been caught between the Germans and the Russians, so if the man looked panicked, he could have been forgiven. 'I suggested to Willy that as he was a West German, it might be for the best if we cleared out. Which we did in due course.'

In due course. Dad has a curiously formal way of speaking sometimes. Not quite like a policeman ('And then, having evaded apprehension, we decamped in a southerly direction'), but with moments of sweetly ill-timed stiffness. I sometimes picture him as a pith-helmeted adventurer lamenting the loss of his legs to a tiger: 'Being a tiger it was rather partial to meat, a fact I am sure you will be conversant with. After wandering into my tent and seeing no readily apparent alternative, it made off with my legs, a course of action which, as you could probably imagine, caused me a considerable degree of discomfort.'

After this glimpse of one of Eastern Europe's revolutions being strangled at birth, Dad found himself – in due course – safely ensconced back at the Red Star, bidding a vase goodnight and preparing for the trip south to Pécs and a revolution of a completely different nature. And a coal mine that was rubbish almost beyond words.

In due course. In good time. I'll think about it. Those were the words that used to drive Mum wild. 'If I waited for him to make up his mind, I would be dead in the ground. He made me want to scream!' (Well, clearly those weren't the only words that drove Mum wild. Sometimes a simple 'hello' sufficed. But 'I'll think about it' had a solid track record.)

As we sat together in the dining car of the Mecsek Intercity, swigging beer in a father–son bonding way while the golden-green countryside scrolled past our curtained window, I kept worrying at the eternal question: how did they *ever* come to be together?

I gazed at Dad's white hair and tried to picture it thick and chestnut brown and framing a boyish face. Geese watched us from yards as we streaked past, paying rather more attention than the bands of chickens scratching around the haystacks and the herd of Great Plain cattle – soft grey with huge, flat horns and laconic expressions – chewing cud in a lush paddock. Storks were out in force, hunting in the reed-fringed wetlands for frogs to drop down the gullets of their rapidly expanding chicks up on their tower and chimney-top nests. Across fields of young, green wheat and sprouting corn, church steeples rose above the clustered roof tops of scattered villages.

'Nothing spectacular, but very beautiful nonetheless,' Dad noted as the conductor checked our tickets. 'Very beautiful indeed.'

I'd travelled on Hungarian trains God knows how many times and never had a problem, with the exception of a plate of slightly dubious gypsy roast once upon a time. Naturally the first time I was going to screw up was going to be in front of my father; Dad seems to exist in a state of constant amazement that I am ever able to find my way anywhere unaided, so the botching of the train tickets probably came as no great surprise.

'Do you not have another part of the ticket to give me?' the conductor asked. 'No?' The sucking of air through teeth. 'Then we have a problem.'

I'd seen him before. He had the quiff and sideburns of a rocker, a mole the size of a radar dome and, beneath eyebrows as thick and dark as bear pelts, an impish glint in his eyes. Just not right now; he had put on a grave expression, one you could comfortably wear to a murder inquest. I was annoyed at myself and embarrassed, rifling through my wallet again for the ticket that wasn't there while my guts twisted a little, just like they did after that gypsy roast.

'So what do you want to do about it?'

'I don't know,' I said uselessly, tipping out the contents of my wallet as if the ticket could be willed into existence. The limits of Dad's Hungarian had been reached and breached, so he contented himself with sipping beer with a look of mild concern.

'You understand that as an employee of Hungarian State Railways, I'm obliged to fine you the cost of the ticket, plus an additional penalty on top of that? That's quite a few forints, you know, quite a few forints. Would you like to think about it for a few minutes?' I half expected him to don his scarlet State Railways cap and begin reciting from the railway code, but instead he went quiet, a trickle of oil oozing into his voice, a gentle, conspiratorial hand lowering onto my shoulder. 'Don't worry, it's not so bad. I'm sure we can work something out. I'll come back soon and –' He glanced about the otherwise empty dining car and softened his voice a little more, '– we'll sort it out. Perhaps you have some dollars, euros? We'll sort it out. Okay?' Then with a wink, he was gone.

'What was that all about, bonny lad? Is there anything I can do to help?'

'As a matter of fact...'

The conductor soon returned, cheered by the continuing absence of an audience.

'Now, what is it to be?' he said, clapping his hands together. 'I have to be able to mark off in my book here that all tickets were correct and accounted for. Would you prefer to pay the fine, or... Or would you prefer to pay something a little more sensible to me so that I can mark things off in my book and we can all relax and you two gentlemen can drink your beer without worry?'

'Sensible sounds good.'

'Excellent, excellent. You look sensible to me. I was thinking to myself, he'll know the sensible thing to do.'

After a quick discussion about exchange rates, a five-pound note purloined from my father's wallet made the world whole again.

'I will make sure Queen Elizabeth is comfortable,' the conductor said, tucking the note in his pocket. Then, with great bonhomie, 'Drink in peace, lads. To your health!'

Dad thought it marvellous. 'It's just like old times,' he said gleefully as the door hissed shut behind the conductor. 'I know that smile of the recently bribed all too well.'

And so it was that we finally rounded the edge of the Mecsek Hills and rolled into Pécs. 'It's a most peculiar feeling, bonny lad,' Dad said as the familiar silhouette of the TV tower hove into view. Then, much closer than the tower, the steeple of the church where he and Mum were married for the second time in a day. 'Even more peculiar.' Then he spotted Bel and Leo on the platform, and Daisy behind them dancing a merry jig to celebrate the arrival of her adored granddad, and he all but flew from his seat.

The Road to Istvánakna

Dad spent much of his fortnight in Pécs in a happy daze, with moments of clarity and recollection piercing through the three decades. 'I don't recall this being here,' was chanted almost like a mantra. So much was different now, of course. Even the glorious Nádor was all but gone, bar the façade.

The Reformation Church, at least, was exactly as he remembered it. The bells began pealing the moment we stood in front of it. ('Curses, I've been spotted,' Dad said.) As the ringing faded, I noticed for the first time that one of the crossroads it stood at was Mártírok utca, or Martyrs Street. Dad found this droll.

We wandered the streets and walked in the woods. We sipped wine and chugged beer, guzzled coffee and inhaled the clouds of purest pong that wafted mercilessly from the thermal baths down the road at Harkány. We went rambling in the countryside where the first of the poppies were raising their scarlet heads and watched farmhands walking to work in the fields with scythes over their shoulders. Sometimes, they carried scythes while riding bicycles, which looked potentially exciting.

The more Dad saw, the more memories began trickling back: the faces and voices of people he'd worked with, and nights of wine and gypsy music at a restaurant called the Rózsakert, or Rose Garden. There were the japesters who'd greet him with, 'Mr Jeffrey . . . Christine Keeler!' – evidently the best known Briton in Hungary at that time – or 'Mr Jeffrey . . . *hat–három*', a reminder of Hungary's Golden Team and its 6–3 trouncing of England at Wembley Stadium more than a decade before Dad first arrived in Pécs. Or when things weren't going so well, the greeting might be a more sardonic, 'Mr Jeffrey, you look like the gypsy who is to be hanged at dawn and says, "The day begins badly."' Dad still guffaws at that one.

Our first attempt to find the apartment that had been his and Mum's was a fiasco, so we had to call in help. Joli, who seemed to know everything and almost everyone in Pécs, declared herself more than up for the task.

We prepared ourselves for the mission with a cake and coffee stop next door to the Nádor's mortal remains. Dad had rediscovered his sweet tooth after a number of celery-crunching years and ploughed his way through Hungary's cakes and ice-cream with abandon. We headed past the Djami and up the hill, buzzing with sugar and caffeine as Joli led us unhesitatingly around corners, along streets and past the house where the composer Zoltán Kodály had lived behind the screen of a dense garden, and came to a squat, but not unattractive, block of flats behind the cathedral. It was three storeys high and painted dark mustard. Dad stared at it blankly for a moment, then came to.

'Oh, yes, that's the one.'

'You lived just up there,' Joli said, 'in the corner on the second floor.'

This was the flat I'd always been told I was conceived in. (It was only later that Mum placed her devastating correction on the record. 'No, it wasn't there at all. Your life started in Budapest. Your farder and I were having a dirty weekend up there. Yes, Jimmykém, you were conceived at the Red Star!') It was also the flat from which my parents had launched their single, half-arsed defection bid. It was part way through what would end up being an eighteen-month battle for Mum to be given approval to leave for England; Dad thought they could perhaps speed things up by heading to Bulgaria and sneaking onto a ship bound for Turkey. Mum, Lac and Eszt remember that the plane rattled and creaked an awful lot, and they remember that the loos at Sofia airport were deeply nasty. They also remember that the ports in Bulgaria were bristling with police and soldiers. So they had a nice beach holiday then headed home.

'Yes,' Dad said, gazing at the block of flats. 'I seem to recall now that there was a doctor who lived above us. Friendly man, pleasant smile. Seemed like a cheerful soul.'

'Yes,' said Joli. 'He killed himself.' Suicide, it would seem, retained its place as one of Hungary's darker national customs, one that has never really been frowned upon. There had been times when Hungary had, per capita, been the world champion. These days, Russia has the winning edge.

'He was just about to move to Algeria with his family to take up a posting,' Joli continued. 'No one noticed anything wrong with him, but he got some sort of poison that only a doctor can get their hands on and he finished himself off. Right there in that very flat.'

It was coal that first led Dad out of Derbyshire and it was coal that eventually brought him to Hungary. As we strolled through the Inner Town beneath belltowers, walls cloaked in sweet clumps of wisteria and cherry trees straining beneath the weight of their fruit, I knew Dad's mind was on a derelict coal mine just out of town. So, partly for nostalgia but mainly because it was the reason

Dad ended up in Pécs long enough to meet Mum, I decided to take him in search of the Istvánakna colliery.

'Oh, God, that mine,' Dad moaned one morning over coffee and a slice of cake big enough to abseil off. 'The Istvánakna directors had told us it was in virgin condition, but when I went there I could scarcely believe my eyes. That mine was a complete and utter dud.' He chewed some cake thoughtfully. 'I was only meant to be there for four weeks, but because it was in such a bloody awful state, I ended up staying for seven months.' Which was more than enough time to meet Mum, get lured onto the dance floor at the Palatinus, fall in love and get married. Honesty might be the best policy, but I owe my very existence to lying commies.

To go out to Istvánakna meant introducing Dad to the car. He eyed the Skoda with suspicion, which I thought an achievement for a man whose own car dates from roughly the same period that steam started to go out of fashion.

'Does it have seatbelts?'

'Yes, Dad.'

'Are there enough seatbelts?'

'Yes, Dad.'

'What are the laws here?'

'Which laws might you be referring to?' I said, the whole time willing the key to turn in the lock of the driver's door.

'The laws pertaining to the wearing of seatbelts.'

Eventually, with our seatbelts safely buckled and the hamster-like roar of the Skoda engine in our ears, we were under way, leaving Pécs behind and rattling up into the enveloping green of the Mecsek. The car was soon awash with the scent of the last of the year's bear onion, and we heard odd buzzing noises from beneath the bonnet. Oaks and alders and the occasional beech stood in walls by the roadside, their trunks almost as close together as the tailgaters' bumper bars were to the Skoda's exhaust pipe. We zoomed straight past the now unmarked turn-off to Istvánakna, passing through the Swabian village of Mánfa.

'I don't remember this being here,' Dad said.

'It's not that recent,' I said. 'There's a church here that's at least twice as old as your school' – Dad's school being about four hundred years old.

We pressed on, pausing on verges to consult the map, eager (on my part, at least) to avoid entering Komló, a little industrial clump in the bosom of the Mecsek that dismays as much as Pécs charms. I once asked Mum about it and she wrinkled her face.

'Komló,' she eventually said, 'that is a *fing hely*. Yes, a *fing hely*.' Drop the 'l' and that's pretty much how you pronounce this useful expression. While in English we might refer to such a place as a hole, Hungarians opt for an expression that translates as fart place. Having been to Komló, I'm still not sure whether Mum's judgement was harder on Komló or farts.

Just as the sign welcoming us to Komló loomed, I swerved to the right, clinging to a vague memory from my small-scale map that a road branched out just before the *fing hely* and, in a roundabout sort of way, led to Istvánakna.

'Are you sure this is the right way, bonny lad?'

'Of course I'm sure,' I lied.

'I don't recall seeing any of this before.'

'Of course you don't.' By now, we'd figured out that we'd passed the main turn-off and I was being retrospectively wise. 'This is a different route to the one you took.' Or that anyone else ever took, judging by the state of the road. At first it simply became narrow, a whimsically thin lane hemmed in by bulging shrubs and low trees.

'Could be interesting if someone comes the other way,' Dad opined. Sometimes when he gets tense, he reacts by understating.

Then the potholes began. Some were deceptively deep puddles, others ruts that jarred our vertebrae and probably did scientifically interesting things to the Skoda's bearings. A few looked deep enough to be home to their own microclimates and possibly even a string of souvenir stands around their brittle asphalt brims. Dad isn't normally one for swearing, but he was prepared to make an exception for those holes.

'It really is quite beautiful countryside around here – oh shit. Nothing spectacular, but it is gorgeous forest and – shit – those hills (any idea whereabouts we are?) are most lovely. Strewth! Should we be turning back now? Ah, listen to those birds. It's a most splendid sound, don't you think? This really reminds me of 1968. Did you know that this is the only country in the world – bloody hell! – where I managed to get three flat tyres in a single day?'

Clutching the steering wheel ever more tightly, I indicated that he may have mentioned it on the odd occasion.

'Well, if – bloody hell, that was worse than the last one – you require – shit – any more words of comfort, let me know.'

I could see another car ahead, a Lada Zhiguli. Unusually for these parts, it was taking the road slowly, threading its way through the obstacle course of craters. The scenery was as bucolic as the road was ghastly. While the Skoda's temperature gauge kept irresistibly standing to attention, we were all but hypnotised by the velvet crush of leaves around us and, whenever there was a break in the canopy, by the rolling, tree-cloaked hills. Enormous snails sailed across the pitted tarmac like ivory galleons.

The only other traffic we saw was a small convoy of quad bikes so thoroughly encased in mud we almost surrendered and turned back, and two men on a cart tugged along by a pair of grey mares. This was Dad's first horse-drawn cart since his return to Hungary and we basked happily in this thought for several more seconds until we hit an interesting yet invisible deformation in the road. In hindsight, it made me think of that little upward curving ramp they sometimes have at the end of an aircraft carrier's flight deck to help planes achieve lift-off. The Skoda floated high on its suspension – the tyres may have even left the ground – then we came down with a mighty whump that knocked our vertebrae even closer together and prompted Dad to use a word I hitherto hadn't suspected was in his repertoire.

And so it was that we finally, achingly, left the woods for the fecund meadows of the foothills and crept through the one-steeple villages of Hird (where a group of beer-swigging gypsies by a railway crossing looked surprised by Dad's friendly wave), Vasas and Somogy. Considering we'd only just been taking a trip up the road, we'd been gone some time.

'Think we might be crossing any national borders any time soon?' Dad asked unhelpfully.

We once again pulled out the map and as we sat lost in wonder at the route we'd managed to take, a taxi reversed up the street and pulled up alongside us. The driver had tinted glasses and a tuft of prematurely grey hair. He puffed nicotine cloud formations as he wound down his window.

'Can I help you?' he asked, a fug of ashtray rolling the short distance from his car to ours.

'We're looking for Istvánakna. Is this the right road?'

'Istvánakna?' He looked surprised. 'Yeah, this is the right road. Keep going straight ahead. You'll pass one intersection, then you'll come to a fork. When you come to that, take the right fork. Do you understand me? The right.'

It turned out he really should have said the left, but the taxi driver's suggestion meant we got to enjoy a road slightly wider than a toothpick, a lot of mud and some bemused stares before miraculously joining the road we should have been on. Finally we arrived in a village altogether smaller and decidedly tattier than the rest.

'It could be Istvánakna,' I said, my eyes swivelling back and forth between the windscreen and the temperature gauge.

'Why don't you ask these two fellers here?' Dad said, indicating two men swaying gently in the street outside the village's only pub.

'*Jó napot kivánok,*' I called, wishing him a good day. 'Could you tell me, is this Istvánakna?'

'*Jó napot.* Yes, this is Istvánakna,' replied the one who was swaying less, sounding even more surprised than the taxi driver. 'Why are you . . . I mean, have you lost your way?' He edged closer and I suspected from his aroma that it had been a long and satisfactory afternoon in the pub. His companion stood silently behind him, wobbling like an ear of wheat in a soft breeze, eyes squinting out from a face that hadn't felt a razor for the best part of a week.

'No, we're not lost. My father used to work here in the coal mine a long time ago.'

'Really?' the first one said. He edged closer and put his face to the open window, all but brushing my cheek with his neat, grey moustache as he got a good look at Dad. I found myself thinking of canaries in coal mines as our new friend – his pub fragrance even stronger at such close quarters – peered into the car.

'Your father worked here? What's his name?'

The other one squinted harder and tried to lean forward to get a better look, but this proved more trouble than it was worth.

'Ian Jeffrey,' I said. 'He worked here in the late sixties and the early seventies.'

'My God, really? I think I might even recognise him.'

Sadly, this soon proved to not be the case, but after we parked the Skoda, we enjoyed a diverting quarter of an hour in the street with Károly, as he introduced himself with a formal handshake and a briefly rigid back. As his companion melted back into the gloom of the pub, Károly and Dad had an entertaining game of 'Does this name mean anything to you?', with neither of them scoring any hits. Behind them, a grey horse stood whinnying in a muddy yard while chickens scurried between its hooves.

'What about Béla such-and-such? Ask your father if he knew him. He was a good bloke.'

Dad shook his head disappointedly and recited the handful of names he still carried in his head, including his long dead best friend, Sándor – or Alex – Kapusi, who used to live just up the street with his wife, Mari, in one of the mine's houses.

'No. None of them,' Károly said cheerily. 'What about Jancsi so-and-so? Good old Uncle Jancsi. His brother became a doctor and moved up to Pest for a while. Might even still be there, though he's probably dead. Surely your father remembers Jancsi.'

'No, sorry,' Dad said through me, before repeating it in Hungarian. He still had quite a bit of Magyar left in his head, even after all these years.

'Is your father sure he doesn't remember Béla such-and-such? He's dead now, of course, but his wife lives just over there by the bus stop.'

'No. I'm very sorry, but it's been a long time.'

'Well, who does he remember?'

We went through the list of names again, but it was as fruitless as before. As Dad and I took our leave and walked towards the mine, Károly called out. 'What about Zsolt what's-his-face? Don't you remember him? How could you not remember Zsolt?'

Trailed by three yapping puppies, we walked to the mine head, passing a derelict building that had been graffitied with the message, 'Sanyi, I am the king of goals.'

The Istvánakna mine complex was looking as good as you'd expect for a place that had been abandoned for the best part of a quarter of a century, but despite the smashed windows, the rusted railings, the crumbling brown concrete, the trees growing from some of the roof tops and the grounds submerged in jungles of weeds and free-range shrubs, Dad recognised it at once.

'Yes, bonny lad, this is the place. Though I daresay it probably looks better underground now than it does on top.' He furrowed his brow as he looked at the stairs leading down to the main entrance; they were so extravagantly riddled with concrete cancer, it seemed they might collapse at the first puff of wind. 'And considering the state of things underground here, that's saying rather a lot.'

Rising above it all was the shaft-head tower, the late afternoon sun shining through its grimy broken panes and huge, still pulley wheels. Looking up at it as it loomed motionless over the decaying, tree-sprouting rooftops of the mine complex, I couldn't help thinking of that scene toward the end of *The War of the Worlds* where H. G. Wells's narrator spies the Martian fighting machine standing dead over the houses of an abandoned London. Then my brain accidentally segued into the most recent movie version, and I wiped a bitter tear from the corner of my eye. I noticed Dad was very quiet, too, but I suspected it wasn't thoughts of Tom Cruise that had rendered him speechless.

'So,' I said, trying to lighten the mood a little. 'This is where you first saw Mum?'

'She may have popped in on the odd occasion.'

I kept looking around trying to picture her here, but it was proving an even more difficult mission than imagining her in England. I pushed for more detail about Mum and the area, but it was no good.

'Bonny lad, my memory's not that crash hot any more. And besides, when I was working here, my fixation was on what was underground. I just don't remember the surroundings that well.'

Beyond the mine, the unbroken canopy of the forest spread across the hillsides to the distant TV tower. As we meandered back along the road, a familiar figure swayed into view. 'Has he thought of any more names yet?' Károly sang out as we drew close. 'What about Béla? Is he sure he can't remember Béla?' He shook his head in disbelief as we confirmed Dad's inability to remember any Bélas with the right surnames. Károly reeled off the names of another half-dozen men, only one of whom, it transpired, had actually worked in the mine, and probably not when Dad had been there.

'None of them? Well, what more can I do?' Károly suddenly brightened. 'Hey, see that house behind you? There's an example of real idiocy for you.' We turned to see a faded mustard-yellow villa in an overgrown garden. It was grander than the other houses of Istvánakna, even if its best days were well and truly behind it.

'The people who owned that place had this plan to restore the king of Hungary, and they were going to do it in that very house there,' Károly said, stroking his moustache. 'Yes, that very house. They called it the King's Cathedral. They even put up a plaque.' He pointed to a discoloured, oval-shaped patch on the little portico. 'And no sooner had they put it up, the gypsies came and stole it. Ha! There was even a bit of graffiti just over there on that pole that said, "For fuck's sake take these people away." Imagine that, eh? The king in Istvánakna.' He attended to his moustache a little more. 'What arseheads.'

A couple of days later, Dad and I visited Pécs's Mining Museum, located in a surprisingly extensive labyrinth beneath a gallery devoted to the father of op art, Viktor Vasarely. Dedicated to Pécs's twin mining industries of coal and uranium, the museum, featuring the recreation of a coal mine, was a shrine to small, muscular, grubby, pick-wielding gods. Dad thought it was magnificent, right down to the frankness of the information boards. 'The Mecsek was considered as one of the most dangerous mining fields of the Hungarian coal mining,' one of them began.

'That makes for a refreshing change from the bullshit the Istvánakna mob fed us,' Dad commented.

'The majority of accidents was caused by gas blow, pit-gas explosion, coal-dust explosion and underground fires,' the board continued in its curious English. 'As a result of the developments taking place in mining and the establishment of large-scale industrial works, there were more and more tragedies demanding a lot of victims – more than 700 victims in the past 200 years.'

Looking at some of the black-and-white photos of miners who'd eschewed safety helmets for the comfort of trilbies while drilling into the rock face, we were able to hazard a guess at the nature of at least some of those deaths.

The uranium boys, on the other hand, looked a whole lot cleaner. They laboured in mines close to Pécs at the other end of the Mecsek in an industry that seemed to excite the communist government's propaganda specialists a whole lot more than coal did, judging by the way mine entrances bristled with more red stars than a row of Christmas trees. There is even a story floating around that at some point in the depths of the Cold War, Washington made an offer to Budapest: sell your uranium to us instead of the Russians and we'll rebuild your entire road system. Needless to say, the Soviet Union kept its supply of Hungarian yellowcake and Hungary kept its whimsical roads.

Uranium mining, one of the museum signs noted laconically, ended due to the change in international relations, 'namely the Cold War ended'. Coal mining followed shortly after.

Dad cast a cursory glance over the uranium mining displays, then happily sank back into the wonder of coal. Core samples, drills, methane detectors, coal lumps, fossilised tree trunks, ventilation shafts and God knows what jostled for his attention.

'Some beautiful samples they've picked out here,' he sighed in ecstasy. The mines might have gassed people, crushed them beneath monstrous falls of rock and slowly devoured their lungs with black dust, but Dad still pined for the industry that had faded here in Hungary and vanished from his home country, too.

He might have been reticent about Mum, but I know he would have happily talked enough to fill a whole book about mining. A thousand pages, bound in leather. But we'll leave it there.

Round the Bend

'AND HOW IS your farder?' Even after being flung halfway around the world, sifted through copper, beamed through the vacuum of space and bounced off satellites, Mum's voice lost none of its power, making the receiver buzz in my hand in the airless phone box. 'Joli says she saw him. I bet it is strange for him to be there after all these years.' I squinted through the grimy pane of the booth and saw Dad further down the street at his café table, peering into the middle distance, quite possibly humming to himself as Mum's voice vibrated in my eardrum. It was probably the closest I was going to get to a Mum and Dad Pécs reunion.

'Now Jimmykém, I have two very important questions to ask you.' I could hear the urgency creeping into her voice, the very particular urgency that usually meant matters of commerce were close at hand. 'One. Do you want to buy my car?'

The car in question was a white barge of a Volvo that Mum viewed in her usual schizoid fashion, teetering between an almost aggressive pride ('It is such a beautiful car. And so safe! Nobody makes cars like Europeans. Nobody!') and an indignantly wailing rage ('Do you know how much it cost to fix the facking alternator? It is not worth having a European car in Australia. Not worth it. So much money, the pigs. Are they not ashamed of themselves?'). I thought it timely to remind Mum of these discussions.

'All cars cost money!' she protested. 'But not all cars are so beautiful. Think how good it would be to put your children in a Volvo. So safe, so European. And it goes like a rocket!'

'Why do you want to sell it this time, anyway?' It was a long way from the first time the Volvo had been in the firing line.

'Jimmykém,' she sighed dreamily, then in almost a whisper, as if confessing an affair, 'I have found a more beautiful car. A Renault!'

'Another European car?'

'Yes, a Renault Laguna.' She said it like a schoolgirl swooning over a movie star. *Rrrenault La-gooonah*. 'Jimmykém, you have never seen a car so beautiful.'

'Wouldn't that mean more expensive parts?'

'It is the most beautiful car I have ever seen. Even Laci looked at it and said he would buy it if he needed another car. It. Is. Like. A. Dream. A dream! Don't you want the Volvo then? Why not?'

I reminded her that we already had a car.

'Oh, well, if you don't want it, is up to you. I am not forcing you to buy it. The second question is do you want to buy my house?'

The house, like the Volvo, was on the white and boxy side of things, albeit without the same comfort factors. It was made of weatherboard and no matter how much Mum Magyarised the inside – shelves and shelves of Hungarian porcelain and fussy little Zsolnay figurines with their radioactive-looking glaze, exotic accumulations of animal fat in the freezer and even a poppyseed-patterned kitchen bench – the house still felt typically suburban Australian. As hot as a kettle in the summer, and come the winter time, as cold as those tubs of frozen fat. And besides, it was a Sydney house, which meant it was worth roughly eighty trillion times the amount of money we could rightfully call our own.

'It's a sweet thought, Mum, but we can't afford it and it's not really where we want to live.' I kept picturing her backyard with the house-encrusted hill rising behind it with all its huge windows staring down like giant surveillance cameras. ('There are thirty-five of them,' says Bel. 'I counted.')

'But why don't you want to buy it? I sell it to you for good price. Then I will go live in a unit in Liverpool and travel the world, not like your farder sitting all by himself in that big empty house with all his money stuck in those bricks and going nowhere. For what? For *what*? Such a stupid. Why doesn't he just sell it and move into a nice cheap little unit somewhere? No, I will go to Scandinavia, I will see the world. And you would have a backyard for the little ones to play in. Do you want to be paying rent all your life? That is chocking money down the drain. *Ja, ja.* Down the drain.' I could sense her bewilderment. 'Why you want to chock it away?'

'How was your mother?' Dad asked afterwards.

'As ever. She sends her best.'

'Oh, yes.'

And so it was that Dad's time in Pécs came to an end. As his daughter-in-law and grandchildren, then the Reformation Church steeple, then Uranium Town and eventually the Mecsek all passed from view, he sat motionless, staring from the train window with a distracted look on his face. But by the time we made it into the bar carriage, he was chipper again, telling me excitedly as we rolled north towards Budapest about how his travel bug had been reawakened after many years spent missing, presumed dead. The more Pécs-brewed Szalon beer we drank, the more robust and enthusiastic his bug became. And so did mine.

It was dimmed again in the Budapest traffic a few hours later, but only in the most fleeting sort of way.

I'm happy to report that after such a cold and sodden beginning, the end of Dad's trip to Hungary was glorious, the sun's rays gilding the trees, the rooftops above the grand squares and the ornate façades with their extravagant platoons of cherubs and lion heads. We walked from the same apartment we'd spent our first night in; as far as I know, the landlady kept her television company through the night once more, but Dad and I slept soundly in a state of almost snoreless bliss.

We walked quietly in the morning light, my mind focused on that first coffee of the day and Dad's eye focused on his wristwatch as he pondered whether or not I would be able to get us to our boat on time.

'Twenty-five past,' he announced. 'Which gives us –'

'Thirty-five minutes?'

'Thirty-five minutes.'

We clambered aboard the number 2 tram, which took us skirting around the edge of the Parliament then clunking along the Danube Embankment towards the ferry wharves. Our mission was to cruise north around the Danube Bend, past Vác and beneath the mountaintop castle of Visegrád to Esztergom. The idea was to visit one of the first places Dad had ever seen in Hungary, the city he'd travelled to with Willy Birkemeier to catch a glimpse of the Prague Spring as it died.

There was the added (and arguably less edifying) attraction of walking across the rebuilt bridge from Esztergom into Slovakia. The beer was meant to be cheaper over there. And better. (No slights intended, but let's face it, Hungary is a wine country.)

I'm afraid to say that at this early hour, no self-respecting café in the fifth district was open, leaving us with McDonald's as our only option for coffee.

'I knew you'd come round to the idea one day,' Dad said as we walked out with our mystery black brew from the house that Ronald built. 'Seven forty-five,' he added as we walked around the corner and spotted our boat, the perky white *Visegrád*. 'Are we going to make it?'

The *Visegrád* set off on time at eight precisely (according to Dad, who checked his watch as she nosed out into the rushing current), Magyar tricolour fluttering from the stern over the gracefully spreading wake. And then, after a voyage of roughly three minutes, we stopped to pick up the second load of passengers, which seemed to consist almost entirely of elderly women giggling like girls. Dad started fidgeting as the boarding party flowed out onto the upper deck in a tide of silver and henna-dyed hair. A solitary man walked with them, helping his wife with her walking-stick as she sat down.

'Go on, love, hit him with your stick,' Dad muttered under his breath. Then as they all shifted to the sunny half of the top deck, 'Oh, dear. Go on then, all move to one side and tip the boat over while you're at it.'

'You're in a vicious mood this morning,' I commented.

'Yes,' said Dad with a proud smile. 'It's my Scottish side showing.'

We glided under a bridge graffitied with two stages of love: LUCIA SZERETLEK (Lucia, I love you) and GYERE VISSZA CLAUDIA (Come back Claudia). Both messages moved the old women deeply as they began opening their bags of cheesy *pogácsa* scones and their carefully wrapped salami and paprika sandwiches with the fastidious speed of military surgeons.

'Oh, Lucia is the lucky one, isn't she?'

'Yes yes yes, but why did Claudia leave the other one?'

'Poor boy.'

'Poor boy. Ha. There is always a reason.'

'That doesn't mean it was his fault.'

'Maybe. Doesn't anyone need extra salami?'

'You really think it wasn't because of the *man*?'

The group's solitary male shifted in his seat.

Yellow trams made their way across the Margaret Bridge which, like every other bridge in Budapest, was a reconstruction of one that had been blown up toward the end of World War II by the retreating Germans. Now the trams – charming in an agreeably creaky sort of way – were in the process of being phased out and replaced by German ones. Europe's full of these little symmetries.

As the women busied themselves with breakfast, more supplies and packets of back-up biscuits kept appearing from small but seemingly bottomless bags. They ate like jolly shrews, feeding every ten or so minutes as if they feared they might lose consciousness if they didn't keep up the intake. Not everything was successful, though.

'These are the shittiest biscuits I have ever bought,' said one as she moved down the centre aisle, proffering an open packet. 'But try them if you want.'

'It really does taste just like she said,' an older one giggled quietly to her neighbour, who pulled a face.

'*Jaj*! This makes me want to eat soap.' This provoked much merry screeching in the group.

'Who wants coffee?'

'I have more biscuits . . .'

'Who has the *pogácsa*?'

Then the oldest one in the group stood up and, dancing slowly up the aisle, began singing to her friends in a high, soft, papery warble. She was a petite woman in rouge with stylishly oversized sunglasses, a sensible hat worn at a rakish angle, and a set of hypnotically large moles that poked up through her foundation like manhole covers on a snowy street. 'When I was a little girl . . .' she began.

Although they were spread out at first, the cool morning breeze blowing off the river soon had them clumping together like penguins in a blizzard, guffawing and pointing out various sights – statues, expensive new apartment blocks, some of the more interesting traffic snarls and, as the city thinned out and eventually ended, fishermen, little beaches, seagulls perched on river buoys, and a stork flapping low over the tree line.

'Budapest is such a beautiful city.'

'Piece of cake anyone? I have some strudel as well.'

'Look at those trees. *Jaj*, so many shades of green. So lovely.'

'Ooh, it's a bit cold up here.'

'Just you wait till that breeze calms down. It will be so delicious sitting out here in the sun.'

As we edged closer to the Danube Bend, they seemed to munch their way through their bodyweight in snacks; it was an awe-inspiring sight. Then supplies began to run low and a momentary dolefulness descended until one of the party emerged at the stop of the stairs with a joyous expression and cried, 'The canteen's open!'

Indeed it was. The coffee wasn't much chop, and the plastic cups it was served in felt like they might melt onto my slowly combusting fingertips, but it did contain caffeine. After just a few sips, Dad was feeling chatty again and eager to talk about Daisy and Leo. Again. As we talked, the *Visegrád* kept pausing at wharves decked out with astroturf and potted geraniums to take on more passengers, many of them children on their last excursion of the school year. They held hands as they were shepherded onboard by teachers who either opted for dowdy dress or a distracting skimpiness, but rarely anything in between. We chugged past Vác with its pretty, baroque skyline, its backdrop of quarry-scarred hills and its prison that had been a torture centre much cherished by both the right and the left. In Ptolemy's time (when the Magyars were moving out of the marshes and fens of western Siberia and probably dreaming of somewhere with fewer mosquitoes) the town had been saddled with the longer name of Uvcenum.

'Make sure you take a photo, young man,' the singing lady told me. 'Vác is beautiful, no?'

'It is,' I said and dutifully performed my photographic duty, wondering whether or not to include the quarry's appalling gash. A solitary egret moved through the shallows with the slightly hesitant grace of an off-duty ballerina, its eyes scanning the water for fish, its slender dagger of a beak poised. A group of children lounged on a wooden pontoon, waving with the languor of kids who have the entire, school-free summer spread before them.

'Daisy would enjoy this,' Dad said. I told him what he already knew but loved to have repeated to him on a regular basis: I adored having children, loved them to distraction. Their births had been marked by the sound of my spinal cord slipping out of my brain and leaving me a mushy-headed, gibbering, grinning simpleton. I thought fatherhood was bloody magnificent. But I also wondered what it might have been like if they were Bel's children and not my own, how I would have felt taking on two kids – and everything that goes with them – who were not connected in any way with my DNA. 'So, Dad, how was it for you?'

'You mean with Eszter and Laci?' He massaged his chin with his fingertips. 'No, it didn't worry me.'

'You were getting married in Hungary to a divorcee with two kids; weren't you even a little nervous?' I was thinking about the time I was incompetently smitten with a woman who had a young son; the idea of becoming a stepfather had tied my guts into award-winning, if slightly premature, knots.

Dad looked at me blankly. 'No.'

His answer surprised me. Was he being blasé in hindsight? Was he unflappable? Or was it something else? Perhaps it was just that he'd become so hung up on László and Eszter's father instead.

'More than anything else, I was probably a little naïve in believing all your mother's stories about Kruller and what a nasty bugger he was and things to that effect.' Dad always referred to Mum's first husband as Kruller; calling him László would have caused too much confusion in a family where a couple of names have been so thoroughly cherished and repeated through the generations. (László, son of László, brother of Eszter, daughter of Eszter, daughter of Eszter, daughter of Eszter . . .) 'Yes, I accepted them as gospel truth when I never should have. Even at the time, I had people telling me that Kruller wasn't among the band of angels, but he wasn't quite as your mother described him, either.'

That was one change I'd noticed in Dad over the years, that certainty he'd done the right thing slowly metamorphosing, through long nights of reflection, into a questioning, then a gnawing sense of wrongdoing and ultimately a leaden feeling of guilt that he'd done another man a terrible injustice.

'I remember how I felt when your mother tried to take you and Olivia away from me. But then I think to myself, I did exactly the same thing to someone else.'

By now, the old women had grazed themselves out and migrated one by one to the rear deck where they lay basking in a state of supreme contentment like a colony of wrinkled seals. The silhouette of a hilltop citadel meant we were approaching Visegrád, once the summer 'capital' of Hungary and the not entirely secure repository of its crown jewels. In 1440, King Sigismund's daughter, Elizabeth of Luxembourg, pulled off the heist of the year when, helped by her lady-in-waiting (or, more correctly, her lady-waiting-in-the-getaway-carriage), she made off with the jewels and raced south to Székesfehérvár to have her baby boy, László, crowned king. The things people do for their kids.

Cameras clicked like a field of locusts as we passed beneath the high citadel and the squat stone keep on the river bank. As yet another wriggling group of schoolchildren was ushered inside the wheelhouse by one of the skimpily dressed teachers, a middle-aged man stumbled to a halt in front of them, lobbed an empty beer can into the river then continued on his way. The further west we travelled, the more money showed in the riverfront houses, simple villas giving way to mansions with sparkling swimming pools and staircases with fat cement balustrades descending to the river. Glossy motorboats as pointy as sharks' teeth skipped past the lumbering barges, leaving white gashes of foam. A fisherman with a bare, well-rounded belly bulging proudly over the top of his boardshorts waved as we passed.

'You do know that Kruller had custody of Eszter and Laci when I met your mother, don't you?' Dad said, almost in passing.

'Eh?'

I hadn't known this. When I was younger, Mum would pause from her diatribes against my snake father (he was always a snake in Mum's more fiery orations) to let me know that she'd been so unlucky in marriage, her first husband had been a complete bastard, too. Possibly even handcrafted by Satan himself. (Once this turned into a trifecta – three bastards on the trot – she gave the game away. Or so she keeps saying.) Even now, when she could barely be bothered with the effort of denouncing a dead man, her sister kept up the sense of team spirit. Once when Joli was talking about Mum's troubled relationship with Eszter and how Eszt was always needling her and picking fights, her tone turned dark, and in a low voice she murmured, 'You can see the Kruller in her.' In a family where the women cling with a peculiar tenacity to the belief that all the good comes from within the tribe and not from those vexing but apparently necessary outsiders who join by marriage, these were harsh words. Not that Eszt would care. Or at least not once she'd gotten a few choice words of her own out of her system.

I'd never actually asked or had it spelled out for me, but I'd always assumed that when Mum and Kruller parted, she'd kept the kids. After all, we're talking about an age when a man almost stood a better chance of being trampled to death by an elephant than winning custody of his children ahead of the mother. And the chances of a woman losing custody twice in two consecutive marriages seemed as likely as getting trampled by an elephant in boots. And the odds of a woman losing custody of two sets of children in two completely different countries with completely different ideologies and legal systems . . . well, we're talking a pretty exotically attired elephant.

And yet, as I learned sitting on that hard little bench as we slowly slid past the lachrymose-sounding town of Szob, Mum had. She was even more remarkable than I'd thought. I'd never known she'd struck such a blow for equal rights.

But then Dad managed to pull off a feat even less likely than death by elephant. After he married Mum, he sued for custody of Eszt and Lac. Looking back now, I can't help but admire his optimism. There he was, a Westerner in a communist country, during the stagnant depths of the Cold War, trying to wrest his wife's children from their Party-member father. Even now, as we cruised beneath the limestone hills of the Danube Bend, Dad looked taken aback as he talked about what unfurled in that Pécs courtroom.

'They carefully weighed things up, but in the end what they said was that it would be better for the kids because they'd have better conditions in a Western country.'

'They said what?' I almost gave myself a nasal enema with bad coffee. 'Are you kidding?'

'Not in the slightest, bonny lad. They said Laci and Eszter would be better off with me because they'd have better conditions living in a Western country.' He gazed across at the north bank where Hungary was coming to an end and Slovakia was beginning. 'I admit I was somewhat surprised to hear sentiments like that expressed in a communist country.' Dad always was rather partial to understatement.

'Didn't you bribe him with a car or something?' Dad had mentioned once or twice in the past that Kruller had received a car when Eszt and Lac left the country.

'It was,' Dad said, slipping into his formal, letter-to-the-editor-of-a-quality-newspaper mode, 'suggested to me by my legal representative that I buy Kruller a car as compensation.'

What sort of car could possibly have been compensation for the loss of two children? As we edged closer to the town that bore Mum's name, Dad revealed that it was a Wartburg ('Don't ask me to remember what colour it was'). Like the even more primitive Trabant, the Wartburg had probably been invented to prove that East German communism had a sense of humour.

'When it was all over, your mother said to me, "No Hungarian would have done for me what you have done for me."' That was a line I'd heard many times before, a few words that somehow managed to convey all of Dad's bitterness about the way things eventually turned out.

We cruised on with Hungary to the left of us and Slovakia to the right, both sides anxiously flying their flags. Ahead of us loomed a massive, duck-egg blue dome capped with a golden cross, resting on a ring of elephantine columns with a pair of domed belltowers perched on its shoulders like epaulettes – the Basilica of Esztergom. Beneath it, five green arches of bridge stretched across the Danube to the Slovakian town of Sturovo. The Vienna–Budapest hydrofoil sliced past with a great fanfare of noise and spray, while behind us, the old ladies were stirring with the first pangs of pre-lunch hunger.

'Shall we have a little something before we go to lunch?'

'I still have some *pogácsa* if anyone wants one.'

'Last chance to grab a shitty biscuit before they go in the bin.'

'Oh, even if they are shitty, it seems like such a waste to throw them away.'

'Yes, that's true. Here, let me take one, too.'

And so we docked in Esztergom. As we walked ashore, Dad gazed over at the concrete embankment he and Willy Birkemeier had seen back in 1968, when Slovakia was still locked in marriage with the Czech Republic and getting a good going-over by the biggest member of the Slavic brotherhood.

'That's where the messages were painted, the ones asking for help,' Dad said. 'On this side of the Danube, of course, you could barely move for uniforms and guns. Hungarian militia were everywhere along here. The Soviets as well, of course.' Dad had a habit of pronouncing Soviet as Serviette. Once when I tried to politely correct him I copped such a blast for being a hair-splitter that I had decided to live with Serviette. And besides, every mention of the Serviette Union was something special; in Dad's mouth, the dreaded Russkies had been turned into little more than domineering napkins.

'Can we just walk across?' Dad asked as we both gazed at the bridge and the cyclists and pedestrians and cars going back and forth.

'That lot don't seem to be having any trouble.'

'Did you bring your passport?'

'Yes.'

'What happens if we get over there and they take our passports and tell us, "Thanks, fellers, your visas will be ready in a week"?'

'Dad, we'll be walking from one EU country to another.'

'I'm just thinking about when I was here last time.'

'From one EU country to another. They'll even let *you* in.'

The Esztergom bridge had been blown up in the war, but unlike its counterparts in Budapest, it had only been rebuilt a few years ago. The original was the setting for the end of *A Time of Gifts* and the beginning of *Between the Woods and the Water*, the first two books in Patrick Leigh Fermor's unfinished trilogy about his 1930s journey through Europe's twilight, travelling by foot from the Hook of Holland to Istanbul (or Constantinople as Leigh Fermor, like my father, prefers) as the continent edged toward war. It was Dad who introduced me to *Between the Woods and the Water*, which follows

Leigh Fermor from his entry into Hungary, down through the vestiges of aristocratic Transylvania, Romania and the Balkan Peninsula to the Iron Gate on the Danube. It was my first glimpse into a Hungary that went so far beyond my mother's world I became almost drunk on its evocative, elegiac power. As we walked onto the bridge's latest incarnation, I gazed across at the basilica and tried to imagine it as Leigh Fermor saw it in the gathering shadows of that distant Easter Saturday, the elegantly clad grandees in their furs and jewelled scimitars awaiting the arrival of the Cardinal of Esztergom and Prince Primate of all Hungary, while above, the storks settled in their belfry nests, forgetful of the great pealing that would soon send them wheeling into the sky.

No matter how hard I squinted, there was no fur and no scimitars, and none of the local storks had had the absence of mind to set up home on the belfries. It was a shadowless June day and the banks of the Danube were awash with shorts and ice-creams and tans carefully acquired in solariums during the long winter and an unseasonably chilly spring. Dad was imagining another Esztergom as well, but his had a lot of nervous fingers on Kalashnikov triggers. The fake tans were preferable to that, at least. Passengers on the top decks of river cruisers waved merrily as they passed beneath the bridge while we walked toward the red line that marked the border, and a sign announcing that we were entering the Republic of Slovakia. I'd never simply walked across a national frontier before; we amused ourselves by taking the obligatory photos of each other with a foot in either country, then I surrendered to childish instincts and sat on the border with a cheek on either side. Then we turned our backs on Hungary and continued across the bridge to the waiting border guards.

'Mum really wanted to leave Hungary at the time you were married, didn't she?' I asked as we approached what looked like little more than a string of toll booths.

'Oh, grief yes. She had said beforehand that she wanted to get out of Hungary. Very much so.'

I was travelling on an EU passport for convenience, and the uniformed guard perused it briefly before sending me on my way. But the sight of Dad's Australian passport with its kangaroo and emu proudly embossed on the cover caused a moment of consternation. Dad put on the terse expression he wore when he knew he was about to be proved right and that things would turn out badly. 'I find the best approach in life is to always expect the worst,' he once explained to me. 'And that way you'll either be prepared or pleasantly surprised.' I think he told me that just before I got married.

As it was, it was merely a matter of the border guards trying to remember which one of their colleagues had last been in possession of the stamp. A series of epauletted shoulders were shrugged until a man with even bigger epaulettes was summoned from the guard house. He strode into one of the booths, reached into a drawer and, with a great sense of ceremony, produced the rubber stamp. Three seconds later, we were officially in Slovakia, standing on a street named after the man Magyars still refer to as the greatest Hungarian – the visionary reformer and eventually suicidal melancholic, Count István Széchenyi. As we walked, I noticed that most of the signs seemed to be in Hungarian, as were the voices. In an eerie sort of way, it was almost as if Sturovo were still the town of Parkány and Trianon had never happened.

We strolled past rendered walls, squat apartment blocks and fussily decorated *fin-de-siècle* buildings that looked as though they should be served on small dishes with silver spoons and coffee.

'What about you, Dad? You'd been in this part of the world for a while by then. Did you want to leave?'

'I'd made a suggestion to my company that I stay on here and be based either somewhere in Eastern Europe or, if that proved unacceptable, in Vienna. But that was rejected. And besides, your mother wanted to leave and given that she was pregnant with you, we both thought it made a certain amount of sense for you to not be born this side of the Iron Curtain.' He glanced back at the river and absentmindedly hummed a couple of bars of 'The Blue Danube'. 'I guess I was happy to leave Hungary for England because I thought I was doing something that made your mother happy.'

'Did it make her happy?'

'Briefly.'

'So when would you say things started to go wrong between the two of you?'

'When we left Hungary.'

'How long were you all in England before Mum started to get unhappy?'

'Not long.'

'Do you remember how Eszt and Lac and Mum reacted at first to England?'

Eszt and Lac were ten and nine years old when they arrived in the West, while I travelled *in utero*. Whenever we talk about those early days in England, the conversation inevitably finds its way to the topic of bananas. They were rarely seen in communist Hungary, turning up only on special occasions to cast their spell upon the masses with their tropical yellow curves, then vanishing again into the realm of the semi-mythical. Suddenly the trio from Pécs were in a country where all the shops seemed to have mountains of them – every day! That was the wonder of the West: shops with bananas.

'I don't recall any particular reaction,' said Dad.

Although Dad normally picked over his long-dead marriage with a certain energy, he was descending into a singularly unexpansive mood. My mind turned towards beer. As we walked down Széchenyiho ulica/Széchenyi utca (as the bilingual street signs had it), most of the frantic advertising seemed to suggest that nearly everyone who came barging across the bridge had little more than beer in mind; I felt a brief flush of shame at how common our motives were. I'd been thinking how flash it would be to walk into another country just to have a pilsener...

A girl huddled over a tiny electric fan in a sweltering booth exchanged my ugly currency for another and I walked with Dad into a beer garden where we were served by a young woman who spoke Hungarian, Slovakian and English with equal aplomb. Despite the much cherished legend, the beer wasn't any cheaper than in Hungary. But it did taste better.

'Not an unpleasant drop,' Dad noted. One long beer turned into two and we eventually ambled out with the haziness of men who've managed to knock off a couple of careless pints before lunch. I could feel my brain quietly slipping its moorings as we walked in the sunshine, the dome of the basilica staring down at us across the rooftops from the Hungarian side of the Danube.

'Well, I can't say I'm feeling particularly thirsty,' Dad said as we stood swaying gently. 'It might be time to grab a bite to eat, though. I was thinking some time before we both fall over.'

After another search for the box with the rubber stamp, we were back in Hungary, sitting at a riverside café, staring at a microwaved hamburger and a lump of fried camembert while a waitress with a tomboyish haircut and a glistening nosestud asked us if we spoke Deutsch. A German couple in motorcycle leathers swigged wine spritzers at the next table and watched soccer on a precariously mounted television.

'I'm not sure all the food has improved a great deal since I was last here,' Dad said, prodding his burger as if checking to see if it might still be alive. As I thought about all the cafés and restaurants where we could have had a decent goulash or bean soup, I felt a quiver of regret. But it had been very important for us to eat. Those pre-lunch beers had hit their mark like mortars.

'So you've come all the way from Australia,' the waitress said as I went in to pay the bill. 'Why in God's name have you come to Hungary?'

I told her I loved it. The waitress exchanged surprised looks with her colleague.

'You do? Maybe you can stay here and your government will let me swap places with you and stay in Australia instead. I bet you can make more money there than here.' The other waitress laughed wryly. I gave my usual spiel about how, yes, pay was higher in Australia, but then so were costs. But given how much prices were spiralling in EU Hungary and how static wages seemed to be, it was starting to sound a bit lame.

'But yes, you're right,' I said in an attempt to jettison the taste of bullshit from my mouth, 'you can definitely make more money in Australia than here.'

'Do you speak English in Australia?' the other waitress asked.

'Oh, I'd go to the beach,' the first one said. 'I'd go sit on that lovely white sand and turn brown while I watched the nice boys on their surfboards. Of course they speak English in Australia. And they have so many long, empty, beautiful beaches, don't you?'

Dad and I walked through the custard yellows, strawberry pinks and lime sorbet greens of the old quarter of Esztergom, watching black birds flit between the trees. High above us, a girl lounged on her windowsill with a book, one bare foot dangling insouciantly over the edge.

'Ugh, that's not good for my vertigo,' Dad groaned as he averted his gaze. Vertigo or not, we were soon following a staircase of cobblestones (*macskakő* or cat stone in Hungarian) that threaded its steep way up through the old hillside fortifications to the basilica. As the Danube dropped away, I found myself out of breath while Dad, who was given to making noises about how I should make allowances for his age and not be in such a bloody hurry all the time, was bouncing up the path as effortlessly as a mountain goat. It couldn't have been the microwaved hamburger. I was amazed. What made it even more galling was that while I was gasping for breath, the bastard was making conversation.

'The thing you must remember, bonny lad,' he called from above, 'is that whatever difficulties I had with your mother had no impact whatsoever on my feelings for Hungary.'

'I didn't think so,' I tried to call back, but it came out sounding more like, 'I nn tingzo.'

'No impact whatsoever. My affection for Hungary was never dimmed, and it isn't now. It's still a very special place and I'm over the moon you've brought me back here. Absolutely over the moon.'

A long black freighter was nosing its way under the bridge as we made it to the top. Tree-cloaked hills rolled into the distance on either side of us as we walked beneath the gargantuan stone arches of the basilica. I asked the old man in the doorway how much it cost to get in; I'd grown used to the idea of paying to enter Hungary's cathedrals, except when I cheated and went during religious services. I once did this by accident in Pécs, tumbling through the creaking wooden door during evening mass as a host of white-robed figures standing at the altar turned their heads in unison. Feeling like the interloper I was, I left them to their worship and slipped back out, almost tripping on the uneven cobblestones of the square as I went.

'Well, not very much for you and it would be free for him,' the man said, nodding toward Dad. 'Am I right in guessing he's over sixty-five? But that's just for the museum and that's closing' – he studied his wristwatch – 'now. But the temple itself is open and that's free. The Good Lord won't be taking your forints this afternoon.'

'He thought you were over sixty-five,' I told Dad as we stepped inside.

'Utter rot.'

I'm not normally one for cathedrals or churches, though I will confess to an irrational love (is there any other kind?) for Orthodox churches that grew during my years of coming and going in Russia – the gilt-edged icons and onion domes and walls blackened by decades, even centuries, of smoke from the sweet-smelling beeswax candles; the worshippers with heads bent low singing their polyphonous devotions; the stern-faced, extravagantly bearded priests floating past in billowing black cassocks, dispensing smoke that uncoiled and spread through those severe, beautiful, pewless spaces and out under the heavy wooden doors to the waiting snow.

That said, the Esztergom Basilica was a cracker. We wandered quietly spellbound beneath the gazes of Gregorius and Hieronymus and a blue-robed Jesus ascending to Heaven between the white marble columns flanking the altar. Light spilled white and brilliant into the dome. Its outside was a simple blue, but its interior was as elaborate and bejewelled as a Fabergé egg. We sat down beneath a bas relief of Jesus on his donkey and an organ as big and daunting as a multiple rocket launcher, capped with a flight of some ecstatic-looking angels, to take in the acres of marble and gold and allow me to finally get my breath back. It was only later that I discovered that the original dome had been destroyed in a fire a few years back and what we were sitting under was every bit as much of a reconstruction as the bridge below. By all accounts, the builders were faithful to the original's unabashed grandeur – this had long been the seat of Catholic power in Hungary and in the twentieth century was revered as the base of Cardinal Mindszenty, a man as despised by the extreme right regime the country fostered as he was by the extreme left one that slipped into its place. Not that any of that was on our minds particularly that afternoon.

'Thank you for bringing me back,' Dad repeated. 'It's been magical, bonny lad, it really has.'

What I still wanted to know was how the magic disappeared. Mum and Dad went from being in love in Hungary to falling quickly out of it when they left. I was born a few months after they settled down to life in Lancashire. Just a few months after that, as I got into a routine of either being pushed around in my pram by my besotted sister or parked on my chubby, nappy-clad bottom on the grass while she and her friend took turns riding in said pram, Dad was already making plans for escape.

'It had gotten so bloody awful and I was so heartily sick of it, I was ready to walk out the door for good. One day I had you in my arms and I was going to leave while your mother carried on yelling from the garden.'

It was probably for the best that Mum moved from the garden to block the door when she did; if Dad had made it out, my little sister, Olivia, wouldn't be around now and I might have grown up as a fugitive somewhere like, say, the Isle of Man. Dad stayed and we all lived in a state of truce, depending on how flexible you are about the definition. It was probably more like one of those dodgy states of affairs you sometimes get in international relations where the United Nations ums and ahs and wrings its hands and ultimately says that yes, it *is* all a bit on the nasty side, but we really mustn't get involved because it's an internal matter. For Mum, it was the Four Years of Tears – 'I cried every night in England. It is thanks to me that we left that rubbish place and came to Australia. *Ja, ja.* It is because of me.'

There must have been some good bits, though. Looking through Dad's treasure trove of slides, I can see a lot of happiness in those pictures; they can't have all been faking it for the sake of the camera. But whatever joy there was must have been intermittent. By the time I was one, Mum and Dad were talking about the possibility of divorce. Or at least Dad was paying lip service to the idea of divorce; his mind was more on what could be considered the divorce equivalent of elopement.

'There were some very specific reasons for that,' Dad explained. 'The odds on a man getting custody at the time were fourteen per cent.'

Okay, so maybe I was a little off there with the elephant, but there was no such fudging with Dad. He was very specific about the number.

'Fourteen per cent exactly?' I asked.

'Fourteen per cent exactly.'

And so it was that the plan to do a runner with me to South Africa was born, living a brief but feverishly enthusiastic life before dying away.

'South Africa? Well, I'd worked there, so there was a certain familiarity. And it seemed like a bloody long way away. Possibly not the soundest choice at the time, but I was desperate.'

Wherever things had gone wrong, it wasn't here. We descended from the basilica, pausing at a hillside public toilet that was preparing for Hungary's still far-off conversion to the euro by charging in both currencies. Judging by the disparateness of the fees, it must have taken quite some creativity and/or *pálinka* to arrive at the exchange rate they were using.

Back in the town, I could tell by the regularity with which he was checking his watch that Dad was starting to get anxious. He fidgeted while I lingered over the strawberries lying in dizzyingly sweet mounds at a string of wooden stalls; they were at the peak of their season and almost embarrassingly cheap so I bought a kilo and got scoffing. It was bliss. Once I'd reassured Dad for the fifth time that I would be able to read the timetable, buy tickets *and* get us onto a bus back to Budapest, he reached a state of semi-contentment.

Dad eventually climbed beyond semi-contentment into the realm of bliss, but it wasn't until a few hours later as the memory of the uncomfortable, interminable bus ride from Esztergom faded into the present of a perfect summer's night descending upon Budapest. We sat on one of the yellow trams that crossed Margaret Bridge, passing over the southern tip of Margaret Island and its promenading, snogging couples, and the fleets of illuminated pleasure boats chugging up and down the river. From Moszkvá Square, we slowly made our way up to the Castle District. It was getting late and the forint-sucking turnstiles that had been installed at the Fisherman's Bastion in recent years had, happily, been switched off. We slipped up the white limestone stairs beneath the bronze gaze of St Stephen and the frenetically mosaiced spire of the Matthias Church, then had our brains malleted sideways by the vision of Budapest at night.

Across the river, behind the spectral glow of the Parliament, Pest spread flat and glittering with its grand boulevards toward the east and the Great Plain, flaunting its energy back up at the more staid Buda and its hills and edifices and monuments awash with sodium light. Even the weepingly ugly Intercontinental and Marriott hotels, erected on the Danube Embankment with the approval of possibly blind planning officials in the 1970s, looked halfway decent.

And there in the midst of it all curved the Danube, light dancing across its rippling, swirling surface from the logjam of boats and the bridges that held the two halves of the city together, especially the Chain Bridge – Széchenyi's bridge that had in 1849 united the two sides of the river and was so wonderfully festooned with light bulbs, it made our retinas contract. While Vienna shuns the Danube, perversely consigning it to the backblocks, Budapest embraces, celebrates and worships it. Except when it floods.

'What you might call a vision splendid,' Dad murmured. He only ever reached for Banjo Paterson during moments of emotional rapture.

We drifted downhill beneath the floodlit walls of the palace along tree-shrouded paths dotted with dogs and their owners, walking towards the festive glow of the Chain Bridge. In just a handful of hours, we would be getting up again with the sparrows and the street-sweepers and Dad would be leaving Hungary one more time, flying to England just to change planes for the inhumanly long flight to Australia – his whole journey from all those decades ago repeated in the space of one seemingly endless day. But we had a few hours yet.

As we passed between one of the pairs of stone lions that guard either end of the Chain Bridge, I paused for a moment and watched Dad quietly walking ahead, lost in thought, white hair and blue blazer bathed in electric light.

Chews Your Relatives

ON THE BAKING EXPANSES of the Great Plain, the summer storms swell above the oceans of sunflowers in purple, flickering columns. Gaunt silhouettes of old wells – long, spindly booms balanced on wooden forks and raised half-heartedly to the sky – dot the otherwise featureless horizon. Tractors haul their loads of hay, leaving little blizzards of dust swirling yellow in their wake, and (at least when we passed through) scythe-wielding women in bikinis tend to their yards. Mum was born out here, but left before she could so much as crawl. This flat country touched off a sense of desolation in her that made her want to hightail it back to the reassuringly rumpled landscape of Transdanubia. All the same, she made the trek east from Pécs in 2001, travelling with me, Bel and Joli to visit Kati, Ica and Piroska – cousins she hadn't seen in decades. And it was there, in my grandmother's home village of Hajdúszovát, that Bel and I learned the greatest peril in Hungary – travelling without children.

The cousins' reunion was a jolly affair, five small women with almost identical dumpling-like builds rocked by raucous gales of laughter and bouts of merry honesty. 'Oh, look at you, you're in good flesh, aren't you?' and 'My sweet Lord, you look just like you did last time, only there's more of you,' and so on. We were in the miniature farm that was Piroska's yard, patrolled by geese and chickens and lazily cropped by cows so round they looked like cement trucks with fur coats. There seemed to be pigs grunting and snuffling behind every door, though a slight dent had been put in their numbers that morning when one had been taken from the sty and converted into sausages.

Amidst the noise, Piroska's son Tibor showed us how to ride a horse bareback, with running commentary provided by his proud older brother, Antal. Once he'd wowed us by standing on the horse's back with the reins nonchalantly held in one hand, Tibor encouraged me to have a go, whereupon I disgraced myself and the family name. To round out the sport, Antal wedged us into his tiny Trabant and took us for a noisy ride around the neighbourhood, dodging geese and bouncing over level crossings at daring, barely Trabi-like speeds of over 50 kilometres an hour.

It was a day of noise and joy, and far too much swine. But it was only after lunch, when the dark, trembling sky finally cracked open with a summer downpour and we sat in the big kitchen by the white dome of the bread oven barely able to move for fear of breaking the floor, that the danger signs began to make their appearance. The talk turned to the subject of grandchildren and after all the merriment, a tone of almost religious fervour crept over the conversation like lava. Of Mum's four children, only my little sister, Olivia, had bothered starting a new generation. Mum adored my niece, Claudia, of course, but for someone who aspired to having as many grandchildren as the average guppy, one was never going to be enough.

As the grandmaternal clucking grew more feverish – why, there was even talk of someone being promoted to the loftiest rank of great-grandmother some time within the decade – I gazed out the window at the plain stretching emptily toward Romania, but it didn't do me any good. It was like the gulag – no fences, but no escape.

'And what about you, Eszter?' someone finally asked. Negligently, I'd only translated part of the proceedings for Bel's benefit, but she noticed Mum wringing her hands.

'Just one!' Mum blurted with a mix of shame and bewilderment. 'I only have one.'

Those women might have only come up to my armpits, but as they turned in unison to bring their collective glare to bear on me and Bel, I felt like we'd been cornered by a ruthless posse of vigilante fertility gods.

'How,' one of the cousins broke the silence, 'could you do this to your mother?'

'How could you make her suffer like this? Grandchildren are the most wonderful thing in the world. In the world!'

'Both of you are so young, why don't you just *breed*?'

I figured it would be different when we made our triumphant return with children. And it was true that when we took Leo and Daisy to Hajdúszovát (much to the dismay of the pigs, who lost another member), the atmosphere had changed. But only up to a point. Amid the circus of child-worshipping and mountains of very fresh pork ('It was still grunting this morning!'), Bel and I were asked, in a very nice sort of way, when we might be planning to expand our little tribe.

'It would be so nice for your mother.'

In Hungary, it's not just relatives who take an active interest in your children. When we arrived in Pécs with Daisy and Leo, it didn't take us long to learn we'd become public property. First there was the Hungarian instinct to worship kids; everyone from beaming old ladies to sozzled bums gently wobbling their way out of the boozer made time to bend over Leo's stroller and wax rhapsodical about what a beautiful baby he was, or to loudly admire Daisy's pigtails and coquettish smile.

The flipside to this was the tendency – usually among women aged vaguely between fifty and five hundred – to offer streams of unsolicited advice, forced through lips either bent into unconvincing smiles or puckered into passable impressions of cat bottoms.

'You're not thinking about taking that child outside in weather like this without a hat?'

'Why have you dressed your child in that?'

'What sort of parent doesn't put a proper scarf on their little one on such a cold day?'

'What sort of parent puts gumboots on their little one on such a hot day?'

'You should be giving your baby chamomile tea.'

'Why aren't you giving your baby fruit?'

'You're giving your baby too much fruit!'

'Why do you carry your baby in a harness like that? It doesn't matter if it is made in Sweden, he will suffocate!'

'Your baby won't be able to move!'

'Your baby won't be able to breathe!'

'Your child will freeze!'

'Get a fever!'

'Catch cold!'

'Overheat!'

'Fall sick!'

'Drown!'

'Get run over!'

'Squashed!'

'Die! Yes, *die*!'

'Or worse!'

'Why do you do this to your baby?'

When such helpful thoughts aren't being offered directly to your face, they are instead ostensibly exchanged with your baby ('Won't you get sick without your socks?') or shared with another woman in the fifty-to-five-hundred bracket loudly enough to make sure you overhear as you pass in the street or the supermarket aisle or as you pause to read a bus timetable. Even on a stinking hot day, if your baby's singlet rides up dangerously above the belly button, you can bet all your forints that some semi-desiccated crone will be on hand to suggest that your negligence as a parent is exposing your poor, innocent child to hypothermia. It's all fun and games, but eventually the novelty of this particular national idiosyncrasy wears off. Putting on a straight face and explaining that it's the custom back home to kill your offspring as a cost-saving measure doesn't get you anywhere.

Besides, there were worse things – like the cycling evangelist who appeared on the streets of Pécs that summer. Dressed in black pants and white shirt, he rode some antiquated piece with a high seat and low wheels along the back streets of the Inner Town, bouncing and rattling where the lumpy, ancient bitumen had worn thin and exposed the fossilised cobblestones beneath. There was an unusual severity to his beard and from his corroded handlebars hung a leather satchel with 'Jézus' emblazoned across it in jauntily coloured letters. The first time I saw him, I was out walking with Bel and the kids. Not what would have struck me as a group that looked in most immediate need of salvation, but we were a slow-moving target.

'*Jó napot*,' he called as rode up alongside me, reaching inside the satchel. 'Can I interest you in this brochure about Jesus?'

'Absolutely not, but thanks for asking.'

He politely thanked me for my time, but returned after a couple of minutes spent haphazardly circling like a tipsy shark.

'Don't be angry, but I'd like to ask you a second time.'

'No, for the second time. No.'

This time he disappeared, the creaking of his pedals echoing off the close walls and their flaking stucco.

'You'd think he could find other people to save,' Bel commented.

When he eventually reappeared, he came cycling at speed out of a narrow side street, zooming past a statue of St Florian and making as though he was trying to head us off before we escaped through the city wall into the outside world. All the little niceties were dispensed with and I noticed his face was flushed. He began shouting in a strange, indignant quaver, like a newly pubescent boy who's just figured out he's sitting on an ant nest.

'I really have to tell you,' he cried as he arced past with trousers flapping, 'about Sodom and Gomorrah!'

This time Bel did the talking and we didn't see him any more that day.

All in all, the nosy old women – judgemental, wannabe mother figures that they were – seemed slightly less unbearable in comparison.

Then my real, actual mother figure came rolling into our lives like a thunderstorm. The build-up to Mum's visit began before she'd even left Australia with phone calls that crackled and rumbled distantly during those languid, early summer days after Dad left. Each time we talked she seemed to have racked up another transaction, and the bigger the deal, the more pumped she sounded.

'Jimmykém, I have bought the Renault Laguna,' she said, sounding even more Zsa Zsa Gabor than usual. 'It is sitting on my driveway; I hope that facking possum doesn't leave its footprints all over it. Did I tell you that little bastard eat all my tomatoes? I try so hard to grow my beautiful tomatoes and that little devil comes and gobbles them up. Then he hides in my garage door. You know how my garage door rolls up – that's where the little bastard hides and the stupid Australian law says I cannot touch him. If we were in Hungary, that little shit would be in the soup by now.' A picture drifted into my head of Mum pushing a brush-tail possum – as big as a cat and full of hiss and spit – into one of her stainless steel pots along with a load of onions and paprika; I was getting used to having hallucinations in that baking phone booth.

'And stop telling me it is because I live between two national parks that I get possums. All I want to do is grow a few tomatoes in my little garden because they taste so much better and I don't want to chock my money away on that robbish at the supermarket. But that facking possum –'

'So you bought the Renault?'

'Oh! I drove it home so fast, that lovely Laguna. I am locky the police did not catch me. Not like that time in your Sigma, remember? It is as beautiful as a dream.' The Volvo, God rest its safe, Swedish soul, was finally history. 'I traded that in. They can keep it. I have my Laguna. Are you not sad you did not buy that Volvo? It was a good car. I am so happy it is gone.'

Then, within days: 'Jimmyként, I have bought a unit. Yes, in Liverpool!'

This had been an even longer lived dream than the selling of the Volvo, but was usually the middle section of a three-part fantasy, the first being the sale of the Heathcote house, the third going crazy with the left-over money. The whole plan always came unstuck on the perplexing reluctance of the house-buying public to agree to Mum's asking price. ('If they won't pay, then' – rude gesture involving one of her brown forearms and albino fists – 'I am not giving my house away for peanuts. For what? I stay here, and that's that. They don't get my house I worked so hard for, for peanuts. No way.') Something was missing.

'Congratulations, Mum. Have you sold your house?'

As we talked, Pécs's latest tourism innovation lumbered past, a tiny car disguised as a steam locomotive pulling a string of wooden carriages filled with sightseers on a tour through the Inner Town. It was staffed by a wanly smiling driver wedged into a cabin with a round, peroxided woman with a microphone, a flat, penetrating voice and a permanently put-out expression.

'We are now passing the Szabó Marzipan Exhibition,' she intoned, as if diagnosing something incurable, 'a wonderful Austrian–Hungarian museum featuring a life-size Elvis Presley made from marzipan to celebrate the King of Rock'n'Roll's seventieth birthday...' One of the main sponsors of the sightseeing train, I couldn't help noticing, was the Szabó Marzipan Exhibition. (I went to check out Elvis and the rest of it weeks later and emerged from the building shaken, a changed man.)

'No, I haven't sold it,' Mum said. 'The bank has given me something called a bridging loan. They give me the money to buy the flat and all I have to do then is sell my house. But first, I will rent out the flat and the money can start coming in nicely.' There was a moment of dark reflection. 'They probably take my pension away, but fack zem.' That last bit never seemed to be delivered in Hungarian. It's not that the Magyar version lacks for blunt-edged potency, but in moments of highest indignation, Mum preferred a touch of Saxon spice. 'Fack all of zem. I don't need their money.'

'Uh huh,' was the most I could think of saying, which even at the time struck me as disappointingly inadequate. Down the street, the tourist train parped its whistle at one of Király utca's more foppish drunks, who swayed out of its path and doffed his hat ostentatiously.

'Then, one day, Eszter will buy it from me. That is what she told me.'

(Eszt wasn't exactly buzzing when we spoke a couple of weeks later. 'I went with Olivia to have a look at it. God, Jim, it's the most depressing place I've seen in my life. And it's so fucking ugly.')

When Mum asked me how the inspection had gone, I fudged around the edges with typical cowardice. 'I don't think it, um, really grabbed Eszt.' Mum was livid. 'Well what does she expect for that sort of money? *What?* She wants to pay rent all her life? You pay all that rent and is gone forever!')

'So are you going to be able to get all the paperwork and stuff sorted before you leave Australia?'

'No, I can leave that with Olivia.'

I felt a twinge for my little sister.

'So now I don't have much money, but I promised I would come to Hungary, so I come. I keep my promises, *ja ja*. Jimmykém, why don't you buy a nice little flat in Liverpool? For investment!'

So it all seemed like business as usual at that end, and somewhere amidst all the fresh, happy commotion in her life, Mum began packing her bags for her return to the fatherland.

The text message Eszter sent me was altogether shorter: 'Don't let her shit all over the paradise you have created!'

A brief word of background: Mum and Eszter have what may be characterised as an overdeveloped inability to get on, yet they still feel compelled to be near each other. It's the sort of relationship perhaps best understood by scholars of Middle Eastern international relations and/or modern explosives.

They share names – two Eszters in the long chain of Eszters the family has produced, which, appropriately enough, sounds a bit like an organic chemistry lesson gone wrong. No one seems entirely sure how many there have been, but I have a vague image of a line of Eszters stretching unbroken back to some time shortly after the first apes began to walk upright and verbally abuse each other. Great Chief Árpád probably used a battalion of Eszters during the conquest of the Carpathian Basin; God knows Mum and Eszt could have cleared a path all the way from Bessarabia to the Danube during one of their blues.

Eszter Jnr and Eszter Snr can behave normally enough when left to their own devices, but let them into the same room together and the pyrotechnics begin. NASA uses a similar principle to send its shuttles into space.

It's normally Eszter Jnr who lights the fuse by going for the pre-emptive strike, but once it's on, it's on. The scabs of old hurts have their tops knocked off, fresh abuse is hurled and genetic composition is questioned – especially at Christmas. There's something about the season of goodwill that brings out their worst and some of us in the family look forward to their yuletide stoushes with a certain perverse glee. With their emotional laceration, their linguistic gymnastics and their general futility, the Fighting Eszters' Christmas displays combine the histrionics of Italian opera with the metaphysical damage of a Dostoyevsky novel, the pointlessness of the Gallipoli campaign, the educational value of a David Attenborough documentary, and the small-scale devastation of a hand grenade.

The actual fireworks that follow a few nights later on New Year's Eve always end up looking kind of small.

It had been years since I'd had any major bust-ups with Mum, and I was looking forward to her arrival. We packed the car and headed toward Vienna. Not the Skoda – it was given a rest in light of its growing fondness for visits to Bandi the mechanic – but a hire car with such extraordinary features as air conditioning and the ability to go faster than a hundred kilometres an hour without feeling like it was about to separate into its component molecules. Bel and I were very excited and poked at all the buttons. Only Daisy was true, harrumphing with a three-year-old's indignation that she liked our yellow Skoda better. After half an hour of air conditioning, though, she admitted she might like this car, too, and promptly fell asleep. Leo wriggled for a bit, dribbled onto his chest, then followed suit.

The driving felt weirdly effortless as we zig-zagged our way up through Transdanubia, performing all sorts of stunts beyond the scope of the Skoda: accelerating up hills, overtaking other cars without having to first calculate if we had enough of a tail wind, and so on. We stopped for ice-cream and coffee in the village of Nagydorog, entertained by the twin spectacles of stork chicks plumply jostling for space in a nest across the road while the café owner circled her coffee machine as warily as a trainee bomb defuser. She eventually managed to turn out a pair of almost but not quite undrinkable cappuccinos, and as she brought them to us, an adult stork came gliding down across the roof tops, wings fanned, legs splayed for landing, a huge frog dangling from its beak. The chicks erupted in a consternation of clacking beaks as their parent touched down on the edge of the nest and set about dividing the luckless amphibian.

We slipped through villages thick with the clanging of church bells and roadside stalls garlanded with scarlet strings of paprika and garlic hanging like chains of big, white molars. The strawberries and peaches were joined by the first watermelons of the season, lying fatly in piles like striped cannonballs. Between villages and dark clumps of forest stretched fields of young sunflowers and wheat flushed with pink beneath a swiftly darkening sky. The first crack of thunder was soon followed by the first white pellet of hail thwacking loudly off the windscreen. The first pellet was followed by another, then something the size of a marble. Pondering Napoleon's thoughts on the effectiveness of grapeshot, I nosed the car under the densest looking trees I could find. Some drivers pushed on into the ice storm, but most didn't – there were limits to Hungarian fatalism after all. The thunder barked and clapped above while the rental car kept getting thumped and I got quivery trying to remember the insurance details (in nearly microscopic type) I'd signed my name to in the rental car company's office earlier that day. But it was all soon over and we were on our way, dent free, windows down and gulping lungfuls of air flavoured with the sweet, herbaceous scent of thousands of freshly shredded leaves. In their exposed nests above us, families of storks were raising their heads over their twig parapets and glancing warily at the heavens.

The traffic grew ever more congealed as we drew closer to Lake Balaton, sardonically referred to as the Hungarian 'sea'. Even some of the tourism brochures banged on in wounded tones about how 'history and geography had conspired' to rob the land of the Magyars of a coastline. Still, they'd managed to hang on to Europe's largest lake, and this acted as a source of consolation.

We stopped at a typical Balaton beach, namely a spot where punters paid money to be let through the outer defence ring of swimwear shops, *langós* stalls, gyros stands and pizza joints (with the obligatory red-and-white checked tablecloths and fake, potted flowers) to a strip of grass at the lake's edge. Bathers splashed in the shallow, tepid water, and beyond the swimmers, children and couples clop-clopped along in paddleboats shaped like police cars and Ferraris. Further out, men rowed to little fishing platforms, where they sat happily for hours hunched over their motionless rods. In the distance, the twin spires of the Benedictine Abbey – the burial place of one of Hungary's first kings and a short-lived refuge for its last – rose hazily from the Tihány Peninsula. Mum and Dad had honeymooned somewhere over there; nobody seemed to remember the exact location any more. ('It was delayed a week for work reasons,' Dad explained. 'We stayed at a weekend house owned by one of the mine officials, eating out, swimming, boating, enjoying the surrounds. Your mother would know more about it than me.')

From Balaton, we travelled north past Veszprém with its castle and coal mines (vastly superior to the one in Pécs, according to Dad), driving through a procession of villages and towns that looked ever better heeled the closer we got to Austria. As dusk gathered in the valleys of western Transdanubia, we headed down through the darkly wooded slopes of the Bakony Hills past the ruined castle of Csesznek, which stood as gaunt as a skeleton against the purple sky, adding fuel to Daisy's princess fantasies, before finally coming to a rest in Pannonhalma at a little hotel below the hilltop Benedictine Abbey. We arrived too late and had to leave too early to visit its vast library with its kilometres of books and its tightly guarded medieval parchments (including the nearly thousand-year-old deed of foundation from the Tihány Abbey, which contains the first known example of written Hungarian), having to make do instead with the sounds of a coachload of tourists getting steadily sloshed over cards and guffawing so hard, I half expected I'd find bits of lung tissue scattered about their table in the morning.

We flicked on the television to be greeted with the sight of George Bush in Budapest to commemorate the fiftieth anniversary of the Hungarian Revolution. He was four months early, but seeing as he was in the neighbourhood (Vienna for an EU–US summit), it must have seemed like a handy time to pop over. As he stood at the podium above the Danube, comparing Hungary in 1956 to Iraq in 2006, I thought Bel – who has a habit of hurling barbed comments at the TV when disagreeable things are being broadcast – might have a stroke.

'What an arrogant, cynical twit,' she observed. It obviously got harder for her as Bush recited the national poet, Sándor Petőfi's, lines – the ones that had helped launch Hungary's war of independence against the Habsburgs – with that oddly simian, eyes-too-close-together smirk of his:

> Here is the time, now or never!
> Shall we be slaves or free?
> This is the question, answer!
> By the God of the Hungarians we swear,
> We swear to be slaves no more!

'You do realise he can't hear you?' I gently asked after one particularly creative piece of invective.

'It had to be said,' Bel harrumphed. 'You can't just be a passive viewer.' She got crosser as Bush went on in front of the simpering Gyurcsány without ever getting around to mentioning how much America had helped Hungary back in '56, which was not at all. She finally relaxed after it was mentioned that unlike the Magyar prime minister, the ceremonial president of Hungary had got stuck into Bush about human rights.

Meanwhile the guffaw-a-thon downstairs continued. I glanced out at one point in the small hours during what must have been a particularly entertaining round, only to see a stoat bounding down the driveway, skirting around the edge of the light and vanishing into the darkness, probably with plans to ruin the night for a family of fieldmice.

We headed off again in the early light with that special sense of bleariness you get when you've emptied your wallet for a nice hotel room, only to get sod-all sleep. The card players were evidently having more luck and the only sounds were a solitary bicycle squeaking past and the early morning symphony of birds. Barely any time after the abbey vanished from the rear-vision mirror, we were sucked onto a motorway near Győr and swept along with a hurtling tide of trucks and cars encrusted with toll stickers toward Austria. Then a dull uniform and a shuffled deck of passports and the Magyar vanished – after all those lazily stretched vowels, gently cushioning y's and windswept accents, the German signage hit like a blunted axe. We slipped away from the motorway to drive through villages where we soon found ourselves longing for a little less polish, a touch of eccentricity: a solitary Trabant or a head-scarfed granny on a bicycle, or even a chimney-top stork nest with a great halo of guano frosting the tiles beneath. After Hungary, it all felt strangely anaesthetised.

'You know what it is?' Bel said as we crawled through the fifth hamlet. 'It feels like we're just driving through the same place over and over again.' She voted with her eyelids and passed out.

I kept thinking about the writer and intellectual András Török's warning that this was the fate that awaited Hungary. 'We have another five years before we become another prosperous, boring little European country with a rich cultural heritage. Maybe ten.'

Mum was herself looking a little on the anaesthetised side when we found her in the arrivals lounge at Vienna airport a short time later, sitting beneath her helmet of auburn hair (recently dyed) next to a suitcase the size of a small ox and another catatonic traveller, both of them staring straight ahead with the hollow, corpse-like eyes so familiar to anyone who has done the flight between Australia and Europe. Mum had only been expecting me, so the sight of Daisy and Leo jolted her agreeably.

'Oh, my beautifuls, my little beautifuls,' she boomed, catapulting her neighbour into full consciousness. To the neighbour's relief, we shifted to one of the airport's cafés, where a procession of women with heavy make-up and white aprons trudged between the tables, taking orders with an air of mild resentment. As the caffeine slowly but methodically bit through Mum's jetlag, she began to get almost uncontrollably excited in the way she does when she's in the first throes of infatuation with a car she's spotted in a dealer's yard.

'I brought this,' she said loudly, waving aloft a big, green Granny Smith apple, then a mandarin. 'And this! Real Australian fruit. Yes, I brought it on the plane all the way from Australia. This one,' she added, showing us the mandarin and turning it in the light to make sure we caught all its best angles, 'is from Laci's garden in Bellingen!'

I didn't know what Europe's view was on the topic of impromptu fruit importation from Australia, but Mum was carrying on like a smuggler who'd not only outwitted her foes, but had gone on to flaunt her success in their very den. The more she revelled, the more I could see *her* mother, who, sadly, failed to enjoy similar success in her own smuggling attempts in the opposite direction. Not for want of trying, it must be said.

Whenever Nagyi was about to set off on one of her periodic visits to Australia, Mum would call her just before the departure date to remind her of the folly and general undesirability of packing her suitcase full of salami, even if it was the really good stuff from Szeged. Nagyi didn't have a phone, so Mum would ring one of her neighbours, who would scurry next door and fetch Nagyi to listen to the usual spiel from her youngest daughter about the severity of Australian quarantine laws.

A couple of days later, we'd be anxiously waiting in the arrivals hall at Sydney airport, watching as all the other passengers from Nagyi's flight came out. But not Nagyi. On at least two occasions, she eventually turned up with a sheepish expression on the arm of a grumpy looking quarantine officer almost double her height, who would make a beeline for Mum, fuming about how her elderly mother had brazenly attempted to enter the Commonwealth of Australia and endanger its fragile agricultural economy with a suitcase full of paprika, salami and sundry meat products, while Nagyi quietly murmured something about it having been the good stuff from Szeged.

Despite the lectures she'd delivered, Mum herself got pinged years later trying to bring back what sounded like half a larder.

'The bastards treated me like a criminal,' she spluttered in outrage all the way to the airport car park. 'Open all your bags! Empty all your pockets! Take off your clothes! *Jaj*, I feel sick with shame. Those bastards treat me like dirt. Ha! But I show them.' She reached into a pocket and pulled out a bag of seeds. 'They did not find this! They think they are so clever, but I have my seeds.'

(That was, of course, a very long time ago and Mum would never even contemplate doing such a thing now.)

There were no grumpy quarantine officers this time around and Mum's tiny fruit shipment was safely conveyed out of Vienna airport and across the Hungarian border, where we stopped for a loo break approximately five seconds after passport control, parking among a knot of trucks, unenticing motorway cafés and money-changing booths with the most shameless rates of exchange I'd seen anywhere in the country. Mum returned to the car with an expression of moral violation.

'They charged me seventy forints just to pee,' she spluttered. This was worth about forty cents, or somewhere over fifty going by the exchange rates advertised around us. 'I don't know this country any more,' Mum said as she climbed back into the car. 'Seventy forints! I could have peed for free in Vienna.'

And so we zoomed ever deeper into Hungary, hurtling along the motorway and zipping in and out of what looked like one long conveyor belt of trucks, while Mum marvelled that such fine roads existed in the land of her birth, and every now and then, when a lorry got especially close, pondered aloud whether or not she should have spent the night in Vienna and caught the dawn train to Pécs.

'Look, Hungary has everything now,' she kept repeating as we passed giant shopping centres, long stretches of sound barriers and clusters of shiny new houses with driveways decorated with equally shiny new cars. 'This is not my country. This is not Hungary any more; this could be anywhere.'

It was just as well then that there was no schmick motorway to Pécs. When we eventually left the dual carriageway for the potholed, village-dotted road that would take us there, Mum relaxed. 'Now I start to feel like I have come home. Oh, my beautiful little country.'

There were also matters of finance to be attended to and as we bounced along in more familiar fashion, Mum opened the ledger book she kept in her head.

'I bring with me two tousand dollars from Australia, and that is it. When that runs out, it's goodnight Charlie. I go home. So don't ask me for any money because I don't have any to give you.' Then, with a pleasingly theatrical flourish, 'Sorry.'

'I didn't ask for any money.'

'And Laci give me *tree hondred bocks*.' She pulled the hundred-dollar notes from her purse, held them up to the light and, almost as if in prayer, smiled beatifically and tenderly murmured, 'Thank you, Laci, thank you.'

I caught Bel's eye in the rear-vision mirror. 'Thank you, Laci,' we repeated in unison.

'Now he is not working, so don't ask him for any money, either.'

'I wasn't planning to.'

'He doesn't have any money to give. He is moving to London, to that terrible, expensive city, and he is not working. I was locky he give me this tree hondred bocks, my poor little boy.'

'Good-oh. I wasn't planning to ask him.'

Mum turned to me with a pitying expression. 'Do you have enough money?'

'Yes. We have enough money. I'm not asking anyone for money. We have enough money.'

'Are you excited about being back in Europe, Eszter?' Bel called brightly from the back seat.

'Yes, yes, yes. It is so different, so beautiful.' Then with a wistful sigh, 'So historical.' Mum pulled a bottle of water from her handbag and took a loud swig, informing us she'd taken it from the plane. 'So, are we still going to England?'

I'd planned a flying visit for us and Joli and Lac to the part of England that had been our home during the Four Years of Tears. I wasn't expecting much in the way of illumination, but you never know. I'd called Mum a couple of times before I booked the tickets to check, then double-check, then triple-check which dates would work for her.

'August, like we agreed.'

This triggered a moan and a look of almost haemorrhoidal discomfort. 'August is so far away. Can't we make it sooner?'

'No. They're non-refundable tickets on a cheap-arse airline.'

'But what if I run out of money before then?'

'Christ, Mum, what do you think we had those long chats on the phone about?'

'Okay, okay, I go then,' Mum sighed, putting on her best martyr's face. 'A promise is a promise.'

'You were excited about going.' Joli certainly was, giggling girlishly every time we talked about it, unable and unwilling to shake from her head the image of us all wedged into the snug of a Lancashire pub, downing pints of bitter.

'How much were the tickets?'

'It doesn't matter. It's my present to you.'

'No, no. I pay you.'

'No, Mum, I said it was a present. It's something I want to give you.'

'I don't want to owe anything to anyone.' She clutched her handbag tightly to her chest. 'How much?'

'Two hundred bucks, give or take.'

'*Jaj*! So much!'

'It doesn't matter. It's a present.'

'No. I am not owing anyone a cent. I am not owing anybody anything!'

'But it's okay for Lac to give you money?'

'That is different.'

'You were just telling us how Lac doesn't have any money,' Bel said.

Mum shrank into her seat, looking like an irritated tortoise trying to pull its head back inside its shell. 'That is different. You have little children.'

'And a job.'

'It is different. I give you the two hondred bocks.'

One of the few certainties in our uncertain family was that out of Mum's four children, Lac was the favourite. In Mum's universe, the boys outranked the girls, and one boy certainly outranked the other. Mum sometimes denied this, but sometimes flaunted it with the openness of someone who sees no cause for embarrassment or shame. Once, at a dinner in Pécs the night before Lac was due to arrive, she gushed to the assembled guests – Bel and me included – 'I am so excited because my favourite son is coming tomorrow.'

Not ideal, but at least she's open about it. Most of the time. Lac deals with it by taking the piss.

Hungary can sometimes feel like a galaxy of steeples, cafés and bad roads. The bad roads at least have the decency to run past an awful lot of cafés (and, for those in need of a higher form of salvation, the steeples, too), but Mum had the strength of character to resist their siren call.

'Why stop at a café and spend your money? I am not spending any money.' She pointed to a bright blue water pump in a park barely bigger than a picnic blanket. 'Stop here please and I fill up my bottle. You can all drink from it and it doesn't cost you anything.'

'She must be very tired,' Bel suggested as Mum trotted over to the water pump and wrestled with its obstinate handle. She returned with a scowl.

'It doesn't work. It has been locked. I don't know this country any more.' Then she spotted a headscarf and the back of a flowery dress bobbing above a garden fence.

'Auntie! Auntie!' Mum cried, using the polite form of address for older women, as she scurried over with her handbag and plastic bottle. 'Please be so kind and give us some water.'

The woman beneath the headscarf looked a little surprised, then led Mum inside the house. Mum came back beaming like a teenager who's just pulled off her first pot deal. 'I have water for everyone. It is so sweet – and it didn't cost me a single forint!'

Chews Your Relatives

Bel decided to fall asleep and we drove on toward Pécs. Mum and I fell to talking about safe topics, such as how Daisy and Leo were thriving in Hungary, and slightly less safe ones, such as Joli.

Before we'd left for Vienna, Joli had come over from Uranium Town to talk to me.

'Jimmykém, I cannot come to Austria. I tried to change my work day from Friday to Thursday – I said, please let me change, my sister is arriving all the way from Australia – but they wouldn't let me change, the rotters. Imagine that, Jimmykém, they just wouldn't let me change it at all. Such foolishness. It's not as if it makes any difference to them if I do the cleaning on Thursday or Friday, it all gets done in the end. But I couldn't change it so I'm stuck working and it is a shame but I cannot go to the airport with you to meet Katika.' Mum's middle name is Katalin, which is frequently converted by Hungarians' relentlessly affectionate system of diminutives to Kati and eventually Katika, and a lot of her relatives call her that to differentiate her from the string of Eszters. 'And because I'm working all day, I was thinking the best thing would be for you and Annabel to take her to your flat where she can have a shower and a rest and a play with her little grandchildren and I will come around to pick her up when I finish. Okay? That's fixed, then.'

I mentioned this to Mum as we drove past the lake at Orfű and began climbing into the Mecsek.

'Joli said that? It doesn't matter if she is working – I have a key to the flat. That was my dear mother's home. (Oh, this forest is so beautiful – you just have to be careful with the ticks. They can send poison into your brain and you die so horribly.) When I went to see her for the last time before she died, she said to me, Katikám, whenever you come home to Pécs there will always be a place for you to stay here. My poor, sweet little mother. That is still her flat, not my sister's. It is *not* hers. She cannot keep me out.'

'I don't think that's what she meant.' Traditionally, Mum and Joli's big blue wouldn't take place until at least the second or third day after Mum's arrival, but I sensed the possibility of a new record.

'Jimmykém, I am so tired from that terrible, long flight. All I want to do is sleep. Just take me to Uranium Town and drop me off and we can all meet tomorrow when I have rested.'

I understood how she felt. Sometimes that Australia–Europe flight can leave nothing in the burned-out remains of your brain but the image of a bed and a pillow. And sometimes a minibar. In hindsight, though, it might have been a good idea to call Joli and let her know about the change in plans.

Mum and Joli have their own particular brand of interpersonal friction, a sisterly thing that seems to be all fizz and precious little bang compared to the thing Mum and Eszter have going. Some of it's what music industry flaks might refer to as artistic differences. Some of it, as our next-door neighbour (and friend of Joli) laughingly explained, is just because they're sisters.

But some relates to Joli's hoarding, her sentimental attachment to every plastic bag and scrap of paper and jar that comes into her possession. With the industriousness of a squirrel convinced the longest winter in history is in the offing, she stuffs bags and whatnot into every nook and cranny, building a rich archive of packaging material from the late twentieth and early twenty-first centuries, methodically draining the little apartment of space. There'd always been a sense of clutter since Joli moved in ('Not while my dear mother was alive,' Mum said. 'She kept it *spotless*.'), but I only started to worry when I arrived in Pécs a few years back and found that Joli had sealed off the living room as if it were the scene of a particularly ghastly crime. It was the biggest room in the flat and was where I'd normally have sat chatting with Joli for hours, while we scoffed our way through cubic metres of pastries and sipped lemon tea or the diabolically strong Turkish coffee she brewed on the stove top that made our hearts vibrate inside our chests. It was also the room where Nagyi had slowly died, announcing in a clear voice on one of her last days that she could see my dead grandfather smiling from the sofa, waiting to take her hand again.

But by 2001, the door was most definitely shut. The sound of my hand on the handle had Joli materialising out of nowhere like a startled genie. 'No, you can't go in there. It's a little disordered just now.'

I wondered how bad it had become. This time she'd gone a step further and had so far managed to keep us away from the flat altogether. 'It's not that I don't want you to come around, it's just that I have to tidy a little there first,' she'd explain when cornered on the subject.

Some of my favourite childhood photos are from that Uranium Town flat, or more specifically from the playground beneath. I was such a chubby little toddler, but Nagyi always looked happy; she liked her grandchildren to have a bit of meat on them, even the pale ones from England.

Following Mum, I lugged her ox bag up that familiar stairwell with its faint, cellar-like whiff of mould and damp cement to Joli's front door, which was labelled the traditional Hungarian way: Merck Istvánne, or Mrs István Merck. Divorce had long since parted them, then István's death a few years back gave things an even greater sense of finality. But Joli still wore his name, even if she had added another label to the door with the family name of Székelyhidi.

'Now we'll see if this key still works. Oh, it won't go in.' Mum crouched to examine the keyhole. 'Look, the key's in on the other side; that means she is home. I thought she was working.'

The sound of the door bell must have been a shock, judging by the look of consternation on Joli's face as she opened the door. She stood before us in a baggy T-shirt, wild-eyed and bathed in sweat, standing almost knee-deep in a drift of plastic bags.

'You can't come in!' she stammered, waving her arms about her in a strange, slow-motion frenzy like someone being electrocuted under water. 'It's only like this because . . . because of the whore mouse!'

'Hello would also be nice,' Mum said.

'The little whore mouse!'

'Did you have a good trip from Australia? You can ask that too, if you want.'

'What, hey? Oh, yes, hello . . .'

'Hello, Joli,' I said weakly. 'Mum said she wanted to come here first.' Mum peered through the door at the chaos in the hallway and the delirious shambles of bags and pots and empty bottles and plates teetering in unwashed towers in the kitchen.

'There is a mouse in the flat, so I've just been unpacking everything trying to find him.'

'Look at it, Jimmykém, can you believe it? You see what my dear sister does to our mother's home? Jolikám, why are you so surprised to see me when you've known for two months I am coming? Look at it. It makes me sick, Jimmykém.'

The new record was beyond all expectations; even the most conservative of observers would have said the ritual stoush of greeting had got under way by the five-second mark, but more accurate witnesses would suggest hostilities were officially declared open in the microsecond or so that it took the vision of Joli's bag avalanche to be converted into a nervous impulse and conveyed up the optic nerve into Mum's brain. I'd barely made it across the road when my phone rang.

'Jimmykém, it's Joli. Your mother would like to speak with you.'

'Jimmykém, get me out of here please. I cannot stay here one moment longer.'

I could hear Joli's voice in the background, quiet, deflated, urging Mum to calm down.

'Please let me stay with you,' Mum said. 'I will pay. I cannot stay here. I can hardly breathe in this pig sty.'

'Really, now, Katika.'

'What else would you call this pig sty?'

'Listen to your mouth running. This is just a little disorder. I was going to have it all packed away before you came.'

'All *this*? My dear sister, it will take a week to clean up this pig sty. Jimmykém, I pay you. Or I am going to stay in a hotel.'

'Don't be so silly. Stay with Jimmy tonight and you can come back tomorrow. I'll have everything sorted out by then.'

'You don't have to pay us, Mum, for God's sake. I'm coming over.'

It wouldn't last long – Mum and Joli's bust-ups never did. Within a day or two, I knew they'd be out together, merrily gossiping and forensically exploring the streets of their home town one shoe shop at a time, then heading back to Uranium Town to drink coffee in the flat that had been their parents' last home.

But first, they had to blow off a little sisterly steam. That's just the way it was with them.

By night, Mum was already anxious to do the whole olive branch thing, telling me she was just exhausted and everything would be fine after a good night's sleep. 'Please call Joli for me. I want to talk to her and see if she is okay, poor thing.'

This time they chatted in more measured tones, Mum only becoming strident when she was outlining a timetable for cleaning the flat. Afterwards she stood out on our balcony with a cigarette, a glowing, orange dot in the darkness. After three years abstinence that had caught us all by surprise, she was back on the gaspers with a vengeance. But now she was rolling her own, reasoning that they were more natural. 'There is so much robbish chemicals in the filters in the cigarettes you buy in the shops. And they are so expensive!'

But she wasn't in the mood to be a tobacco evangelist now. She just stood there taking long drags, blowing smoke out into the night.

'So strange to be back,' she murmured, staring out to where the tiny bats squeaked and skimmed over the tiled roofs. 'Sometimes I don't know where I belong. Perhaps the best place for me is on the plane somewhere in between.' The dot glowed fiercely for a moment as she drew another lungful, then a low, contented exhalation. 'Is easier for your farder; he never missed England.' Then a small fit of coughing. 'I will give up this bloody smoking again, you will see.'

Mercury and Melons

Summer fell on Hungary like a wall. This came as something of a surprise to the locals, who had been listening for weeks as their meteorologists gently prepared them for the worst of all possibilities short of a major meteorite strike – a cool, damp summer. Even worse, a cool, damp summer with a token week or so of warmth to remind everyone fleetingly what it was they were missing. It was all so shatteringly disappointing; it didn't sound like summer, it sounded like England. Pah!

According to Bel's Hungarian textbook, Hungarians don't particularly regard the weather as an agreeable topic of conversation, but during the moister, more frigid stretches of that spring, they could scarcely shut up about it. And after such a severe winter, too, frozen by a cold front from Siberia. Bloody Russians again. It was just one more episode in Hungary's centuries of misfortune.

But then one morning the mercury stirred inside thermometers across the country, rousing itself from the mid-teens at which it had congealed and marching up through the twenties and carrying on to the mid-thirties, where it seemed to lodge for the next six weeks or so, give or take the occasional dalliance with forty. Roads softened, flowers and Trabants wilted, and the leaves on some of the more resolutely European species of tree browned as surely as chickens in an oven. Within days, adults who had sounded on the verge of succumbing to the national enthusiasm for suicide because of the cold sounded as if their will to live was being weakened from another direction altogether. In contrast, the children thought it was marvellous. In Pécs they got busy stripping down to their underwear – or in the case of toddlers, nothing at all – and clambered into the fountains in front of the theatre and the cathedral. Perhaps the extreme heat had fused shut the panic centres in the adults' brains, as for once the Magyar conviction that children will catch cold and/or drown given the slightest opportunity was put on hold and the grown-ups smiled indulgently at the little ones as they splashed and squealed in the water, walking away with a twinkle in their eyes before going home to ponder death once more.

Not Mum, though. Or at least not at first.

'You think this is hot? This is nothing.' On those first few jetlagged days, her see-sawing ambivalence about her home country kept surfacing in odd places.

As we sat at our regular tramp-magnet café, she roundly rejected the waitress's suggestion of carrot cake.

'For what? We already have carrot cake in Australia for years.'

The waitress's comment that it was almost insufferably hot was similarly shown the door. 'This? Ha. This is nothing. Thirty-five is not hot. In Australia, we have forty-five. Isn't that right, Jimmykém? Forty-five!'

Luckily, a tramp interrupted proceedings. He wasn't one I recognised and he moved with a slightly less shambolic gait than most of them. His clothes looked as though they'd been dug up out of a bog – possibly along with the rest of him – but he carried himself with a certain swagger. He stopped to chat to our bemused neighbours across the geraniums, prompting the waitress to become stern.

'Go away or I'll call the police.'

'But why? What have I done, my good lady?'

'You're bothering the guests.'

'Bothering? You think I'm bothering them?' He turned to our neighbours with a look of altar boy innocence. 'Am I bothering you? No, we're just talking, just a few people talking to each other on a beautiful summer's day.' He issued a small burp whose size belied its potency; I was surprised the geranium closest to him didn't immediately drop all its petals.

'I'm calling the police now,' the waitress said, putting her hands on her hips to show she wasn't to be trifled with.

'Just look at that – isn't she a cheeky one? I stop to have a little friendly chat and she's already trying to call the cops.' With a little flourish, he wished us all a pleasant day and wandered off past the Lyceum Church and the bench that served from time to time as a sort of open-air drunk tank. He waved at its booze-ravaged occupants slumped in the sunshine and they stirred faintly in response, looking so deeply buried in their tattered layers it was possible they hadn't yet noticed summer had arrived. The expression of dissatisfaction on Mum's face solidified.

'I have travelled all this way for this.'

There were times it was hard to escape the feeling that for all her talk – talk that could at the slightest provocation gush from her with the volatile persistence of a punctured airship – Mum liked the idea of Hungary more than she liked Hungary itself. Or at least for the first few days while the jetlag monstered her. I mentioned this hypothesis on the phone to Eszter.

'That's just how it is with her,' Eszt said. 'She keeps telling you how homesick she is, then the minute she gets off the plane she can't wait to get the fuck out of there.'

Lac, on the other hand, tended to suggest taking everything Mum said with a fairly generous helping of salt.

I decided the best tactic would be to pander to one of Mum's obsessions and suggested we check out a bit of local real estate. I saw the first flicker of enthusiasm around the edges of her oversized sunglasses and we headed off to fetch the Skoda. This necessitated leaving the Inner Town, and as we walked, the standard of aesthetics, plasterwork and dustlessness quickly tumbled.

Mum made a face. 'You want to stay here? For what? You say you like it? This dirty, dusty place? I don't understand.' Evidently, this part of Pécs failed to breathe any history whatsoever.

Dad, on the other hand, who had never expressed any sort of longing for England, was as happy as a dog with two tails when he returned to his home town of Bolsover. 'If you looked out from the back of the house, you had the view of Bolsover Castle. If you looked out the front, there was this tremendous slag heap . . .' All said with misty eyes.

'No,' Mum said, 'I do not want to come back to this. I don't understand why you want to bring your children here. Your farder was happy coming here again?' Admittedly, we were walking along a particularly unpleasant stretch of one of Pécs's least lovely thoroughfares – a part of Rákoczi Road arcing through a neighbourhood dating from the period when communist regimes across Eastern Europe harboured a special grudge against the sighted. But still.

I suggested to Mum that this represented something of an about-face from her long-term campaigning for all of us to pack up and return to Hungary. Mum made a dismissive noise and we walked on.

(A few weeks later, she was telling anyone who listened that she would move back to Europe in a shot – in a shot! *Ja ja* – if only her obstinate children wouldn't insist on living in Australia. Then she delivered a brief dissertation on why Hungary, with its relative state of racial homogeneity, was better than Australia which had all those bloody migrants. Her own status as an immigrant was not raised. She moved without pause to a heartfelt soliloquy about how she couldn't wait to get back to Australia to drive her Rrrenault La-*goo*-na.)

Mum's tone softened a little when we crossed to the patch of wasteland where we parked the Skoda. It wasn't the Skoda that moved her, but the elegant green-cupolaed edifice of the university that gave Rákoczi Road its only visual reprieve. It was the university that had given my grandfather a job, luring him and his family, including my infant mother, away from his hometown of Debrecen.

Mum was born in Debrecen in 1943, around about the time that the Hungarian government realised it had yet again joined the wrong side in a world war. When my grandfather was born there, the city – the capital of the Great Plain, two-times temporary capital of Hungary, Calvinist stronghold and the site of Kossuth's declaration of independence from Habsburg Austria – was deep within the Kingdom of Hungary, comfortably close to the fringe of the fairy garden. But in 1943, it was close to the Soviet frontier and ever closer to the devourer of men that was the Eastern Front. Then there was that big patch of northern Transylvania nearby that Hungary's right-wing regime had reclaimed from Romania with the help of Nazi Germany. Now the Russians were on their way and Hitler was reminding Hungary of its debt. There was no possible way any of this was going to work out well.

Luckily, Nagypapa accepted a transfer to the Medical University in Pécs and moved his family across Hungary from the mirages and dust devils of the plain to the hills and vineyards of southern Transdanubia. The Red Army reached Debrecen shortly afterwards, then Hitler dispatched the Luftwaffe. The Hungarian phrase for carpet-bombing has exactly the same combination of incongruity and random devastation as the English. Debrecen was all but flattened.

'That was where my dear father worked,' Mum said as we rattled past in the Skoda. 'My poor, sweet father.' If anything, Mum seemed more tormented by the death of her father than of her mother. She'd been able to spend time with Nagyi during her final months, but Nagypapa went to the grave during the poisonous thick of Mum's custody battle against Dad. She was told it would be unwise to leave Australia even for the short time it would take to go back to Pécs and throw dirt on her father's coffin. Mum has never made her peace with that.

We drove down the road that runs past the long cemetery wall with its encampments of flower sellers and stretches south from Pécs toward the Croatian border and the spa town of Harkány, which seems as thick with Germans as it is with hydrogen sulphide right through the summer.

I'd first visited Nagyi's and Nagypapa's graves on a crisp November night ten years before. It was the Day of the Dead and the cemetery was filled with a constellation of grave-top candles that made the whole place dance with shadows and bathed the tombstones and crucifixes (and the neighbouring encampments of Red Army and Wehrmacht graves with their regimented rows of red stars and black crosses) in a light that somehow managed to be both warm and eerie. The air had that pinching edge that suggests the first snowfall of the winter isn't far off, and families filed through the gates in coated clumps with fresh bouquets for dead relatives, grumbling about the gypsy kids who were doing a roaring trade outside, selling flowers they'd just pinched from the cemetery.

Mum called hello to her parents as we went by, looking on the verge of tears but managing to stay dry. We headed past roadside stalls all but buried beneath mounds of watermelons and boxes of strawberries toward the village of Kökény, which not only manages to provide a measure of childish amusement by being pronounced a lot like cocaine, but has also been a bit of a real estate fantasy hotspot for Mum and me.

Straddling the crest between two gentle valleys, Kökény is one of the prettier villages around Pécs, with lakes on one side and farmland bucolic beyond the call of duty on the other. The first time I went there was on a house-hunting mission with Mum, aware the whole time of a dangerous sense of wistfulness thickening around us like fog as we ogled houses with wine presses and fruit-festooned orchards. There was one house that was particularly dangerous as we floated in that sweet void between daydreams and reality. It perched on the hillside with whitewashed walls, wine press and cellar, sporadically ordered ranks of apricot, peach, cherry and apple trees, a view that seemed to stretch halfway to Croatia, and, for security, a floppy-tongued, floppy-limbed vizsla puppy with a tail that wagged and thrashed away like a chestnut whip. The whole package was on offer for a shade over $20,000 and it capsized our brains. We strolled afterwards in a conspiratorial frenzy by the lake where ducks paddled with fluffy lines of ducklings in tow. Baby water snakes wriggled in the warm, reedy shallows, terrapins with yellow cheeks and glittering eyes basked on exposed willow roots with their webbed toes outstretched, and frogs that looked as though they'd been rolled in chocolate and mint, then carefully glazed, leaped at our approach; our walk was marked by an almost metronomic plopping.

It all came to nothing, of course. Mum was in the midst of a property settlement ('Yes, a house! In Liverpool!') and when it came down to it, Bel and I, having just thrown in our lowly paid newspaper jobs in Australia for a carefree life of freelancing in Eastern Europe, had neither the money, the energy nor, ultimately, the desire for the sort of anchor that such a house represents. Even if it was only twenty thousand bucks. I still kick myself once every six months or so.

Mum and I were both curious to see if the place was as nice as we remembered it. After some faffing about and moments of misnavigation, we found the ramshackle road that slenderly led away from the centre of the village – with its solitary shop, bus stop, roundabout and crucifix – through an avenue of mulberry and sour cherry trees heavy with fruit and a meadow buried deep in chamomile blossoms. Mum was definitely warming to Hungary once again; at this rate, she would be a dedicated Europhile poo-pooing Australia within a week. We stopped to smell the chamomile and raid the fruit. The mulberries were still a little on the tart side but the cherries were spot on. Mum reasoned that any fruit on branches sticking across fences into public land was public property, and we gobbled the whole way up the road, contentedly firing volleys of cherry stones into the flowers until we reached the house. It was still there, looking almost as lovely as it had stayed in my dreams, even if the owners had installed a small above-ground swimming pool in a deeply unsympathetic location. The next-door neighbour poked his face through a dense wall of cherry trunks to say hello. A young couple had bought the place, he told us, artsy types from Pécs. Mum asked if there was anything available in the village for that five-year-old price and the man chuckled.

'Ah, no. Those days have already gone. Such prices are just a memory now, and it will get even worse when the euro comes.'

There was one house for sale at the bottom of the road – an unappealing two-storey place that looked only partially formed – but Mum headed straight for the first open window she could find and roused the owner. As he led us through the house, he explained that the ground floor with its bar, tiles, terrace and generous supply of stools had been a village pub that hadn't made any money, serving its last drink to a paying customer a year or so before. Upstairs, though, was filled with unfinished bits and temporary solutions; someone's dream had run out of steam or dough or both. Mum made excited noises in every room we entered, fantasising out loud about all the lovely things she would do if she lived there, things we both knew she had no real intention of ever doing.

Our other mission in Kökény was to look up an old schoolfriend of Mum's. She couldn't remember the street name, but that didn't seem to matter all that much as Kökény wasn't a whole lot bigger than a postage stamp.

'It was definitely this street,' Mum said, sounding less than completely convinced. 'But was that the house there? Or maybe it's this one, though I don't remember it having a roof like that.' She pulled her water bottle from her handbag and pondered the possibilities between slurps. 'I ask those men there.'

Mum waddled over to one of the houses where two men with bare chests were shovelling away in the front garden and asked if they could tell her where her friend lived.

'What did you say her name was again?' one of the men asked. Mum repeated it and they shook their heads.

'Never heard of her,' the older one said, wiping a hand across his greying moustache. 'Are you sure she was in this village? I know almost everyone who lives here, but I don't recognise that name.'

'Yes, she definitely lives here,' Mum said, emptying the bottle down her throat. 'In this very street.'

'I don't think so,' the man ventured. The younger one had stopped shovelling to grin in Mum's direction.

'I am positive she lives in this street. Only . . .' Mum's eyes swept the street unhappily. 'Only her house has disappeared.'

'Disappeared?' the older one cried, throwing me a wink. 'You think it's disappeared? Even in Kökény, houses don't tend to vanish into thin air.'

'Unless it's disappeared behind weeds,' the younger one suggested, but this was a little too prosaic for his companion's tastes.

'Perhaps weeds,' he shrugged. 'Or perhaps there's a Kökény triangle, just like the one in Bermuda!'

Mum began to sense some piss was being taken and she tartly thanked them for their time.

'Idiot peasants,' she commented as she climbed back into the Skoda. We drove out through fields of wheat where a small brown hawk hovered above the yellow ears with tail fanned, then made a pit stop at one of the fruit stalls on the way back into Pécs. Mum soon had the stall keeper lugging his biggest melon over to the car and putting it in Leo's baby seat, which proved to be the perfect size and shape for melon transport.

'Look, is such a beautiful melon. There's plenty of melon for everyone. Anyone who goes with me does well; I am not stingy,' she informed me as we crossed the railway bridge. The Inner Town lay before us, a sea of terracotta spreading up the Mecsek's lower slopes, the dome of the Djami a big, blue button in the middle.

We collected Bel and the kids, and even carrying this extra load, the Skoda only overheated once as we drove out of town again, this time through the hills.

The issue of houses weighed on Mum's mind through the afternoon as Bel and I took Daisy swimming at the lakeside pool in Orfű, only surfacing from that tepid soup of g-strings and inflatable mattresses to hack sweet, sodden red hunks out of the melon. In between phone calls to Joli and bursts of fussing over her grandchildren, Mum once more rued the way that Kökény house had slipped through her fingers.

'You could have bought it, you know,' she added accusingly.

I agreed that it was a shame. I wasn't immune to wistful daydreams that involved Bel and me wandering about our country house, plucking peaches in our orchard or idly wiping the dust from the bottles in our cellar. But five years ago, there'd been so many reasons.

There'd also been all those voices warning us of the dangers of going rural. 'You go back to Australia and leave the house empty and you know what will happen – the gypsies will move in. Then what? You're not allowed to just kick them out. And what will they do if you ask them to leave? They will laugh and spit in your face, that's what.' Or at least that's what Mum and Joli told us.

'Never mind,' Mum said as we headed back toward Pécs, the Skoda heeling distractingly as we negotiated the hairpin bends down toward Uranium Town. 'Don't feel bad because you haven't bought a house yet. I did not buy a house until I was fifty.'

'What about the house you bought with James's father?' Bel asked innocently.

'That,' Mum said, 'was not mine.'

There are times when you should really go against all instincts and instead pay attention to that insistent little voice in the back of your head that's telling you to either shut up, change the subject or make a cup of tea.

'What do you mean, Mum? There was a property settlement with Dad and you got half the value, didn't you?'

'No,' Mum said flatly.

'For the love of God put a sock in it!' The little voice was starting to sound less little.

'But you did.'

'You know what I get? I get twenty tousand bocks, that is all. Twenty tousand! That is not half a house.'

If only the little voice had physical powers as well, it would at this stage have done me the service of removing my tongue.

'That's almost half what you'd paid for the house just a few years before.'

'Look. I get twenty tousand bocks. When you and Olivia were bigger I buy you second-hand car for eleven tousand and for Olivia for nine tousand.'

In a weird coincidence, Bel was also deaf to the little voice – perhaps this was due to the change in air pressure as we came down the hillside. 'That's big-hearted of you, Eszter,' she said, which really didn't help things any more than my words had so far.

'Don't you understand? I get twenty tousand, and I spend it all on you and Olivia. I owe you nothing.'

'I think you're missing the point,' I said. 'You were saying you didn't buy a house until you were fifty, when we know that's not strictly true.' I'm sure I heard a thud as the little voice killed itself. This at least spared it the vision of Uranium Town as we entered its modestly unlovely concrete chasms.

'I. Owe. You. Nothing.'

'It's always about money with you, isn't it?'

'You and Olivia have my twenty tousand. I owe you nothing. Nothing. Absolutely nothing. You get nothing more from me.'

Bel's little voice must have topped itself as well, judging by the thoroughness with which she released her emotional handbrake and expressed some frank and deeply held opinions with a surprising economy of language.

Mum chose not to contest any of her points. She got out of the car and extracted Joli's bewilderingly heavy Soviet-made vacuum cleaner from the boot without a word, along with the gutted carcase of the watermelon. I didn't notice until later that she'd forgotten her shoes and I drove them to Uranium Town that night, stretched somewhere between anger and a desire for things to be vaguely normal again.

Mum was stretched between nothing. 'Why have you come here? Why do you spend your money on the petrol?'

The façade of civility soon dropped and we raised our voices disgracefully, putting Joli in agony because she knew how well sound travelled in that little apartment block.

'Please, what if the neighbours hear?' she pleaded while Mum and I hurled poison at each other. I must have seemed a disappointingly novice adversary after Eszter, but I gave it what I could.

'We were so looking forward to you coming, then you carry on like a demented cash register.'

'You are not going to see me now. You are not going to see me ever again!'

'Please,' Joli grimaced.

'I will change my ticket and fly home on Wednesday. I come here for nothing. I spend my money for nothing. I will leave forever!'

'No you won't,' Joli said as calmingly as she could, then to me, 'She won't. She's just talking.'

'I never see my grandchildren again.' Her voice slid up a few tones to a more suitably melodramatic pitch. 'They will jost be a memory for me. A memory, that is all.'

'Good-oh. Cheerio, then.'

'And why is Annabel putting her nose into matters that happened twenty years before she ever met you. She is nothing between us!'

It had been years since Mum – who was generally on war footing against the partners of her offspring – had attacked Bel. With all the memories from that foolish episode welling up inside me, I returned fire. All in all it was the sort of exchange where you just want to hit the erase button the whole time. I had a sudden image of Eszter in the corner somewhere behind Mum, dressed in Yoda's robes and sadly shaking her head, muttering, 'A Jedi you are not.'

Mum must have sensed my distraction and she grabbed for her trump card. 'You,' she huffed, 'are just like your farder.' These were the most hurtful words she kept in her arsenal. '*Exactly* like him.'

Uncharitably, I recalled the old legends about pipers and their propensity for attracting witches. As I moved toward the door, Joli came with me, asking Mum whether or not she was going to come downstairs.

'What for? There is nothing to go downstairs for. You'll be okay on your own, Jolikám. No gypsy is going to attack you.'

As I drove away I thought that it was probably for the best that no one mentioned the property settlement from Mum's third marriage.

I ran into the sisters by accident a couple of nights later, Mum calling out from their bench opposite the theatre fountains. Dad used to loiter bashfully in this square, waiting for Mum to glance out from the shoe shop she'd come to work in since leaving the mine. Joli was sporting her emotionally worn expression, but Mum was all smiles.

'Come, Jimmykém, I buy you an ice-cream. They are Italian and so delicious; Joli and I just had some.'

'Thanks, Mum, but I'll pass for now.'

'Are you sure? I buy it for you – you don't have to pay.'

I sometimes found myself wishing I had half of Mum's capacity to build her little bridges and move on. I also sometimes wondered how much salt it was that Lac had in mind. All in all, it seemed as good a time as any to escape to a bagpipe camp and squeeze a goat. They say it can be very cathartic.

A Gathering of Goat Squeezers

THE FIRST SONG that Andor taught me had a straightforward message – if I wanted to learn to play the Hungarian bagpipe, I would have to go to hell. (This is, in true Magyar style, a reversal of standard Western practice of learning the bagpipes first and then being told to go to hell.) As promising as this sounded, we agreed that an upcoming *duda* and folk music camp in the neighbouring county would be an acceptable alternative. The village of Szenna sounded surprisingly picturesque for a Hades substitute; it even had a lovely Calvinist church, which, as some people are unkind enough to suggest, is what you should expect in the real hell.

I'd first stumbled across the Szenna bagpipe camp on the internet during a particularly productive bout of procrastination at work the year before. I'd had no idea Hungarian pipers got up to such things; I didn't think there were enough of them. (Unlike, say, uilleann pipers who tend to descend upon their gatherings in droves, driven half bonkers by the prospect of a full week of uninterrupted boozing and squeezing, jigging and reeling in the company of likeminded fanatics. Scottish pipers, on the other hand, allow themselves to get overly distracted by the tossing of cabers and the like.)

But there it was in vivid colour on the computer screen – a goatskin bagpipe summer school an easy drive from Pécs. There was even a photo of Andor with one of his dead flock under his arm and I read greedily in between checking over my shoulder to make sure my section editor didn't catch me engaged in extracurricular activities, particularly as I was meant to be researching luxury treehouse accommodation around Australia.

Mum asked again where I was going, and when told she smiled the eyes-screwed-shut smile she used when acknowledging I had said something and the words had reached her ears but she didn't know what the hell it was I was talking about. A bagpipe camp? *A whole week?* As a lifelong dabbler on the piano, Mum thought the bagpipes were lovely in principle (especially the Scottish ones – such smart uniforms!), but sometimes wondered why I hadn't, in practice, tried a more sociable instrument. The piano, for example. The piano could lead to a career on the stage. Then fame! Travel! Riches! But the bagpipes, my sweet Lord and his mother too, what could they bring but tinnitus? Or witches?

Even the Hungarian music thing was a source of some ambivalence for Mum, although she did once put on an impromptu display of pole dancing at a traditional dance house in Pécs that had quite an effect on the audience; there haven't been many times I've wished I had a feather boa to give Mum to complete her natural sense of cabaret, but that night, as the racing violins slowed and stumbled, was one of them.

For Mum, Lehár was good in bursts and Liszt was perfectly fine (though she preferred that Pole, Chopin), but Bartók seemed too much like hard work. Why didn't I listen to this, she'd say, popping on a CD of Imre 'Jimmy' Zámbo, a helium-voiced balladeer with a great cascade of curls, a collection of leather waistcoats, and a morose, goggle-eyed face that always made me think of a drowned frog.

Imaginatively known as the King ('Four and a half octaves! Almost as many as a piano!'), Zámbó sold a lot of angst-ridden, quavering, love-gone-wrong records in Hungary and lived in a manner befitting his nickname. Or at least he had until one champagne-soaked New Year's morning when he took out his monogrammed pistol to show his mates and accidentally blew his brains out – apparently not as difficult an achievement as you might think. Mum was devastated and the rumours didn't help. Certainly not the persistent story (denied) that hospital staff quietly snipped off King Jimmy's absurd locks and sold them for an unimaginable number of forints to a fan deranged with grief. (Not Mum. I checked.) When you know how little doctors and nurses get paid in Hungary, the story makes sense. Certainly more sense than voluntarily heading out into the sticks to spend a week in the company of pipers.

With Bel ensconced in her favourite position in the passenger seat (shoes off, feet on the dashboard and a fresh set of toe marks on the windscreen), we headed off.

'I'll just stay for the first night and the concert, then I'll head back to Pécs with the kids,' she'd explained beforehand. 'I think it will be better for you to really immerse yourself in the piping and talking Hungarian without us getting in the way.' I suspected she was using diplomatic language to dignify her wriggling out, but it was tricky to prove. Besides, we had agreed in earlier discussions that I would have difficulty sitting through a full week of her favoured wind instrument – the French horn – so I couldn't really take offence. (And yet not impossible. I sometimes worried about my bouts of tetchiness, but when I read Péter Esterházy's line about the overriding pride of the Hungarians and their eagerness to take offence, I consoled myself with the thought that this particular character flaw was at least a sign of my deep-rooted Magyarness. This warmed me for at least five seconds until it occurred to me that Esterházy's line also perfectly fitted Dad, who is as Hungarian as tofu. So it was back to the drawing board.)

We took the long route to Szenna, worried that the shorter, steeper road through the Mecsek would finish off the Skoda on such a hot day. Hills they might have been, but the Skoda – especially when creaking with a full payload of family, luggage, nappies for Leo's ever more productive bottom, and a portable cot so heavy we almost needed a winch to get it in and out of the boot – made the Mecsek feel like the Himalaya. (It didn't actually grind to a steam-billowing halt until weeks later on the Great Plain, where the only mound of any significance for miles around was the belly of the cimbalom player at the Hortobágy Csárda.)

Just down the road from Pécs, we stopped near the spot where Suleyman the Magnificent, four decades into his successful program of bludgeoning Hungary into the Ottoman Empire, died of a heart attack while besieging Szigetvár in 1566. It was twenty-three years after the Turks had more or less strolled into Pécs and forty since Suleyman had overseen the slaughter of the Hungarian army at Mohács. And then a heart attack during the night as he slept in his tent; it's possible he'd started eating Hungarian food.

The Sultan's death was kept quiet in a bid to keep the team spirit undented, his body propped up in a chair overlooking the scene. The Hungarians – outnumbered in even more drastic style than usual – eventually lost the month-long siege in style just two days later, the handful of Magyars under the command of Miklós Zrinyi charging out into the 60,000-strong Ottoman army for a shortlived bout of hand-to-hand combat. Zrinyi's grandson Miklós Zrinyi, himself a celebrated general and poet – a combination not emphasised anywhere near enough in modern military training – converted the siege into verse. It was the sort of defeat the Hungarian heart seems to clamour for even more than victory.

As for Suleyman, his dicky heart was buried a kilometre away and a marble mausoleum built. It was apparently a splendid thing, but it was torn down on the orders of some minor Habsburg official almost the moment Szigetvár was retaken in 1693 and a Catholic church built in its place.

These days, no one seems quite so grumpy any more. A Hungarian–Turkish Peace Park was created on the site in 1994 at the behest of the Turkish government, and a big, bronze, po-faced bust of the Sultan erected. He was joined three years later by a bronze Zrinyi, also donated by the Turks. Or at least he looks bronze until you tap him with your knuckles. I don't think this is strictly encouraged at such monuments, but it is fun to try. Suleyman the Magnificent responds with a pleasing sort of bonging sound, but tap on Zrinyi and all you get is a measly little pok-pok-pok. It turns out that Zrinyi was fashioned from the less magnificent material of fibreglass and then painted a bronzish hue. Somewhere along the way, the story goes, someone pocketed the difference, probably viewing it as de facto compensation for the 150-year occupation of Hungary.

Bel and I entertained ourselves for a while with poks and bongs, also noting gleefully that only Suleyman was shimmering in the baking heat. We stopped our experiment as another car rolled into the tiny carpark and disgorged a family. Which was probably just as well, because they were Turks. The three of them – mother, father and little slip of a girl – walked together wearing matching shades of blue and matching stern expressions.

It turned out that the father was an engineer four months into a six-month stint working in Budapest. He was very curious when he found out we were Australian.

'Did you have any relatives at the Dardanelles?' he asked, his face instantly softening. 'I had several.'

I had to tell him no, but that my family was represented on both sides during the Great War. He nodded and smiled as though that was just to be expected. We gazed across the field to where the little church stood in place of Suleyman's mausoleum and I expressed regret that such an unexceptional building had replaced the Ottoman marble.

'Do you know of Suleyman?'

'Yes, I do,' I said, reeling off some of his successful exercises in empire building, adding that even in Hungary, a country that suffered at his hands, there seemed to be a respect for him.

'He was one of our greatest leaders,' the Turk said. He handed me a camera and asked me to take a photo of him and his wife and his little girl as they stood stiffly holding hands beneath the bronze and fibreglass busts. I decided against encouraging them to do the pok–bong comparison.

I ENROLLED IN MY FIRST ever bagpipe camp in the Szenna school library and was the object of much curiosity. Brigi, one of the organisers, who had been on the receiving end of my emails (in which I hope my enthusiasm made up for my erratic Hungarian) was keen to introduce me as the special foreign visitor. Not only was I all the way from Australia, I'd found out about Szenna on the internet. There was much thoughtful aahing about how wonderfully small computers had made the world and I was effusively welcomed. Then Bel walked in with Leo and Daisy and the room went into the predictable meltdown of child and baby-worshipping.

'Your wife is very beautiful,' someone murmured during a momentary lull in the frenzy. 'She looks almost Hungarian.'

We were shown to our accommodation (two bedrooms, bathroom and a kitchen the size of a hangar) and asked if it would be big enough, while Daisy got busy bouncing the beds in. After several rounds of squeaks and hallelujahs, we eventually meandered down to the restaurant next door where all the musicians were to muster for breakfast, lunch and dinner. The looks on the faces of the seasoned drinkers at the adjoining pub suggested they were ambivalent, at best, about this annual influx of folkies into their village.

'You must be James Jeffrey from Australia,' said a voice as we sat down.

I looked up to see a young man with a narrow, tapered face top heavy with brows as thick as fingers.

'Yes, I am James Jeffrey from Australia,' I replied, surprised into mimicking his tone.

'I read your name on the list as I was registering.' He was leading another man by the hand. 'I'm István, and this is also István. But a lot of people call us Pisti,' – pronounced Pishti – 'It's very exciting that you've come so far.'

'Yes, how did an Australian get involved with the *duda* of all things? How the hell did you wind up here?' The second Pisti was shorter and much rounder, his eyelids closed. When they momentarily parted, it was to reveal a narrow, glistening whiteness. I didn't know if it was the same here, but in the Celtic world, there is something of an aura around blind pipers and I felt a brief and probably deeply incorrect rush of excitement. Both the Pistis were fine pipers, but Pisti the Rounder was also a cross between an encyclopaedia and a folk music jukebox. Pisti the Slender had a sunny earnestness about him and a *duda* which, thanks to some accident in the curing process, had see-through skin. Pisti the Rounder, on the other hand, had a laugh like a ribald old aunt and passed the time by parodying the singing styles of different performers, often while throwing in some musical tidbits: 'Well, that's how he did it on such-and-such a record, but if you listen to track seven on such-and-such, you'll hear some real Nógrád touches he's added in the second measure.' Or something along those lines.

'He's amazing,' Andor said later that week. 'Pisti can tell me exactly what tracks I've done on what CD, even stuff I've forgotten about. So I go home and check, and he's right.'

As the bell tolled seven o'clock, we drifted across the road in the yellowing light toward the Calvinist church for the opening concert. The church stood in the middle of a museum of peasant houses, its white belltower ringed by thatched roofs and capped with what looked like a pair of burnt radishes on a spike. The performers followed in a trinity of moustaches, bagpipes slung over their shoulders with horn-tipped drone pipes hanging over woollen sacks bulging with whistles and shepherd's flutes. As the pipers shook hands with the minister (who, with his shock of white hair, humble moustache and faint sheen of sweat looked oddly like a waxwork version of Father Lajos, the priest who'd married my parents) the bagpipes' carved goat heads peered at us from behind the pipers' backs with impudent expressions as though they were sneaking into church.

During the service (punctuated by the minister's penetrating, magnificently atonal singing – another echo of Father Lajos), we were reminded that traditionally, the shepherds and swineherds who tended to dominate the *duda*-playing demographic were invited into church to pipe for the pleasure of God once a year at midnight on Christmas Eve. One by one, the three pipers puffed their instruments to life. First came the deep hum of the drone, followed by the wail of the chanter and then the up and down pulse of the contra pipe, each instrument a miniature and wonderfully unrefined orchestra that unleashed its noise like a swarm of wasps on helium. Glancing up at the church's ceiling of illuminated wooden panels, chief piper Zoltán insisted that the *duda* was the perfect instrument for church because when you stopped playing, the last breath of wind through the reeds from the deflating bag made it sound as if it were wheezing out, 'Je-sus!' Throughout the concert, I listened hard for any appeals to the Son of God, but these particular instruments emitted nothing holier than indignant squeaks – like rats that insist on having the last word – followed by the dribbling fart of backflushing valves, which gave Daisy the giggles. Leo merely dribbled, but we couldn't tell if he was excited or just teething.

No holy claims were made for the Croatian *gajde* that was later produced, its chanter sporting a huge wooden bell that looked as if it should immediately be stuffed with tobacco and smoked, nor for the long shepherd's flutes that were held with almost inhumanly splayed fingers and stretched from the lips to halfway down the thighs. Powered by the voice as well as the breath of the player, they filled the church with a tremulous moaning, like the wind from a gathering storm sighing across a chimney top. Then a human voice joined in, a woman with hair as black as octopus ink and a hard, almost keening edge to her voice as she sang and yelped and whooped into the night.

Across the road at the Szenna tavern, a young man was serving beer with an air of resentment to men who took it in the same vein, scowling into their glasses between swigs. I felt their eyes upon me as I took my seat with a dubious lager and my notepad (I'd told Bel I would be doing research) and made what was probably an unconvincing effort to look manly in the terse silence. It was finally, mercifully broken when a man in camouflage pants and an uncamouflageable belly stood up, peering through the bottom of his glass and booming, 'Hey, do you actually clean these?'

As a brief but heartfelt discussion about hygiene standards shifted the focus of attention, I glanced around at my fellow drinkers. Apart from a genuinely old man working the fruit machine in a sweat-stained cloth cap, there was a prematurely aged, ruddy faced, shrivelled look about them, as though they'd been locked overnight in a sauna then beaten with sticks. That's not to say they'd entirely given up health concerns, or at least not the pair standing closest to me.

'You know you shouldn't be drinking beer,' the more withered one said over a glass of red to his mate.

'What?' Gulp.

'I said you shouldn't be drinking beer.'

'Why not?' the beer drinker demanded, a little startled.

'Because it will push your nose out,' the wine drinker said, taking an ostentatiously long sip of his plonk. 'Like a balloon.'

'Hey? Who said that?'

'Look at it. It's already started.'

The pipers set up camp on the grass outside, sending in a delegate with the drinks order.

'Good day,' he said jauntily as he strode through the door.

The barman fixed him with a weary look. 'Good evening.'

'Or evening.'

There was a brief barrage of noise from outside as a couple of local hoons went hurtling past on the fastest horse-drawn cart I've ever seen, laughing like drains as they vanished into the dusk. I went upstairs to report my findings to Bel, who decreed that she and the children would like to stay for the whole week.

Later, as the children slept, Bel and I crept out the door into the warm night and walked the few metres to the forest, slipping along a trail winding its way between the dark walls of trees. The only sounds were a soprano saxophone, then a shepherd's flute, a small chorus of crickets and the sporadic barking of dogs passing messages of varying degrees of urgency around the village. There was even a solitary, mistimed crow from a rooster. Bel and I held hands, as dementedly happy as puppies but saying little, pausing to kiss and gaze up at the stars glittering in the narrow, ragged stretch of sky between the black curtains of leaves, while all around us fireflies floated like green lanterns among the darkened trunks.

Bel said yes, she was definitely staying for the whole week.

This necessitated a dash back to Pécs the following afternoon for extra supplies, especially nappies, something the one shop in Szenna didn't stock with any enthusiasm or, on closer examination, at all. The semi-itinerant Andor had yet to arrive in Szenna to take up his *duda*-teaching duties, as he was still performing at some festival in England. A couple of weeks before, it was Albania and Macedonia. Then, after Szenna, he was off to Germany with his sackful of pipes. So we had time.

We headed off to the sound of violins and drove home, a journey so short that only the Skoda (or, at a pinch, a pogo stick) could lend it any sense of the epic.

If we were in Pécs for an hour, maybe an hour and a half, that would have been it. Long enough to run into Mum, who was still keen to know why I didn't want that ice-cream. She was in the same spot as last time, just near the fountain. She seemed to be gravitating to that area a lot.

I muttered something about being in a hurry, but she pressed me for details about Daisy and Leo – were they well, how were their appetites, did they miss their Nagyi – while pointedly not inquiring after her daughter-in-law. Bel, who had been all but canonised a few months before for yielding a grandson ('Oh thank you, Annabel, oh, thanks God') was now unmentionable.

'They're fine, gotta go,' I mumbled, scuttling away with Mum's voice booming, 'I kiss your children,' down the street as I went.

We drove back to Szenna in moonless black, the kids sleeping with their mouths open in the back seat as we passed floodlit steeples and wound our way through the forest. Tiny pairs of eyes glinted redly at us from the verges, and around one bend we came upon a deer cropping grass next to a stag with antlers big enough to hang at least a dozen hats on. From Kaposvár we took a back road that proved a lot less straightforward than it looked on the map, stopping to ask for directions and heading down avenues of poplars that flashed in the headlights in faint bursts of silver. After passing a small lake glistening with starlight, we stopped on top of a hill and turned off the headlights and engine, letting the night lapse into silence, give or take the odd bat and Leo's contented, rhythmic breathing. Bel and I climbed out of the car to see the soft yellow of Saturn and the pink of Mars above us in a sky ablaze with the Big Dipper and the Great Bear and all those other constellations you can't see in the southern hemisphere. Or in much of the northern hemisphere, for that matter. The only other time I'd seen those constellations with such clarity was one drunken night when I was on my way home from a ceilidh in Scotland. I'd clambered (badly) over farm gates, giggling and humming tunes from the night as I staggered through a field as black as the bottom of a well. Then I stumbled into a flock of sleeping sheep. In the commotion that ensued, I slipped, landed on my back and looked up into a shimmering spread of stars. The sheep baaed a lot.

As we stood by the car outside Szenna that night, it felt the same, only sober and less woolly. And there was a bonus in the form of a shooting star, blazing across the sky as bright as a magnesium flame, flaring madly before burning out.

'Not just Szenna,' Bel murmured. 'I want to stay in Hungary.'

I GATHERED WITH my fellow pipers in a classroom where the blackboard, like all the blackboards in the school, had been gaily chalked with the word 'Vacation' by students shortly before they vanished into the summer.

Andor was holding forth from among a pile of flutes and bagpipes and lengths of cane, telling us what an advance it was that piping students such as us could take it for granted that their teacher would turn up.

'Pipers used to go missing all the time,' he explained as he began cutting reed pipes for us beginners to practise on – six finger-holes and a vibrating lip sliced from the side of the cane. 'They'd stop and play in a tavern on the way, or they'd go off chasing girls, or they'd end up in a wine cellar. All sorts of things. I'm not that sort of piper.'

And then he put us to work learning songs, which we would then transfer to our fingers. The first one went like this:

> Whoever wants to be a piper
> Has to go to hell
> There they have to learn
> How the bagpipe must be blown.

('Track one on *Dudásom, Dudásom, Kedves Muzsikásom* – Andor plays on that CD,' Pisti the Rounder noted.)

Not all piping ditties advise a passage to hell. Others suggest that aspiring pipers head to villages with an abundance of dogs. These aren't quite as relevant today as the hell ones; no one makes bagpipes out of dogs any more, or at least no one admits it.

'I once went to see an old piper near Balaton,' Andor said as he scraped away at the cane with a blade. 'A famous piper, he was, full of at least three lifetimes of tunes. But when I sat down with him, he leaned across and said to me, "So, have the witches been bothering you yet?" And that's all he talked about for the next couple of hours: witches. I can't even remember now if he played a single note.'

Szenna itself proved to be fairly witch-free and not at all hellish, but it did get bloody hot during that week of music, hot enough to soften the bitumen on the roads and make it stick to the tyres of cars as they passed through, sending a soft, tearing noise snaking up through the windows, through the urgent wail of the violins and the sighing of the long shepherd's flutes. But when the zither class started up, it was difficult to hear anything but the zithers. And once the bagpipes buzzed into life, you couldn't even hear the zithers.

Despite vague promises my *duda* would be ready in time for the camp, I had to make do with one of Andor's spares. There was no goat's head on this one, but there were other touches of the beast. I ran my fingers along the skin, noting the occasional bristle and the faint odour, which managed to be sweet and rank at the same time.

'That's one of the things that's changed,' Andor explained. 'They used to have a reputation for giving off almost as much stink as they did noise, but now they hardly smell at all.'

We really do live in a world where it's best to count your blessings. Thinking that the piper's motto ought to be, 'If music be the food of love, FORTISSIMO!', I filled the bag with air and squeezed.

In between my decibel-rich, tone-poor struggles with the *duda* and trying to retrain my fingers to only move one at a time instead of getting up to Celtic-style shenanigans, there were lectures to attend in the nearby culture house, a strikingly and surprisingly bland building that was rescued only by the wooden arch that had been feverishly carved in the Transylvanian Szekler style and loomed over the path to the front door. I found the two Pistis sitting up the back while the moustachioed lecturer held forth on the topic of traditional dances across the old Kingdom of Hungary, occasionally digressing to share tips on secretly recording gypsies ('I'd hide the microphone in my sleeve and make like I was scratching my ear') and making soap from pig fat. He then put on a black-and-white film of a group of mostly old men and women stiffly dancing in a forest clearing. It played in ghostly silence, apart from the faint burr of a lawnmower floating through the open windows and the soft murmurings of the lecturer. The men were dressed mainly in black – waistcoats, trilbies, trousers and long, gleaming boots – with a blaze of white shirt, though some of them eschewed trousers for billowing white pantaloons. The women were in headscarves, possibly bulletproof white stockings and dark skirts that swirled and flounced despite looking like they weighed half a tonne each. Once in a while the projector played up, flinging the film into fast forward and sending the dancers with their sticks and slapped boots and the pots of honey balanced on their kerchiefed heads whirling erratically around the clearing, much to the approval of the lecture audience.

I noticed Zoltán on a bench at the side, sitting next to a small old man who smiled beatifically, wooden whistle in his hand and the most elaborately carved walking-stick I'd ever seen laid across his lap.

'That's Uncle Lajos,' Pisti the Slender whispered. In Hungary, uncle – like auntie – is an honorific happily unbound by any need for family ties. 'He's one of the really old folk musicians, like a village elder. He's got millions of songs and tunes stuffed away in his head and others go to him like they'd go to a well.'

During the course of the week, I was touched by the veneration shown Uncle Lajos, escorted wherever he went with his slow but never shuffling gait. Almost every time he took his seat at the restaurant, people hungry for stories and music came to pay their respects. Later in the week, he bestowed his stick on a visibly humbled Zoltán.

Free time was given over to pootling about the countryside in the Skoda or heading over to the neighbouring valley to swim in the lake, while the nights belonged to the *táncház*, when the culture house became a folk dance house. This was partially under the command of Charlie, a moustachioed folk dance loon who spent a lot of time togged up in traditional clothes, imparting dance moves and stories in a voice so rich and deep it begged to have a radio microphone shoved in front of it. The Hungarians were joined by Croats, who were everywhere in these parts of Hungary, and the Swabians, descendants of Germans who were invited by Empress Maria Theresa to help repopulate parts of Hungary emptied by the Turks. They drifted down the Danube on barges deep into Hungary, bringing with them viticulture (good) and some stiff folk dancing (not so good).

During the Swabian dancing, I crept past the bearded violinist, his face surly enough to eat children for breakfast, and the accordionist, who wore the wry, amused expression of a man fully aware that he's playing the piano accordion. A thunderstorm earlier in the evening had left a smell of fresh grass and wet asphalt. I was walking to the phone booth with the idea of calling Mum and trying to normalise things when I noticed two toads perched on the post office step. One was as big as my fist, its companion half that size. They sat there dappled olive and red, gulping side by side with sardonic expressions like grumpy old men. I forgot about the phone and crouched on the path, trying to photograph the toads. They glared at me with unimpressed yellow eyes. The little one eventually lost patience and hopped away into the damp grass, then the big one turned its back on me. Muttering curses never really designed for the ears (or indeed tympanic membranes) of amphibians, I prodded the toad to get it to turn around. The toad gave what I took to be an imperious glare before turning its spotted back again. Deciding that another prod would constitute serious wildlife harassment, I got up and almost walked straight into two of the ruddy faced drinkers. One of them was the camouflage pants guy. I don't know how long they'd been watching my amphibian modelling session, but the looks on their faces suggested they hadn't come to give their blessing.

'Um, good evening,' I said, hurrying past them.

'Good evening,' one of them said dryly. They both turned to watch me go. As I made it to the Szekler gate, I glanced back and saw them standing in the same spot and staring in my direction. I had the feeling I'd only confirmed their suspicions about folkies.

Perhaps it was a toad curse, but I was blitzed the following night by one of those brisk fevers that plays havoc with your senses for a few hours then takes its leave. Sweating, shivering and half addled,

I sat on the windowsill, listening to the music softening to nothing at the *tánchás* and watching a tide of stout old ladies in full folk regalia streaming out through the Szekler gate, chatting boisterously as they floated down the street in a swish of heavy frocks and embroidered cotton, glowing serenely as they drifted through the pools of streetlight.

'I THINK WE'VE HAD enough time in this classroom,' Andor declared on the last afternoon. 'Let's have our class on Grape Hill.'

We walked out of Szenna to the sound of whistles and pipes, drawing the locals out of their houses and startling a horse as it lugged a cart loaded with its owners and a mound of hay. The path left the road and meandered between fields of wheat and corn, turning muddy in parts. We hid our shoes in a corn patch and walked on through the dust and the mud, frogs scattering before our feet in glistening salvos. We sang and piped and stuffed our faces with sour cherries and mulberries hanging from the trees. And as Andor pulled out a violin from his seemingly bottomless bag and went to work on it, we idly wondered if there was any instrument he couldn't play.

The final *tánchás* of the week was a fairly exclusive event. Most of the camp participants had headed off, which was a good thing as it meant my first public *duda* performance wouldn't claim too many victims. While Bel photographed madly, I stood in row with my classmates, pumping and squeezing and filling the room with a pungent squealing. Which felt good. Much later in the night, as we sat around slopping a mystery wine into plastic cups with diminishing accuracy, Andor declared that it was after midnight and therefore time for all of us to go swimming in the lake. Everybody immediately agreed that this was a sensational idea.

By then we'd been in Szenna for almost a week and even I was starting to contemplate the unusual thought that perhaps, just perhaps, a little break from folk music would be in order. But as we piled into his tiny car for the drive to the lake, Charlie turned the key in the ignition and the car stereo filled the night with *duda*s and violins.

'Listen to that, children,' Charlie declared as we set off. 'Because it is good.' There were so many of us crammed in, it was hard to see much other than the backs of heads and the occasional stray limb as we drove the winding road over the hill and down to the lake. Charlie had barely parked the car when he jumped out and began disrobing. The rest of us still jammed inside were greeted with the singular vision of his bare-chested form striding in front of the car, his pantaloons almost blinding in the headlights.

The car's ceiling light was left on to give us something to aim for as we swam back. We wandered down to the lake's edge, stripping to underwear or swimmers and surveying the utter blackness of the lake rippling gently beneath the moonless sky.

'Think of it as pipers' team-building exercise,' Andor said. 'Midnight swimming is a bit like piping – most people don't do it.'

'Of course,' Charlie intoned as we waded into the warm blackness, 'we Hungarians belong in the water. Some people say the Magyars are really from the lost city of Atlantis.' This provoked guffawing. 'I think they were pushing that sort of idiocy about the same time the Nazis claimed to be related to the high priests of Tibet.'

And with that thought, I pushed my feet against the muddy bottom and swam with the others, starlight skating across our ripples. Andor and Charlie talked the whole way across the lake and back again; I was happy just being able to draw enough breath. Afterwards, we rested on the shore, the group taking it in turns to squeeze a final couple of *duda* tunes into the night air. It was only when the early morning milk truck went rumbling past that we decided it might be time to head back.

Andor finally finished my *duda* a few weeks later. Pleasingly, the transaction was conducted out of his car boot in a supermarket carpark in Uranium Town, just like a drug deal. Don't ask me why, but it felt right.

Land of the
Long Black Pudding

As the summer continued to defy the predictions of the gloomy meteorologists and grow ever more molten, the festivals came to a temporary end, the stalls were packed away and the population of Pécs drained slowly but surely in the direction of the Croatian border and beyond to the irresistibly sparkling Adriatic. Every second Hungarian we spoke to seemed to be heading off, driven half demented by the siren call of those blazing white limestone cliffs and the deep blue sea.

At an official propaganda level, Pécs likes to blushingly call itself the 'City of Mediterranean atmosphere', brushing off the pesky absence of the Mediterranean as a detail. ('If it wasn't for those whore pricks in 1920, we'd still have a coastline, you know,' I was informed during one historical discussion.) But no one was buying that now. Even waitresses at cafés who were strangely keen to lift their shirts to show off their tight little bellies and the tans they'd been carefully working on during weekends spent at Balaton happily admitted they couldn't wait. Balaton was fun (in a cheesy sort of way; even Boy George was doing concerts there now), but Croatia was the real thing. After all, the war with Serbia was long finished, the monster Milosevic was safely dead, a newly completed motorway made driving there seem less like a dance with death or Croat lorry drivers (which can amount to pretty much the same thing), and didn't the *New York Times* and Lonely Planet just declare Croatia the travel destination of the year? Thank the Good Lord it wasn't Romania that pulled the title...

As much as I adored the Dalmatian coast and its almost criminally beautiful archipelago – all those sweet little restaurants and crystalline harbours filled with pretty boats bobbing above the heads of glittering fish and succulent octopus – it was also a luxury having Pécs if not entirely to ourselves, then near enough.

Days were happily whiled away wandering the Mecsek trails. The flowers had all but vanished, replaced by dense green banks of leaves. Birds scratched industriously for worms and bugs, while about us buzzed enormous green and gold dragonflies and the more delicate damselflies trembling in shades of electric blue. Butterflies fluttered through the dappled light in a tranquil blizzard of colour, some like snowflakes, some like humbugs and some like chips of amber. Others rested on leaves with gently heaving wings as orange as bushfires.

On the nights we could get a babysitter, Bel and I would slip out for a couple of hours, tripping across the cobblestones feeling sublimely contented. Some evenings we sipped *tokáj* at a bar on the hill behind the basilica and watched the moon float from the horizon beside the eastern towers in a blaze of tangerine, fading to apricot as it slowly vanished into the low cloud before reappearing between the towers, metamorphosed superhero-like into a disc of chaste, papal white. The neighbourhood's cats passed beneath the busts of the Arad Thirteen – generals executed by Vienna for their role in the War of Independence in 1848–49 – in a flurry of writhing tails and silent paws, interrupted only by a solitary stoat that bounded past like a dark, furry missile. Closer to home at the 24-hour convenience shop, a pretty girl with bags beneath her eyes and a rose tattooed across her shoulder blades in a painful swirl of green was losing patience with her customers in the evening heat.

'God!' she cried at a customer who'd asked for a bottle of Jaffa. 'They stopped making that twenty years ago. Do you hear me? *Twenty years!*'

'Really? It's gone?' asked the customer, a middle-aged woman with an erratically cropped head and a note of genuine surprise in her voice. 'What tastes like it then?'

'Here,' said the rose tattoo girl, smacking a bottle down on the counter. 'It's called Fanta. I hear it's the same colour Jaffa used to be. When they still made it.'

'All right then,' the woman said, hunting for coins in her purse with a troubled expression. Then to herself, 'Who would have thought it? They stopped making Jaffa.' She took her Fanta, but as she stepped out the door, her farewell – *Viszontlátásra* – was not returned, a terrible slight.

'She's mad,' the girl said afterwards. 'Always coming in to bother me. Jaffa indeed. Where did you learn Hungarian, by the way? It's very nice. You're not after Jaffa as well, are you?'

Night was drawing its thin veil around the city and as I walked toward home to the sound of tolling bells and a faint tremble of thunder, a pair of minuscule bats worked the street, frenetically flitting between the pools of light from the lamps that hung over the middle of the road. That's where the moths went on warm nights like this, hell-bent on getting drunk on the light, only to be slaughtered by bats that looked scarcely bigger than their prey. It was close to perfection, but I figured the short jaunt to Lancashire with Mum and Joli would prove an antidote.

LOOKING BACK NOW, it seems obvious that it was only large-scale terrorism that ever stood a chance of making Mum and Joli downgrade their plans to smuggle salami into England. For the best part of the month before we left for our brief family nostalgia tour through Lancashire, the sisters had been preoccupied with how to cut costs while travelling in a country as notoriously pricey as England. They found the solution staring them in the face every time they opened the fridge.

'We figure it out, Jimmykém,' Mum announced one day, sounding like an alchemist who has finally produced something that can be measured in carats. 'We take all our food with us!'

'Salami!' Joli chirped brightly.

'Sandwiches!'

'*Pogácsa!*'

'Paprika!'

'Gherkins!'

'Maybe not gherkins. They might be a bit messy.'

'Okay, no gherkins,' Joli agreed. 'But cheese we can take.'

'Yes,' Mum said, rubbing her hands. 'A nice big block of cheese. Jimmykém, we will have so much food we won't have to buy any in England! Such an expensive country and such robbish food. We will be clever instead and take so much good, delicious Hungarian cheese and salami we will live like kings. And we don't have to spend our money.'

'And eggs. We can boil some eggs.'

'*Jaj*! Eggs!' Mum was ecstatic. All her frustrations at Australia's quarantine system and its humourless, by-the-book enforcers were being purged in this traffickers' frenzy of planning.

'Will you have any room left for clothes?' I asked.

'Of course. But we can wear most of those on the plane.'

'Shall we take two of those big salamis?' Joli inquired.

'At least two.'

A few days before we were due to leave, the sisters raided the local supermarket and, judging by their haul of booty, had a fairly solid crack at emptying it. This just left them with the practicalities of how to wrap everything and make it fit in the luggage, the whole time labouring in a fog of vagueness about British quarantine laws, something that seemed to add a certain frisson of excitement for Mum.

Then, two days before departure, England went into meltdown. A terrorist plot was foiled and as the police got busy arresting an extraordinarily large number of suspects, the British airport system ground to a standstill. Almost every flight was cancelled and as the airports there filled with stranded passengers, it seemed touch and go whether we'd be leaving Hungary at all.

The sisters watched events unfolding on television in Uranium Town and were beside themselves, especially Joli, who was nervous about flying at the best of times.

'What do you think, Jimmyként?' Mum clamoured. As much of a panic merchant as she could be sometimes, I often got the feeling that, on some levels, she enjoyed a bit of crisis. 'Are we still going?'

Not so Joli, who was trying hard to be stoic. 'Is it safe?'

'What happens if we get over there, and then we can't come back?'

'Will we be okay?'

'My God,' Mum gasped, holding a hand to her mouth, 'what about the salamis?'

This was a sobering thought as we gathered at the Magda cake shop for a mission briefing. There was confusion about what could and couldn't be packed, and whether hand luggage would be allowed. Joli confessed to crying with the stress of it all, but Mum was swinging between anxiety about whether she'd be able to make it back to get her flight home out of Vienna and a pig-headed determination to get those salamis into England.

Then I opened my map of Britain and the panic abated. The sisters' heads almost touched over Lancashire and they excitedly called out the names of towns from all those years ago: Wigan, Southport, Liverpool, Manchester, Bolton. Even Blackpool got a mighty cheer, something that drew a bemused reaction when I mentioned it to Dad later. He couldn't imagine why on earth I wanted to take the sisters to Lancashire. 'It's not like they'll remember anything,' he said, trying his best to be unhelpful.

But give or take the odd heart palpitation, Mum and Joli couldn't wait. It was entertaining listening to Mum getting almost poetic about a part of the world she used to speak of as if it were a gulag. But then again, even Solzhenitsyn seemed sort of pleased when he finally went back to Siberia. Mum's eyes reddened as she trailed her fingertips over the regrettably small-scale map from the Lake District down the coast to Liverpool.

'Oh, beautiful England,' she sighed. 'Did I make a mistake, Jimmykém? Was I wrong to make us move from there? Perhaps we would all be better off if we had stayed instead of going so far to the end of the world.' I suspected it wasn't going to be a straightforward few days.

After much umming and aahing about which route we would drive if our flight wasn't cancelled, and much wistful sighing whenever Mum's eyes were able to discern another familiar town or village in the map's microprint, we headed our different ways to pack.

I called them late that night to let them know I'd checked on the internet and that our flight number wasn't on the long cancellation list, so we'd be leaving at dawn. The sisters informed me that in deference to the terrorism situation, they would be leaving one of the salamis behind.

As we headed off from Uranium Town in half-hearted drizzle and slowly congealing grey light, we agreed that the weather had a certain thematic appropriateness. I'd been too excited to sleep and was now placing my faith in a pair of medically inadvisable jolts of coffee that Bel – fresh from bed, sleepy eyed, warm – had made just before I left home. The sisters, on the other hand, seemed to have been up for much of the night making enough sandwiches to feed one of Jesus's bigger audiences. The cheese and salami, they assured me in their matching denim jackets as we stuffed their bags in the Skoda's modest boot, were safely packed. We wouldn't have to spend a penny on food, *ja, ja*.

'That is where our father's vineyard was,' Mum cried as we left Pécs, pointing to the vine-clad slopes of the western Mecsek. 'The wine he made there was so delicious.'

'And strong,' Joli noted.

'So strong, if you drank a glass it stood you on your head, *hu ha*.'

Nagypapa was nothing if not scientific in his approach and used to sample his super-strength wine in a fairly empirical manner, and then somehow navigate his way home on his wobbly bicycle with the assistance of gravity. Dad remembered him arriving home a number of times wearing the smile of a man who's found the answers.

'Such a beautiful vineyard. Now we don't even have that any more.'

With the radio on the blink and my brain not too far behind, I had been worried Mum and Joli would nod off, leaving me with nothing but the buzz of the engine and the erratic squeak of the wipers to keep me awake. Which was a foolish thought. The sisters talked the whole way to the airport, almost without drawing breath, striding purposefully and almost seamlessly from topic to topic, ranging through the price of Mecsek vineyards; possible question marks over the paternity of a number of young acquaintances; the real estate savvy of the Dutch; the benefits of building with timber; the pros and cons of living on houseboats; conditions for conscripts in the days of national service; a woman with supernatural powers Joli once knew; the likelihood of a giant salami being mistaken for explosives as it passes through an airport x-ray machine; the likelihood of the Skoda making it all the way to the airport without chucking a wobbly; and the value of going to jumble sales in a shop in Pécs where you could buy clothes by the kilo as long as you didn't mind fighting off rival customers.

Once Mum and Joli got talking, it was like watching two pistons in the same engine. They talked and laughed and talked through the still-shuttered villages, the already stirring towns, the dripping forests and the valleys with their ragged drapes of mist, then laughed and talked some more, treating silence with a radio broadcaster's fearful disdain and whipping each other into a state of ever greater, ever more talkative excitement. What made it droller was that, privately, both sisters were at pains to make it clear that it was the other who was the real chatterbox. The only break in the wall of sound came in the small town of Marcali, where I pulled over to check the map and Mum leaped out to smoke a cigarette beneath the shelter of someone's eaves, observing between puffs that most of the storks' nests were empty now.

There was more excitement as we neared the Croatian and Slovenian borders and passed the turn-offs to Zagreb and Ljubljana ('You see, Jimmykém. *This* is Europe. Everything is so close, not like in Australia.') and the road suddenly and gratifyingly improved in quality. We zipped along past the bottom of Lake Balaton and the sisters expressed their loud approval at the pulchritude of the hills looming over the northern shore in a dim haze of purple. I was meanwhile calculating that if the Skoda finally gave up the ghost, it would be an affordable taxi ride to the airport from here. The appearance of signs advertising the proximity of the unsnappily named Fly Balaton airport provoked near rioting among the sisters.

In its previous incarnation, Fly Balaton was a Soviet airbase and, it can safely be said, had no signs pointing to it whatsoever. Even now, with the Russians gone and the no-frills airlines filling their shoes, it's still the most invisible airport I have encountered. You need to turn off the main road to Keszthely and the more postcard-worthy northern shore of Balaton and head to a village called Sármellék. Once there, turn down a small side road (just near the Russian-owned petrol station) and head past a long and very solid wall of trees. These days, of course, there's a sign to tell you to turn down one of the otherwise easily missed roads that leads through the trees – and, more importantly, there's no one waiting with a Kalashnikov to machine-gun you to death. The road zig-zags its way through the clusters of camouflaged bunkers that once kept MiGs safely hidden from NATO's eyes and suddenly deposits you in front of a shiny new airport terminal that looks like it was made from Lego.

At our first sight of the Lego, there was more whooping and cheering, and Mum, who'd promised the Skoda a great big kiss if it got us there, kept her word. Then it was time to pop the boot and start scoffing some of those sandwiches.

'We don't have to pay for that expensive food on the plane,' Mum said. I'd warned them that flying on a budget airline meant paying for inflight snacks. 'We outsmart them – they won't get our money that easily.'

Joli was still nervous. Happy, but definitely a little on the twitchy side. Naturally, she was the only one taken aside by security for a thorough check of her baggage. There was a touchiness now even about bottles of drinking water and shampoo – the terrorists in England had been planning to use liquid explosives, so Joli was asked to open her bottle and taste its contents in front of security officers. Joli got gulping like a camel at the end of a particularly arduous trek until one of the men held up his hand.

'That's fine. Don't drink it all here – you'll want to keep some for the road.'

Mum snorted. 'I have more water than she does and they don't even ask me.'

The salami went through without a question.

•

IN OUR FAMILY MYTHOLOGY, or at least in the Book of Eszter Snr, Hungary plays the role of the lost paradise while England in general, and Lancashire in particular, sound more like the sort of place Dante would feel comfortable writing about, a kind of damp, dank Hades with relentless rain in place of fire and black puddings in place of brimstone. No position taken was ever entirely consistent or immune to sudden, whiplash-inducing reverses of emotion, but that's generally the way it is in the Book of Eszter Snr. Sometimes Hungary slipped in the rankings, especially when Mum pondered all the lovely cars and possessions she'd enjoyed living in the West – 'I would have none of this if I had stayed there.' And sometimes England rose, usually when Australia was being disowned for being too hot/too far from Europe/not breathing enough history, or, occasionally, when the Queen did something nice. But these shifts were only ever temporary. Mum seemed most at ease with an England that was hell.

'But that was only because of the weather,' she said. 'And some other things.'

The last time she'd seen it had been a June afternoon in 1976 as we stood on the deck of the good ship *Australis*, streamers arcing through the air like paper fireworks as we edged out of Southampton at the start of a journey that would end in Sydney Harbour four weeks later.

I had toyed briefly with the idea of returning via Southampton, but ended up ruling it out as too tediously symmetrical and even more tediously expensive. Lac thought this wise. 'You're not really missing out on much,' he said. 'These days it looks like they had a concrete glut in England one year and solved it by sending the lot to Southampton.' That said, I'm not sure that Stansted – the lager louts' choice of airport, judging by the number of signs warning that drunken, abusive behaviour just isn't on – was necessarily the best substitute, but that's where we went anyway.

The sisters kept up their strict regimen of cheering and generally carrying on as the plane squelched down onto the runway. If anything, the weather looked bleaker than it had in Hungary, which pleased Mum.

'You see!' she cried as we walked the few sodden metres between the plane and the terminal, pointing excitedly to the dingy, seeping Essex sky. 'That is why we left this country. *Jaj*, this is exactly how I remember it.'

Passport control provided a moment of excitement. Both sisters were travelling on their Hungarian passports and while even recently this entailed obtaining finicky visas and being made to feel like a member of a European underclass, it now meant joining the queue for EU nationals and being whisked through with barely more than the most cursory glance and ejected into the shambles of the arrivals hall. As unceremonious as it was, the ordinariness came as a moment of almost weeping relief to a lot of so-called New Europeans. I'd seen Andor just a few weeks before when he came home from a trip to London and he was buzzing. 'I showed them my passport and they just had to let me in. They couldn't say a thing!'

As it turned out, quarantine laws didn't seem to apply to flights originating within the EU, so that was a bit of an anticlimax, except for one brief moment as Mum stood near a customs officers, squinting at a poster, then bellowing, 'Jimmykém! Is it okay if we bring in our boiled eggs as well?'

Stansted is an unsettlingly busy place on an average day. On an unaverage day such as this one, when handfuls of flights had been cancelled, security had been escalated through the roof, the terminal was swarming with enough police to invade a small country and the airlines were struggling to clear the backlog of exhausted, wilted passengers, it was nasty. I spotted Lac with his dark quiff, the greying sideburns his girlfriend was lobbying to have removed and a copy of the *Daily Telegraph* folded under his arm, which I reasoned he only had because he hadn't been in the country long enough to figure out which newspapers were worth reading. His was the only perky face in the crowd – it was obvious he wasn't a passenger.

'Where are the boilers?' he asked with a smile. Mum and Joli might have been as round as rockmelons, but at five feet tall, they vanished easily into crowds. Or at least until they opened their mouths. 'Lacikám!' Mum boomed, ending the mystery with three piercing syllables. The sisters popped from the wall of human flesh like a pair of denim cannonballs, and there was much emotion.

We waded through the sullen throng, marvelling at the hefty guns the multitudes of police were carrying ('They never had guns when we lived here,' Mum observed), and then struggled with the bewilderingly byzantine paperwork of the rental car company – a five-minute process with the same firm in Hungary – while Lac shared his candid thoughts on what passed for customer service in the UK. Then after a break for cigarettes and freshly imported paprika sandwiches in the carpark, we were on our way into England.

'I hope we've got unlimited mileage with this,' Lac said, casting his eye over the dashboard with the predatory look he reserved for rental cars. 'Cause we're gonna give it some wellie.'

We slipped through a series of roundabouts encrusted with police cars and big cameras and were soon surging north along the motorway.

'How beautiful the roads are,' Mum said.

'Not a single hole,' Joli added with a tone of marvel.

Then Mum suddenly sang out, 'I can smell Yorkshire pudding and roast beef.'

'Where?' said Lac.

'Out there. England is full of Yorkshire pudding and roast beef,' Mum declared, peforming a little dance number from the shoulders up.

The sky looked morose and heavily padded with dribbling clouds close enough to graze our heads – I kept thinking of Billy Connolly's story about showing his home town of Glasgow to his small children and them asking, 'Daddy, why is the sky so low?' – but there were fields of soft green and faded gold crisscrossed with stone walls and dotted with stone houses and it was lovely. We passed turn-offs for Cambridge and Leicester and let the names trip from our tongues. We saw Birmingham in the distance and felt our bowels contract. We stopped for cigarette breaks at motorway cafés and while Mum and Lac puffed like factories, I perused the vast spread of newspapers to see how they were reacting to the terrorism business. My attention was particularly taken by *The Daily Sport*, whose front-page headline alerted readers thus: 'TERROR SUSPECT'S SISTER TOPLESS'. Mum and Joli examined everything on the shelves and their price tags with forensic care and marvelled at some of the signs of multicultural England – men in turbans and women in hijabs – before we carried on toward Lancashire, with every road sign that yielded up a familiar name setting off a joyous roar in the back seat.

As we got closer to our old home, Mum and Joli spilled over with excitement and fear. 'Strange things happened in that house,' Mum warned. 'Things would move by themselves. Just like that time in my flat in Gymea when we saw the onion jump out of the basket. Sometimes, we saw two red eyes just floating in the air.' Her voice shrank to a whisper. 'Jimmykém, sometimes when you were a baby, those eyes floated above your cot.'

Joli clapped her hands together. '*Jaj!*'

'Above your cot! Look, I am shivering. My skin gets goosebumps.'

So was mine by this stage.

'They were red like blood. Sometimes they followed us.'

I could see Lac smiling quietly to himself. He'd heard the stories before.

'And things happened to Joli, too.'

'Yes, when I went to visit you in 1973. Jimmy wasn't quite a year old. Katika and Ian didn't say anything to me about the house at first, but I could sense something wasn't right. One night I woke up with my heart bashing against my ribs. My skin was cold and I felt like my face was covered in a spider's web.' Joli shuddered in the back seat, ejecting a pained *jaj* at the memory. 'The next morning they asked me if everything was all right and I told them what happened. They said, yes, we know about it, we just didn't want to say anything because we didn't want to scare you.'

'Oh, and there was that time Zsuzsa and Pali stayed,' Mum said. My uncle and aunt had come to stay with us when they left Hungary shortly after Mum did. 'Zsuzsa could hear someone brushing their teeth in the bathroom and she thought it was Pali and she called out to him, but he didn't say anything.'

Joli shrank into her seat, asking in a small voice, 'Did she go look?'

'She called out again, but he just kept brushing his teeth. Then when Zsuzsa went and looked, there was nobody there.'

'*Jaj*. Oh my God, my God.'

'The bathroom was *empty*.'

'Good to know the ghosts were into dental hygiene,' Lac said.

I wanted to ask about the story Mum had told me and Eszter over lunch earlier in the year, about the time in the Parbold house when she'd been woken by an unseen presence creeping into her bed and ravishing her while Dad slept beside her. ('Your farder's skin was so cold. I couldn't wake him, no matter how much I shouted.') At the time, it had been enough to make even Eszter put her spoon down, but now I found myself unable to form the words. Somehow, I just couldn't find the right way to ask Mum about being rogered by a ghost.

'Um,' I ventured dimly instead, 'how could the house have been haunted when it was brand new and we were the first people to live in it? Do you think something happened there when it was for sale?'

'The land!' Joli and Mum chorused.

'Eh?'

'The house was new, but the land it was built on wasn't,' Joli said. 'Anything could have happened there.'

'Anything,' Mum agreed.

'You can never know what terrible things may have gone on.'

'It was a lovely house, though. A show home!'

'Yes, very nice,' Joli agreed.

'It already had all the furniture in it.'

And so it was that after three decades absence, we returned to Parbold.

Parbold existed in my head as a couple of streets, a small, dull village under a grey sky near a grey industrial town. So I was a little surprised when the last leg of the journey took us along quiet country lanes with hedgerows, verdant meadows speckled with powder-puff sheep, and small, terribly inviting pubs whose modest advertising boards placed a happy emphasis on the availability of cask-conditioned ales. One of them stood at the entrance to Parbold, and the noise in the car was deafening. Lac slowed right down and we gazed in wonder as we cruised past a trinity of pubs, a pair of steeples and rows of nineteenth-century houses with gabled roofs. There was an old stone windmill that had been turned into an art gallery towering solidly over a canal filled with long, brightly painted boats. This wasn't at all what I'd been expecting.

'Oh my God,' I said. 'It's . . . it's really *nice*.'

Even Lac, who was the only one among us who'd been back more recently, was surprised. 'It's a hell of a lot nicer than I remember it being when I came up with Eszt a few years back. Mind you, it was winter when we were here. It seemed really bare and dark. It's looking pretty good now.'

'Children,' Mum cried from behind us. 'We should never have left. I am so sorry. I make us leave from here, I am so sorry. Please forgive me.'

We dutifully examined the first school Lac had been dumped in and the Anglican church where I was christened. After circling it and making admiring noises, Mum and Joli scurried off to have a pee in the bushes. We checked the main school up the road where Lac and Eszt had eventually been sent and where they really started learning English. It was now, in a happy piece of symmetry, a language school.

'I have no great memories of this place,' Lac said, pointedly grinding a smouldering cigarette butt beneath his shoe just inside the gate. 'It didn't turn my crank at all.' Surprisingly, he said he wasn't picked on all that much, even though he must have stuck out like a pork knuckle in a bowl of beans.

'I got roughed up a bit in the playground because I was the new kid. Someone called me a Hungarian sausage, a fight got arranged just outside the school, the kid hit me, I made his nose bleed and that was that. Sorted.'

Hungarian sausage. The innocence of it.

We also went to the hospital where Olivia and I were born, but this took a little more finding. The hospital had been closed and Mum was fuzzy on its location.

'Is that it?' I asked as we drove past a semi-derelict site that looked suspiciously hospital-ish.

'No, no, no, no, no,' Mum said. 'It wasn't in a place like this, no.'

Eventually we turned back and this time noticed a sign that said it was the site of the former Billinge Hospital.

'It *is* the hospital, Mum.'

'That is what I said.'

After being allowed in by a pair of friendly security guards who called me and Lac 'loov' and warned us there were trainee police dogs about, we stood around taking more photos while Mum reminisced about the agony of childbirth. Moved by the emotion of it all, Joli and Mum scurried off to the bushes to have another pee.

'It's funny watching those two, the way they do everything together,' Lac observed. 'Could be even funnier if one of them squats on a police dog.'

We went and stood in front of our old house, of course. There were many attractive homes in Parbold, but our house wasn't one of them. It was a deeply ordinary semi-detached hutch built at a time when pebble-dash was looked upon with inexplicable favour. The garage had been turned into another room since our time, the area around the front door – which had been the setting for so many of our family photos – extended and enclosed in dimpled glass, and a small grey satellite dish stuck on the wall under the grey roof. It was dinner time on a Saturday evening, so we resisted the urge to knock on the door and contented ourselves with taking way too many photos of each other from different angles in front of the house. It would have been a little unnerving for the inhabitants if they'd peered out through their vertical blinds.

'We should have stayed here,' Mum all but sobbed.

Lac looked at the street where he used to wash cars for 20 pence a go, then at Mum, then at the breathtaking blandness of our old house, then back at Mum again. 'Are you kidding?'

ONCE WE WERE SAFELY BACK inside Hungary a couple of days later, warming our skin next to Lake Balaton while the softest of breezes ruffled the rushes, Mum agreed she may have been a little overexcited. We stopped at a roadside stall so she could stock up on melons while Lac and I took photos of a family of storks standing severe and erect in their nest high above the traffic. The chicks were now indistinguishable from their parents; it wouldn't be long before they were flying south across the Mediterranean towards Africa.

'Ha, imagine how much this would have cost if I'd bought it in England!' Mum chortled as she hoisted her fruit into the Skoda. I turned the key and pulled out into the eastbound traffic. I felt like I was driving home.

Coming, Going

O NE EXCELLENT PLACE to not learn about early Hungarian history is the dud cinematic duo of *The Conquest* – about the arrival of Chief Árpád and the seven tribes in the Carpathian Basin and the tremendous fun they had before converting to Christianity – and *Sacra Corona*, the sequel that depicts the infancy of the Magyar nation and the turmoil leading up to the coronation of King László I. Both films are the work of Gábor Koltay who, in his efforts to bring to life some of the epic, pivotal moments in Hungary's history, appeared to spare all expense.

I'd missed *The Conquest* but was lucky enough in 2001 to not only be in the country, but to be in the Uránia Cinema in Pécs for the national premiere of *Sacra Corona*, which featured a speech from Koltay himself. He stood before the audience, flanked by his sheepish looking leads, speaking a little nervously into a microphone. Word was already out that *Sacra Corona* was a dog of considerable magnitude (which, it should be said, raised no eyebrows whatsoever among connoisseurs of *The Conquest*), but the house was packed.

'I hope you enjoy it,' he entreated the audience. 'And even if you don't, tell everyone you loved it, anyway.' I'm still convinced they had an escape helicopter waiting on the roof, or at the very least a hotted-up Trabi idling on the street. As the opening credits rolled, Koltay and his cast vanished as quickly and completely as if they'd been beamed up by the Starship *Enterprise*. But even if they had, it still wouldn't have been quite as wondrous or as mystifying as what unfurled in that cinema over the couple of hours that followed. Pitifully tiny bands on horseback galloped across the screen accompanied, fancifully, by the thunder of a thousand hooves. Lips moved magically out of time with the dialogue (the sound had been recorded afterwards and dubbed with endearing ineptitude), and in the battle scenes the same blokes died over and over again from slightly different angles. Embarrassed tittering spread through the audience as the truth became inescapable – the infancy of the nation had been turned into a Monty Python sketch.

The question was, would Koltay go on and make it a trilogy by tackling the Turkish invasion? It was a troubling thought as we wandered the streets of Mohács. Now a drowsy port of three steeples on the Danube near the border with Serbia, Mohács was the scene of what is still regarded as Hungary's most calamitous defeat. Late in the summer of 1526, after years of unsuccessful marauding and being repulsed by the Transylvanian general János Hunyadi and his son, the Renaissance king Matthias Corvinus, the Ottomans finally broke through, meeting the Hungarian army – led by the young King Lajos II – on a field near Mohács. By the time the battle was over, the outnumbered and ineptly organised Hungarians had been annihilated and 25,000 lay dead, including Lajos who survived the battle only to die ignominiously in the retreat, falling from his horse and drowning in a creek.

('Ah, poor Lajos,' Joli lamented one afternoon at the cemetery as we watched a red squirrel bounding between the headstones. 'So young and dying like that.' She said it as if it had happened only the week before and the sense of hurt was yet to soften.)

Of more immediate importance to me, Mohács was one of the last places I visited in Hungary as a child, back in the days when I would trek back and forth with Mum between her cherished but blighted homeland and the faded promise of England. Andris and I flung stones into the Danube (actually, flung may be putting it a little strongly for me; I was three), watching them splash in the swirling water of the biggest, wildest river I'd ever seen. My grandmother – soft, round, wrinkled, strong – moved like a mixed weather system of smiles and chuckles and overlapping scowls and my grandfather beamed indulgently, his probably not especially white teeth gleaming from that impossibly brown face. By then they knew we were moving even further away from them. Australia may as well have been the moon.

Now, as Mum began packing her bags in Uranium Town, she swung back and forth about Australia, unable to decide whether it was the moon or home. Whether she was in ecstasy about heading back to her weatherboard box and the Renault in the carport, or on the verge of tears about being dragged away from her dear little country by the relentless, untameable forces of fate really depended on which particular minute you talked to her. As for those small matters of family friction, there didn't seem any point in talking any further. Mum either carried on as if nothing had happened, or if it had, then it had been purely the doing of others.

Lac stuck around until just before she left, but, afflicted with a stronger sense of familial obligation than I was, he was soon run ragged by the conflicting claims on his time from Mum and the various relatives ('No, Laci, it's out of the question that you should stay with anybody but us'). After just three days, I saw a look I rarely saw on his face, something verging on exhaustion.

'Ah, mate,' he sighed. 'I feel like I've entered in the Family Olympics. I'm not winning any medals, either.'

He left a couple of days later, looking forward to the relative peace of London. Mum departed a couple of days after that. I took the kids down to the train station to see her off. We found her pumped, swigging excitedly from her water bottle as she sat on a bench next to her ox bag and Joli. We talked, but not about anything in particular, apart from Daisy and Leo, whose heads she carpet-bombed with kisses. Andris turned up with his wife, Évi, and their brood, and Mum was obviously chuffed to have such a send-off. We lugged her bags into her compartment and before we knew it, Mum was standing above us in the doorway, eyes glistening.

'Thank you for coming,' she boomed. 'Thank you all for coming.' For a moment, I pictured her on the deck of the *Australis* as it pulled out of Southampton, lumbering out into the Channel at the beginning of the four-week journey to a new life in Australia. I blinked and Mum was blowing kisses like a diva. I half expected someone to throw flowers, but then the door hissed shut and, with a string of dull thumps, the train began rolling toward Vienna.

MUM HAD LEFT by train back in 1972, as well. The authorities in Budapest had surrendered in their eight-month struggle and issued Mum with a passport and exit visa. Nervous that some faceless official might change their mind, Mum packed in a hurry and with Lac and Eszt in tow, and me growing in her belly, jumped on the train for Budapest, then a plane bound for England. Dad was already there waiting for us.

That weekend, László Kruller made what would be the last of his regular trips to Uranium Town to visit his two eldest children. He knew they were going – he'd signed off on that; taken his payment of one Wartburg – but he still had time with them, still had time to say goodbye. Or so he thought.

'No,' Nagyi told him when she opened the door, all but flinging the words in his face. 'Eszter and Laci aren't here. They have already left Hungary.'

According to Nagyi, László stood there, his face growing redder and redder. Then, without a word, he turned, slowly walked back down the stairs and out the door into a twenty-year silence that would only be broken the afternoon his brother Jancsi came knocking. 'You'll never guess who rang.'

We all began drifting back in the end, caught in that little country's emotional gravity field. Mum was the first to return, leaving Australia for a handful of weeks at a time to look after Nagyi in Uranium Town. Mum's ambivalence about living so far from Europe grew into torment as old age finally blunted Nagyi's tongue and reduced her to little more than a shrivelled chrysalis by the time she died. In Australia, meanwhile, some of Mum's Hungarian friends watched as communism faded from their homeland and, deciding that they'd been in exile after all, began pulling up their shallow roots and heading home. Not all of them: for some, Hungary had changed too much to stir anything more than a muted anguish, but some wrapped themselves up in all of it – the language of their parents, the smell of the air on late autumn mornings, the springtime that meant the coming of storks, the sense of being where they were meant to be. Then there were the others who went back, only to discover complete happiness lay in neither place.

Once the danger of Lac being dragooned into the Hungarian army to do his national service had passed, he and Eszter began heading back as well. But it wouldn't be until later that they decided to close the circle and find their father. Eszter said she'd thought about making contact, but what finally pushed her to pick up the phone was the experience of a colleague who'd had a falling-out with his father, only for his father to die before they'd had the chance to reconcile.

When she made that call to Uncle Jancsi, the family at the other end of the line was shocked. 'In a good way,' Eszter explained.

'I was sitting there with the receiver in my hand and I was so nervous. I didn't know what to say after twenty years. I didn't say sorry. I told Uncle Jancsi we'd like to see our father. When I rang back a little while later and heard my father's voice for the first time, it was surreal. It was like talking to a stranger. It certainly wasn't, "Oh, Dad, I missed you, I want to see you." No, it wasn't like that; it was a detached, cool, polite conversation.' As Eszt was telling me this, I remembered what Attila told me about that day being one of the only two occasions he'd ever seen his father cry.

'So anyway, we set the wheels in motion to go over to visit him. I got scared at one point and I was thinking about backing out, but once Lac was on board, we just kept pushing each other until we got on that plane. It was a fun trip, but the closer we got to Pécs, the more nervous I was. We'd made a date to see him; when the day arrived, Lac and I went and sat in a bar and had a beer before we went. God, I was so nervous. It was good to be with Lac because I reckon I would've chickened out if I'd been alone. As the time got closer, I got quieter – and you know me; I ain't normally quiet – and then Mum's rants against our father came flooding back. I could hear her voice so clearly in my head. You know, "Arsehole! Poisonous viper!", that sort of stuff. The same way she used to carry on about your father.

'Anyway, we finally went. He and Rózsa were still living in the same flat where we'd lived with them. I remember it so clearly, walking up those five steps in the stairwell and knocking, and waiting, and hearing the steps on the other side of the door. Then he opened the door. He was in tears; no sobbing, just tears. He invited us in to the kitchen. I didn't know what to say. He sat there, staring at us over the kitchen table with tears running down his face. And you know, the man I saw wasn't the father I had left. He was just some old, sick stranger. But then the conversation started flowing. We went for a walk around the neighbourhood so he could show us some buildings he'd designed. Lac and he were walking together as I drifted further and further back, and it hit me that Lac wasn't just Mum's favourite child, but his as well. But then he stopped and pulled me closer, saying, "Why are you walking so far behind? Walk with me."

'We stayed with him and Rózsa, but that evening, we went out with someone – I can't remember who now – and we didn't get back until midnight. Our father answered the door. He'd been sitting up, waiting for us at the kitchen table. He looked half dead – he was pretty sick with cancer – but the light that shone in his eyes when he saw us! We talked until three in the morning, trying to condense twenty years into a few hours. We all knew he was dying.

'As soon as Lac and I got back to Australia, I wanted to go back to Pécs. I guess I was still seeking my father's approval. And we did go, and he took us to Jancsi's holiday house by the Danube. I think I got further with him the second time around. But after we came back home and I heard that he'd died, I didn't feel very much. I certainly didn't feel like I'd lost a father. I went to see his grave a couple of times up on the hill next to his vineyard, and felt absolutely nothing. I just stood there, looked at the stone and thought, that's my father's name. And that's it.

'But then I think back to that night first time around, when we were up into the small hours. You could see he was struggling, that every minute was costing him dearly. But he wouldn't go to bed. He wanted to see us so badly.

'I asked him if he thought there was life after death. He laughed. "I don't believe in any of that shit," he said. "When I die, I just disappear." But I made him promise to appear to me if he could. He just laughed.'

•

WHEN I FIRST asked my boss in Sydney if I could have six months off to go to Hungary, he agreed immediately. I realised I'd made a mistake: I should have asked for twelve months or, more sensibly, forty-eight. As it was, I was given six. And besides, there were weddings to go to in Australia and a ravaged bank account to replenish.

Summer was on its way at home. Cicadas would be stirring into life, grandparents clamouring for their grandchildren. The sun, rising ever higher in that diamond-bright sky, would be warming the sea, and thunderstorms splitting the humid nights open in wondrous, Old Testament style.

If Bel and I couldn't stay in Pécs, then maybe we could find a way to be in both places.

Perhaps.

Our six months raced past so fast, you could almost hear the air slam shut behind them. Suddenly it was September, and Pécs, having had a break of a few weeks from any sort of festival, was revving up for its biggest annual shindig, the *Pécsi napok*, or Pécs Days. As the Mecsek began to blush with the first autumn tinges of yellow and orange, tents and stages and tables and pigs on spits erupted across the town. Bel and I tried to divert our thoughts with friends and family and by ceremonially handing the Skoda over to Attila, then we slowly began to pack, realising that parts of our brains had already migrated ahead to Sydney and started dealing with the ordinary day-to-day matters that would be waiting for us. Sweetly, we had plenty of friends ready to point out the shrinking days and regale us with tales of the ghastliness of previous Pécs winters. 'You're going at just the right time.'

There were some distractions along the way. Far away in Budapest the population was going into meltdown over a leaked tape of Prime Minister Gyurcsány telling his Cabinet that the economy was screwed and that they'd been lying morning, noon and night to the electorate.

'No other country in Europe has done anything as boneheaded as what we've done,' he added by way of explanation. As democracy hadn't been around long enough in Hungary for apathy to set in, the said electorate made a very public show of being cross. While this was mainly restricted to peaceful protests and bad songs, some went crazy, imagining they were reliving 1956 – the fiftieth anniversary, in a neat piece of synchronicity, was just a few weeks away – by setting alight cars, smashing windows and storming a TV station, carelessly picking the one with the country's lowest ratings. After forty-nine years and eleven months of good behaviour, Magyars were getting rowdy.

In Pécs, the protests happened on a mercifully Pécs scale. No one smashed any windows or even set fire to a car. (Which is probably just as well; if anybody had tried to burn a Trabant, half the town would have choked to death on its fumes.) Széchenyi Square filled nightly with disgruntled citizenry, waving flags, singing and calling on Gyurcsány to resign in a number of colourful ways. One night, while Bel was introducing Daisy to theatre, I took Leo along to the square, figuring he was ready for his first political action, and he cooed happily at our fellow protestors while some bearded professor boomed into a microphone.

'When Gyurcsány took power, he spoke of the great honour of the office of prime minister, he spoke of the great honour of leading his ten million fellow Hungarians.' Jeers rippled through the crowd. 'He said he would do a good job, or die trying. What I want to know is, who held him back?' The crowd roared with laughter, and Leo got excited, flapping his pudgy little arms.

'Resign! Resign!' the crowd chanted, and Leo gurgled loudly. Two protestors broke off from the chanting to make a fuss of him. As they told him what a beautiful baby he was, oh yes, such a beautiful baby, a less polished voice sounded over the speakers.

'It is, is, yes, you know, yes, this is sad, terribly sad.' I looked up and saw, to my glee, that one of the Király utca bums had somehow materialised on the stage and got his hands on the microphone. The protest organisers were squirming at this lapse – 'These fucking Pécs drunks are always causing trouble,' one complained as he came close, but not close enough to snatching back the microphone – but it was too late.

'Such, such sadness, yes, sadness in the eyes of the Lord,' the man slurred to the delight of the crowd. 'I think, yes, that it would be for the best if we all sing a song now.'

As that frayed husk of a voice spread across the Inner Town, the crowd slowly joined in. Leo and I quietly slipped away from the square, past the soft green gleam of the Zsolnay fountain and down the backstreets, the song echoing off the stuccoed walls to follow us home.

A FEW DAYS LATER, Andor rang to tell me that for the Pécs Days, he'd helped organise Hungary's first ever national bagpipe festival and he would get his hands on a set of Scottish highland bagpipes if I agreed to play them on stage. When the day came, I was excited to see that my name – perhaps accidentally – had been printed on the program with my surname first in the Hungarian way. And as I stood on stage in front of the Djami, with borrowed drone pipes across my shoulder, glancing over at the façade of the Nádor where it had all begun, I smiled at the thought of Mum and Dad. Their marriage could only have happened during one of those moments when the normal laws of the universe held their breath. But in Hungary, it seemed, the normal laws of the universe were a little more inclined to look the other way from time to time, which was just as well.

I gazed down and spotted Bel with Daisy and Leo among all the Magyar faces, so many familiar faces, and Andor introduced me as an English Hungarian from Australia who'd come back to his spiritual home in Pécs.

'Sounds about right to me,' I thought as I inflated the bag and, sparing a passing thought for the *duda* witches, let rip.

Captions

Page 4: The turkeys of Nagykozár ask us to leave.

Page 14: Outside the Pécs Reformation Church in 1975 for Olivia's christening. From left to right: Joli, Eszter, Laci, Dad (holding Olivia), Nagypapa and Nagymama. Andris and I are in the front, being sullen.

Page 54: One of our swine is missing; Piroska's pigs looking justifiably concerned in Hajdúszovát.

Page 80: Trabant on Széchenyi Square, Pécs, with the Ottoman Djami in the background.

Page 90: Have kerchief, will travel.

Page 112: Andor gives my goat a workout.

Page 122: The Hungarian Parliament seen from the Chain Bridge, Budapest.

Page 156: Dad returns to the mine at Istvánakna. Festive locals not pictured.

Page 240: At home in Pécs with Bel, Daisy and Leo.

Page 270: Slow traffic in Villány-Kövesd.

Conceived in Hungary, born in England and raised in Australia, James Jeffrey lives in Sydney with his wife, Annabel, their two children and five bagpipes. He has been a journalist for *The Australian* on and off since 1998. He holds an honours degree in Russian Studies from the University of NSW, and spent a year working in the post of deputy business editor of *The Moscow Times*. A constant traveller, James keeps gravitating to Hungary, Russia and the Australian outback. This is his first book.